EXPRESSIVE THERAPY

EXPRESSIVE THERAPY

A Creative Arts Approach to
Depth-Oriented Treatment

Arthur Robbins, Ed.D., A.T.R.

Creative Arts Therapy Department
Pratt Institute, Brooklyn, New York
Institute for Expressive Analysis
New York, New York

Prepared in collaboration with colleagues of
the expressive therapy professions.

 **HUMAN SCIENCES PRESS, INC.**
72 FIFTH AVENUE,
NEW YORK, N.Y. 10011

Library of Congress Cataloging in Publication Data

Robbins, Arthur, 1928–
    Expressive therapy.

    Bibliography
    Includes index.
    1. Psychotherapy. 2. Creation (Literary,
artistic, etc.)—Therapeutic use. 3. Art therapy.
4. Dance therapy. 5. Music therapy. 6. Movement, Psychology of—Therapeutic
use. I. Title.
RC480.R63   616.89' 165   LC 80-13005
ISBN 0-87705-101-1
        0-89885-279-X (paperback)

CONTENTS

CONTRIBUTORS

ARLENE AVSTREIH, M.A., D.T.R.
> Coordinator, Dance Therapy Program, Creative Arts Therapy Department, Pratt Institute, Brooklyn, New York.

DONNA BASSIN, M.P.S.
> Faculty and supervisor, Creative Arts Therapy Department, Pratt Institute, Brooklyn, New York.

JULIE JOSLYN BROWN, M.P.S., A.T.R.
> Supervisor, Creative Arts Therapy Counseling Service, Creative Arts Therapy Department, Pratt Institute, Brooklyn, New York.

MARY DEVINCENTIS, M.P.S.
> Art Therapist, Hospital Audiences, New York, New York.

MICHAEL EIGEN, Ph.D.
> Director of training, Institute for Expressive Analysis, New York, New York.

ANNA FALCO, M.S.W.
> Formerly supervisor and faculty Creative Arts Therapy Department, Pratt Institute, Brooklyn, New York.

EMANUEL HAMMER, Ph.D.
> Visiting professor, Creative Arts Therapy Department, Pratt Institute, Brooklyn, New York.

KATHERINE IRISH, M.P.S.
> Art Therapist, Bowery Project, New York, New York.

MARILYN LaMONICA, M.P.S.
> Supervisor, Creative Arts Therapy Department, Pratt Institute, Brooklyn, New York.

CARMELA LUONGO, M.P.S.
> Art Therapist, Cumberland Hospital, Brooklyn, New York.

FRANCES LYSHAK, M.P.S.
> Art Therapist, Bronx Children's Psychiatric Center, Bronx, New York.

JANE MATTES, M.S.W.
> Director of clinical services, Institute for Expressive Analysis, New York, New York.

RUTH OBERNBREIT, M.P.S., A.T.R.
> Supervisor, Creative Expressive Program, New York Hospital-Cornell Medical Center, Westchester Division, White Plains, New York.

MAUREEN RENEHAN, M.P.S.
> Art therapist, Rye Hospital, Rye, New York.

ARTHUR ROBBINS, Ed.D., A.T.R.
> Professor and chairman, Creative Arts Therapy Department,
> Pratt Institute, Brooklyn, New York.

ALTHEA ROSE, M.P.S.
> Private Practice, New York, New York.

ALICE SHIELDS, D.M.A.
> Assistant director, Columbia-Princeton Electronic Music Center, Columbia University, New York, New York.

ELAINE V. SIEGEL, D.T.R.
> Director, Movement Therapy Department, Suffolk Child Development Center, Huntington, New York.

ANNE STERNBACH, M.P.S.

Formerly faculty and supervisor, Creative Arts Therapy Department, Pratt Institute, Brooklyn, New York.

AMELIA STRAUSS, D.T.R.

Supervisor, Creative Arts Therapy Department, Pratt Institute, Brooklyn, New York.

FLOYD TURNER, Ph.D.

Psychologist, Rutgers Medical School, Piscataway, New Jersey.

MARGARET WILSON, M.P.S.

Art Therapist, Elmcrest Psychiatric Institute, Portland, Connecticut.

ANN WINN-MUELLER, M.S.W.

Social Worker, Rutgers Medical School, Piscataway, New Jersey.

PREFACE TO THE PAPERBACK EDITION

The culmination of many years of practice as an art therapist and psychoanalyst resulted in the initial publication of *Expressive Therapy: A Creative Arts Approach to Depth-Oriented Treatment*. Five years have now passed and I am aware that the term "expressive therapy" has become a more acceptable piece of the psychiatric nomenclature in the mental health field. Coinciding with this development is an awareness by mental health professionals of the importance of an overall creative arts therapy theoretical framework that unites rather than separates the practitioner. I also observed an increasing number of job lines that contain the title, expressive therapist, as well as the formation of professional organizations and conferences dealing explicitly with the issues cogent to an expressive therapy approach.

Since the initial publication of this text, I have lectured and conducted workshops in various parts of the United States as well as Europe and the Far East. In virtually every professional visit the exercises elucidating the various theoretical issues that underlie the work of an expressive therapist have cut through the very formidable language and cultural barriers. I have also observed a hunger for a depth-oriented approach that resonates with the complexity of the work of an expressive therapist.

This text supports the notion that one does not require formal artistic training to understand and apply the approach of an expressive therapist. The increasing flow of literature regarding the aesthetics of therapeutic communication mirrors this position. I am pleased, therefore, that this book continues to be available as a guide to the therapeutic artist who works towards helping patients in finding the artists within themselves.

Arthur Robbins

PREFACE

This book addresses itself to the mental health practitioner who wishes to study the creative process as it applies to depth-oriented psychotherapy. A good therapy session contains many of the characteristics of a work of art. Both share a multiplicity of psychic levels and a release of energy that radiates along the axis of form and content. Therapeutic communication, like art, has both a sender and a receiver and is defined by psychic dimensions that parallel the formal parameters through which art is expressed. In any one session, we can detect in patient-therapist communications both verbal and nonverbal cues that can be examined within the artistic parameters of sight, sound, and motion; that is, in rhythm, pitch, and timbre; in color, texture, and form; and in muscular tension, energy, and spatial relation. These elements of therapeutic composition will have their own principles and will require the utmost of skill in therapeutic management. This complex field of energy will become transformed during the process of treatment as the perceptual fields of both patient and therapist go through the process of differentiation and fusion, much as the perceptual field of the artist ebbs and flows. The expressive therapist relates and responds to this complex matrix and develops the tools to contain and organize communications that may resist reduction to the linear logic of words. Moreover, the expressive therapist must have the talent to create metaphorical interventions that bridge fantasy, dreams, and play with the world of reality.

The essence of expressive therapy lies in process rather than in technique, for the therapy occurs through the vehicle of psychic play rather than in the actual products of artistic production. Dance, art, or music, as well as other expressive modalities, can facilitate this process, but the actual use of a particular art form will depend on the special talents of the therapist and on the particular receptivity to that art form of a given patient. What is crucial, however, is the therapist's availability to hear and attend to the dance, music, and visions of his patient's communications.

Expressive therapy will be presented primarily within a psychoanalytic orientation, although the process can easily be adapted to function within a humanistic, gestalt, or transactional orientation. Common to all these therapies is the goal of creating congruence between the patient's inner world and his outer behavior. Treatment in expressive therapy not only can be expressed only through the medium of words, but also through gestures, sounds, visions, and fantasies. These rich communications, combined with the necessary ego supports, work towards strengthening the patient's capacity to risk making his inner dream a reality. Expressive therapy, therefore, is psychoanalytic in perspective in its use and understanding of mental structure, transference, and psychic development; it is field oriented in its approach to space and energy, and holistic and humanistic in philosophy.

Chapter 1

INTRODUCTION TO EXPRESSIVE THERAPY

Arthur Robbins, Ed.D., A.T.R.*

Any discussion of expressive therapy requires clarification and understanding of the byproducts of primary process communications. Fantasies, dreams, art, and play, the organizers of our primary process, contain the raw affects of our inner experiences. According to Susan Langer (1942), creative manifestations originating in part in the unconscious utilize visual and auditory images presented simultaneously rather than successively in time, and thus through association in time acquire inner relationship and meaning. Discursive symbolism on the other hand is the language of conscious rational thinking presented consecutively in time according to the conventions of grammar and syntax. The expressive therapist, then, creates or discovers through verbal metaphor bridges forming a link between nondiscursive and discursive communications.

Gestures, postures, styles of movement, tones, and inflec-

*I am indebted to Alice Shields, whose editorial work made a significant contribution to this chapter.

tions of voice, all are like fantasies, dreams, art, and play; fueled by drive and muscular tension, outwardly shaping and forming these inner postures of primary process. Primary process, then, serves to promote self-continuity and identity (Noy, 1968) and is potentially available through the conscious regulation of the ego as perceived in productions of the mind and bodily expressions. On the other hand, secondary process communication gives us feedback and validation for our perceptions, and is used for all functions aimed at encountering reality. Both primary and secondary processes vary in level of organization and integration and are manifested through different cognitive ego states. We will attempt to demonstrate in future chapters how primary and secondary process are expressed through different cognitive modes, one being a right hemisphere orientation that is essentially holistic and spatial, as contrasted to a left hemisphere mode that is more synthesizing and analytic. Expressive therapists, then, are trained to be open and receptive to both primary and secondary process modes of communication, through an enlarged capacity to shift ego states. Thus they can be at home with a very holistic, intuitive, and receptive orientation that is essentially spatial, or be ready at any given moment to shift to a more synthesizing mode in which the precision of words gives structure and definition to nonverbal flow. This ability to synthesize and articulate the multiplicity of levels in the patient-therapist dyad is the process of creativity in depth-oriented therapy. Implied in this position is a very basic shift from the classical psychoanalytic mode of treatment: not everything can or should be converted to words. Thus experiences cannot always be reduced to direct verbal expression, for behavior is a product of a multiplicity of cognitive, affective, and perceptual states whose properties are often spatial and contiguous, rather than direct and linear and therefore verbal. It is the artist or poet, rather than the psychologist, who then captures the authentic meaning of a phenomenological act, because art, in the larger sense, is not restricted by the usual boundaries of verbal syntax or logic.

The role of the therapist is often reduced to two levels: the art, dance, or music therapist is considered a specialist in non-verbal expressive therapy, while verbal therapists are usually trained to work solely on the direct, verbal level of communication. Patients are usually assigned to their expressive therapist on the basis of that therapist's particular modality. Yet we see that verbal, visual, spatial, kinesthetic, and aural cues constantly intermix within any one therapeutic dialogue, and a patient's receptivity to these different modalities can fluctuate widely within any one session. Thus in our view, a therapist must be trained to be receptive to both verbal and nonverbal cues.

Within this multidimensional orientation the expressive therapist, though not necessarily a dancer, artist, or musician, is sensitive to movement, vision, and sound and can play with his or her patients on these levels. The perceptual mode, then, becomes a frame or container through which the expressive therapist meets his patient's communications. Thus the patient is encouraged to make an inner reality find concrete expression in the outside world. This responsiveness to a variety of sensory and perceptual cues is the crucial determining factor in an expressive therapy relationship. But whether the expressive therapist in actuality paints, moves, or sings with his patient is not particularly relevant, for the choice of modality is contingent upon a variety of considerations ranging from characterological resistances and the patient's lifestyle, to his particular sensitivity within a given modality.

An expressive therapy orientation adapts itself to a variety of clinical populations. For instance, the neurotic patient, who is often on the couch, usually does not require a nonverbal modality simply to facilitate verbal expression, although in some instances, he may need to be assisted to bypass his verbiage so that both parties can move onto a more experiential level. For the most part, however, the neurotic patient's nonverbal behavior will be received and responded to by the therapist through the use of creative and paradoxical metaphors. For instance, the therapist may share with the patient an image stimulated by the therapeutic discussion, an image that may capture far more of the complexity of a given conflict than could be said in a linear fashion. What comes to mind here is the case of a young woman talking about her pain and loneliness in a fairly depressed and disconnected family. The father is grimly held onto as an idealized object in spite of his many lacks. As she speaks about his death, an aural image comes to the mind of the therapist. Floating into his consciousness is the aria "Un bel di" from *Madame Butterfly*. Puccini expressed in this aria a subtle mixture of pain, sadness, resignation, sweetness, and subtle, bitter rage that simply cannot be reduced to mere words. The sharing of this image seemed to bring both therapist and patient into greater harmony.

The expressive therapist, then, works within a humanistic orientation, while at the same time he does not discard the valuable constructions of psychoanalysis or other depth therapies. There are, however, many complex issues underlying his training. A sensitivity to the creative process usually requires some direct experiences in creative work. Besides analytic training, areas of knowledge from literature, philosophy, and academic psychology would be most relevant for the expressive therapist. We have also found that personal analysis is simply not enough in unlocking a therapist's creativity in work with patients. Group countertransference workshops, a midway station between group therapy and supervision, have proven to be most useful in training therapists to utilize their inner resources as a response to patient communications. Here the therapist shares his inner imagery and feeling inductions to patient communications, while the group takes on the function of a psychodramatic screen for the externalization of self and object representations, which are being stimulated by the patient-therapist matrix.

This training will hopefully expose the expressive therapist to the complex, protean nature of his work. In this light, the process of therapy seems to take place in a fluctuating energy field of positive and negative vectors associated with projected and introjected identifications. The nature of this ever-changing field is communicated through nonverbal imagery, physical sensation, and affect mood states, as well as verbal metaphor. In treatment this complex field of energy ebbs and flows, going through a process of gestalt reorganization. How the therapist responds to the spontaneous reorganization of his own inner field, of his own ever-changing gestalt, and how he utilizes his own conscious and preconscious symbolism is the very essence of his creative work.

Viewed in another light, this energy field is itself part of a complicated network of communications.

Ernst Kris (1952) views art as a communication in which there is a sender, a message, and a receiver. In the therapeutic communication, patient and therapist continually exchange their roles of sender and receiver, while the message that emerges is the product of their interaction. Therapy, then, can be an artistic expression of the two parties involved, and can be an invitation to a shared communication in which two minds intertwine on the deepest level of psychic existence.

However, in order to arrive at this profound level of communication, the therapist must employ an enlarged capacity to respond to nonverbal cues. This capacity on the part of the therapist may originate in his early relationship with his mother. René Spitz (1965) offers us valuable information on the quality of this early sensory-motor dyad. He describes perception in this relationship as multimodalitied although primarily visual. The mother-infant relationship, then, is experienced primarily as one of looking and being looked at, often accompanied by touching and cooing. Further, the pattern of communication characteristic of the early mother-infant field is modeled on what each party brings to the interaction. As Noy (1968) points out, primary communication is mutual. Thus what each party brings to the subtle cuing and recuing reinforces and structures a primary network of communication. Further, the quality of the mother-infant relationship is coenesthetic; that is, at such a very early level this network of responsiveness is still under the control of the autonomic nervous system, and therefore has a visceral and unconscious quality. Some adults retain this capacity for visceral responsiveness, in which communication stays on a subtle, intuitive, preconscious level, and is attuned to a host of sensory cues. The expressive therapist has this ability to see, hear, and experience his patients on a coenesthetic, visceral level.

COENESTHETIC EXPERIENCE IN ART AND IN THERAPY

At this point, it is necessary to compare in some detail the nature of the creative experience in art and in therapy. Being a sculptor as well as a psychoanalyst, I see many parallels between art and therapy. As a sculptor, I work with metal, stone, or wood. Each medium engages me through its own particular rhythm, motion, and texture. The act of welding, for instance, is dramatic and absorbing; while doing it, my body is intensely alert, and there is no time to plan or organize, only time to respond. Molten metal actually crackles, it becomes alive and electrifies my entire being; the hot metal literally dances before my eyes, and as I work on it I have fleeting memories of childhood play with erector sets.

Therapy, just as welding, taps the part of me that wants to construct or build. There, too, one at times plays with white-hot molten metal. In this context I am reminded of the action orientation of a difficult and provocative adolescent entering a therapy session. I feel both our bodies taut, as if stretched out to a fine line. I see that he is ready to explode, and I draw back, attempting to meet his heat with my cool. He is ready to spill over, and I try to offer words as a means of giving him some form of release and expression, but his aggressive impulses are too powerful to be harnessed by words. We quickly mold and shape a clay model of a snake that gives him some degree of mastery, control, and release of motor energy. In the artistic process words now find room to communicate his experience. Our emerging multifaceted relationship gives structure and containment to raw affect, and yet gives enough space so that I am experienced as nonintrusive. Containment, nonintrusiveness, and motor expression provide the shifting figure and ground of new patterns of communication. In these new patterns are the positive and negative valences of hate and love ready to be played out in the transference-countertransference. The intensity of the tension between us, the nature of the sensory nonverbal contact, gives energy and rhythm to our communications.

As a sculptor, stone offers me the greatest challenge and demands the utmost in perseverance and persistence. I look intently at my stone, until I virtually become part of it. I scan its texture, feeling its many crevices and cavities and its rough edges, in general immersing myself in a sensory experience. Slowly my energy is brought into play, as vague impressions begin to come into consciousness. My body soon finds a rhythm that harmonizes with the energy of the stone. I experience a sense of timelessness and complete immersion in my work. I literally get lost in stone. At first the work is fast, as I remove large chunks. Suddenly, out of nowhere, an unexpected irregularity in the stone demands a new course of action. The unpredictable becomes an open door into something new and exciting. Instead of feeling defeat because my original conception has changed, I feel mastery and power. But this is not always the case, for often I find myself on an endless plateau. Everything seems dismally the same and I feel discouraged, as the image that I once held is now somewhat blurred and I cannot see much ahead of me. I suffer the pain of giving birth, and I swear that I will never do this again. But, finally, I learn not to fight the stone, for at these times I must play with my image and find a different perspective. As the stone takes shape, images that speak of the stone's potential shift and change like frames in a moving film. I try to avoid premature closure, not settling for too easy a solution. By the same token I struggle with my tendency for over-elaboration and learn to walk away from my own perfectionism and grandiosity. I move in and out of various cognitive states: now I am lost in my work, now I move back and take perspective. At times I feel calm and whole inside, centered and complete. With the emergence of the sensation, and the imagery and the affect inherent in form, comes a new synthesis that follows the laws of balance and harmony, a synthesis that has released in me a certain sense of power and force, and is very much a personal statement.

A similar creative synthesis characterizes a good therapy session. There is often a honeymoon period that literally pushes the therapy work ahead. But soon the inevitable resistances and fears slow the process down. The resonance and intuitiveness of the therapist are then called into action. Surprise, paradox, mirroring, or confrontation—in the language of expressive therapy containing, framing or visual, spatial, and aural play— are some of the tools that may facilitate the return to therapeutic movement. But these techniques can be reduced to clever maneuvers if they do not develop organically: ultimately it is his employment of and receptivity to preconscious imagery rather than clever techniques that will be important in overcoming resistance. Authentic therapeutic interventions will be discovered through this deep form of relatedness.

At times, a therapy session becomes totally engrossing, and there appears to be a loss of time and space. Thus, when therapist and patient are working well, they are finely attuned in resonance, yet are distinctly separate. Further parallels between art and therapy come to mind. As with the stone, we try to avoid premature interpretations, or going against the patient's rhythm, and move towards areas that are more pliable and accessible and less resistant. The field of communications is constantly being altered in terms of figure and ground: there are new and different configurations with subtle shifts in affect between therapist and patient. On other occasions the therapist's ego challenges, or gives structure and definition, as well as perspective, to this very complicated matrix of visions, sensations, and perceptions.

In short, as therapeutic artists we oscillate between two different cognitive styles or ego states. One such style can be described as a right hemisphere orientation wherein attention is suspended, a rational goal orientation fades, and a receptive state prevails. Psychoanalytically, as we shift from secondary to primary process thinking, the ego gives up control and allows the deep, bottomless core of existence to intrude into consciousness, a core of existence that can be likened to our early experiential form and state, in which energy is diffuse and consciousness nondifferentiated. Neurologists refer to this condition as the alpha or theta state. We will elaborate upon such neurological and cognitive parallels in another section of this text. Jungian analysts use the term archetypal images that connect our inner symbols to this state of timelessness. Reaching this state is not an easy process. For some, play functions as a way of suspending ego controls and moving towards unconscious imagery. For others, repetitive stimuli or meditations are necessary. Involved in this shift to right hemisphere orientation is power released by the abandonment of societal mores. There is often a sense of arrogance or even grandiosity when we are propelled by the enormous energy that is unblocked in this process, but if this newly found power is to have any meaning, it must have a communicative value. Therefore the shift to a reality perspective governed by order and logic, harmony and balance, must take place. Gradually for some, suddenly for others, the shift into another cognitive style occurs. By means of this cognitive style, our observing ego challenges, perceives, confronts, and at times surprises our patients. We help patients integrate splits and put polarities together. Through this process, hopefully, our worlds have been made afresh so that we are now in a new left hemisphere orientation, discovering creative ways with metaphor that the ordinary come alive with organic richness. Through this process, we aid patients to risk exposing the core of their vulnerability so that the inner and outer realities find some congruence. Often, when the symbols of both participants in a therapeutic dialogue emerge, a new field of force is discovered, in which lie the developmental tasks of separation and individuation. This mutual coenesthetic experience sometimes makes therapy a transcendant experience.

SOURCES OF EXPRESSIVE THERAPY IN THE PSYCHOANALYTIC LITERATURE

In light of the above descriptions of the process of expressive therapy, we will trace how the tradition of psychoanalytic thought enters into expressive therapy theory and technique. In expressive therapy we make extensive use of such concepts as mental structure, primary and secondary process communication, the ego as a force for organization and adaptation, and the critical importance of object relations as a binding link between inner and outer reality. As a review of the literature is contained in each section of this text, we will here briefly mention landmark studies that become critical guideposts for further explorations and understanding.

THE IMPORTANCE OF THE EGO

Hartmann (1958) and his collaborators play a pivotal role in our understanding of ego psychology as it relates to the expressive therapist. Concepts of human adaptation, involving autoplastic modification of the self, alloplastic modifications of the environment, and the effects of these ongoing processes, become the study and province of ego psychology. Within this framework, we see patient/therapist interactions as a subtle and continuous mutual adaptation of one another through the vehicle of verbal and nonverbal communication (Langs, 1978). The elasticity and flexibility of the therapist's ego to synthesize (rather than introject or project) difficult and complex stimuli from his patient's projective identification will be of the utmost importance in determining therapeutic change. Thus the expressive therapist's employment of a modality for containment or framing of intense affects that facilitates a more orderly assimilation of patient communications may preserve and sustain the therapeutic integrity of the patient-therapist alliance. For in many instances, the direct expression of raw unneutralized affects can be very disruptive to the therapeutic alliance. Examples of the use of an expressive modality to contain or tame intense affects will be presented in the chapter by Avstreih and Brown (Chapter 9) while Shields (Chapter 15) will place musical expression in a mathematical frame in which intense affects will find a container for expression and holding.

Thus visual or aural play can often give a patient the distance and protection to see, hear, and understand his inner projections, and temporarily take refuge in play so that he can avoid being overwhelmed or threatened by the intensity of primitive affects. Different modes of expression offer more elasticity for patient responsiveness and lend structure and accommodation depending upon the patient's particular ego deficiency. Examples of the different modes of expression offering different protections and accommodations will be described by Avstreih and Brown.

The therapist is trained how to help patients shift from one ego state to another. Thus many patients require a very calm presence on the part of the therapist in which excessive verbalization from both parties is minimized. In this quiet, however, the therapist listens with an intense concentration on his patient that bears a close similarity to meditation. In time, the patient may also feel the presence of the therapist and this intense concern. We believe that this may be one of the properties of a healing experience, and it is basically nonverbal in character. On other occasions, by contrast, the therapist's ego is brought into play: he augments the patient's capacity to cope with his outer and inner worlds. In these instances, the therapist's emotional investment is very much in his own ego sphere, and consequently there is a concentration in effort towards helping the patient attend, ask questions, investigate, contrast, and, in short, objectify his perceptions. This implies a hooking up of what we see and feel with what we know. The borderline or psychotic hides and takes refuge in primary process communication, while the neurotic may be fearful of intense affect and fantasy. The therapist and patient, equally, must maintain harmony and balance while shifting back and forth from primary to secondary process communication. However, the dynamics of shifting from one ego state to another still need much study and elaboration. What do you do when the patient is too fluid and scattered in energy? How do you help another patient to organize and synthesize some of his nonverbal intuitions into a goal-directed response? The creative therapist needs not only to understand the problems, but the methods to remediate the ego functioning that help people to be more creative. Discussion of such methods will be found in other chapters.

OBJECT RELATIONS THEORY

Often, artistic work becomes the transitional means to cope with object loss. Here the artist recreates in his work the lost object and finds a safe space to repair the damage of intense injury by investing his energy into creations that represent images of the past fused with the pain and dread of the future. Thus creativity is inextricably connected to self and to object, and on a suprapersonal scope, to symbols and images that become affective codifications of our intrapsychic life. The problems of wholeness or splitting can either be resolved in or interfere with the process of artistic or therapeutic creation. Self and object representations are complex spatial, perceptual, and affective configurations that are not easily reduced to linear thought. Therefore expressive therapy has something very special to offer, for it dares to concretize the nonverbal language of object relations into a nonlinear frame that can be externalized and communicated.

Expressive therapy finds a theoretical home in the works of Winnicott, and, consequently, his material will be extensively quoted in many sections of this book. Winnicott offers the expressive therapist a map that gives some overall perspective to the development of inner and outer space. He views development at the very start of life, in which the mother by nearly total adaptation affords her infant the opportunity for the illusion that her breast is part of the infant. Thus, according to Winnicott (1971),

> From birth, therefore, the human being is concerned with the problem of the relationship between what is objectively perceived and subjectively conceived of, and in the solution of this problem there is no help for the human being who has not been started off well enough by the mother. The intermediate area to which I'm referring is the area that is allowed to the infant between primary creativity and objective perception based on reality testing. This transitional phenomenon represents the early stages of the use of illusion without which there is no meaning for the human being in the idea of a relationship with an object that is perceived by others as external to that being (Winnicott, 1971).

As regards this necessary adaptation on the part of the mother, our understanding is that borderline and psychotic patients have a basic deficiency in this primitive resonance. The work of the expressive therapist, then, becomes very close to Winnicott's definition of therapy:

> Psychotherapy takes place in the overlap of two areas of playing, that of the patient and that of the therapist. Psychotherapy has to do with two people playing together. The corollary of this is when playing is not possible then the work by the therapist is directed towards bringing the patient from a state of not being able to play into a state of being able to play (Winnicott, 1971).

Involved in this therapeutic play, then, are two minds attempting to make contact on a prelogical symbolic level. Influenced by Winnicott's work, Mary Milner (1952) offers a narrative of 20 years of therapeutic work with a patient with whom Winnicott's transitional dimension of therapeutic space emerged through the vehicle of drawing as well as vision and touch. Milner, discussing the importance played by the frame, states:

> The frame marks off the different kinds of reality that is within it from that which is outside it; but a temporal spatial frame also marks off the special kind of reality of psychoanalytic session. As in psychoanalysis it is the existence of this frame that makes possible the full development of that creative illusion that analysts call the transference (Milner, 1952).

Utilizing this frame, the expressive therapist formulates the goal of treatment as mediating a congruence between the inner life of the patient and his outer reality. Inherent in this formulation of treatment is a modification of Freud's classical definition and aim of psychoanalytic treatment: Where Id was, there Ego shall be. Rycroft drastically modifies this position:

> The aim of psychoanalytic treatment is not primarily to make the unconscious conscious, not to widen or strengthen the ego, but to reestablish the connection between disassociated functions so that the patient ceases to feel that there is an inherent antagonism between his imaginative and adaptive capacities (Rycroft, 1962).

Masud Khan (1974), however, cautions that in order to accomplish this goal and mitigate the inherent antagonism between imaginative and adaptive capacities, the therapist should enable the patient to have freer access to his unconscious, stemming from a stronger ego capacity within himself. According to Khan, this shift in treatment emphasis from the traditional psychoanalytic mode is reflected by such theoreticians as Deutsch, Erikson, Greenson, Sorrels, and Lange. Treatment within this new context becomes a total mind-body experience in which imaginative communication is more than simple reporting; it demands an affective involvement on the part of the patient. To quote Khan:

I am using the concept of knowing in a rather complex way. Knowing is more than just mental reporting and self-awareness or verbalization of memories of life experiences. There is a distinct quality of ego cathexis plus imagination added to the remembered facts or to the mental representations of past experiences. For experiences of knowing to crystallize, it is one of the basic functions of interpretation to sponsor this particular imaginative affective ego cathexis in the patient in her own self-awareness (Khan, 1974).

Thus, for the expressive therapist treatment becomes a total experience in which perception, affect, and sensation join cognition at the same point in time and space.

To summarize, as through nonverbal communication, the analyst makes contact with the most primary and basic core of his patient; he experiences the subtle expressions of pain, loss, and loneliness that are unfolded in his patient's stunted capacity for relatedness (Balint, 1965). Within a therapeutic relationship of play, the subtle symbolic representations of self and object move into a new world of meaning. The various splits and part objects, with their attending affects of love and hate, need to be touched, heard, and visualized. But most importantly, the therapist must himself experience and make contact with this early developmental field in order to reproduce a transitional space for reparation. In this transitional space there is room for resonance and dialogue and for complex affective and perceptual systems to become increasingly integrated. We believe that such a process is nonverbal and demands the utmost on the part of the therapist in his ability to play, symbolize, and employ a variety of sensory-spatial modalities. Examples will be given throughout this text describing this process in detail.

THE PSYCHOLOGY OF THE SYMBOLIC PROCESS

If we speak of ego and object, we must also explore the language of symbolic expression through which these two systems make contact with one another. As we have seen, the subtle shifts from primary to secondary process are the language of both the artist and the therapist. The imagery they share is the raw juice of a therapeutic dialogue.

Within a developmental context, imagery may be expressed within varying levels of perceptual differentiation. Some sensations and affects have minimal shape and form, and are at the vague beginnings of taking on the framing qualities of perceptual clarity. These vague and as yet incompletely imagized affects or sensations are referred to by Arieti (1976) as endocepts, which we may consider as a disposition to feel, act, or think; a disposition that is repressed, yet continues to have indirect influence on our lives. In its preimagized state, then, an endocept cannot be shared. The therapist must find an expressive medium for the communication of an endocept, an image that ultimately can become a bridge to secondary process communication. However, before we reach this bridge, the image may go through many stages of transformation. In some instances, we may see part or split images requiring higher levels of perceptual integration. Other images require affective cathexis as well as elaboration. At times, even, the expressive therapist may himself provide the sensory experience as the raw building block for imagery and symbol formation. We see this process of image building as a basic tool for the expressive therapist; images are needed especially for patients with poor impulse control or those in whom object constancy has not been established.

Jungian analytic treatment has much to offer in developing a framework of symbolic imagery for the creative exploration of a patient's unconscious. In this context, the creative act of imagination is a meeting ground for patient and therapist to explore the unconscious. The use of artwork and symbolic expression, then, has been extensively employed by Jungians in a depth-oriented approach (Hochheimer, 1969). Jungians also provide an adaptable theory to explain extrasensory phenomena in terms of archetypal symbolism and the collective unconscious. Our chapter (Chapter 11) utilizing Castaneda's work as a frame to explain such phenomena may be of interest to expressive therapists to see how Don Juan invests an extraordinary amount of energy into symbol formation, which ultimately becomes transpersonal in character.

THE CREATIVE USE OF THE THERAPIST'S RESOURCES

The expressive therapist's strength lies in the subtle interplay of inductions and countertransference and the harnessing of these affects so that they can be used in the service of the treatment process. How we share, communicate, and explore a multiplicity of feelings with our patients and how we use our imagery to overcome barriers and fears make treatment more than simple linear communication. Indeed, therapy becomes an act of creation when fear is changed into self-affirmation. The literature in the countertransference area is both rich and extensive, and will be reviewed in our chapter on countertransference. However, we may note here that Searles, especially, offers us a container with which to utilize countertransferential material (Searles, 1955). The countertransferential field for engagement is with introjects; our goal is the disentanglement of self and object from the preverbal matrix. The Spotnitz-Nelson group (1969) and Lacan (1953), as well as others from the French school of analysis, speak of the nonrational countertransferential components of the therapist-patient communications. Racker's work (1957) is crucial in this area and will be used as a central reference in our countertransference chapter.

We have consistently referred to field theory as being an intrinsic part of an expressive therapist's framework. We distinguish a field theory orientation from gestalt therapy, which has its own separate techniques and point of view. Field theory, however, is not antithetical to a psychoanalytic position. In expressive therapy, as in psychoanalysis, the patient-therapist relationship is seen as an unfolding field of mutual perceptual differentiations. The subtle use of field theory principles would seem to have tremendous bearing in working through transference and countertransference relationships. As the therapist becomes a part of the patient's world, experiencing the patient's self and object representations, the subtle shift in figure and ground becomes a paramount issue in working through the transference/countertransference. A short clinical vignette is offered to highlight the subtle interplay of transference/countertransference.

A new patient enters my office. She is well-built and muscular, and is strikingly blond. A quick and easy smile covers her face, filling the room with eroticism and excitement. I see that her walk has a sense of assurance and direction; the space she fills is very large. I soon become aware of her body tension; her muscles are tight and held back, particularly around the midpart of her spine. I see underneath her controlled exterior an explosive quality that is tenuously held back and pushing against her own tautness. She wears a business suit that seems almost like armor. The tension in the room soon mounts. She is there because of her son. She speaks with a voice that is choppy and that seems to erupt from a deep part of herself. It soon becomes apparent that she has not come because of her son. It's because of her marriage: it is awful. Her husband, a police officer, is assaultive and abusive, and she wants out of the marriage. As her story unfolds, I am immediately engrossed and excited. I feel like an accomplice ready to enter into a murder plot. An old movie crosses the periphery of my mind, *The Postman Always Rings Twice,* a murder story with a double indemnity twist.

The patient's voice and mood, as well as her action, communicate a multiplicity of impressions. The emerging field that comes into our room is sharp and clear. She is very much the figure in our field, and I am in the background. I see her as a cornered cat ready to claw. For many sessions I will remain very quiet, for that is how she wants it. I offer her complete control and by so doing establish a workable field. Over the course of the next five years, this field changes both in affects, direction, transference, countertransference, mood, and texture. Each of my responses moves this field towards a more differentiated and complex pattern. I experience myself as Pygmalion, teaching a dirty street waif elegance and refinement. Later on I experience myself as a German soldier coming home from battle to his fräulein (singing to myself "Madeline"), and with each stage of transference/countertransference, I find a greater latitude, interpretive breadth, and communicativeness. In psychoanalytic terms, I change from a narcissistic appendage to being more object related. And with each degree of greater clarity and differentiation there is an exchange of anger and rage as the texture of our patterns becomes more thoroughly demarcated.

Our nearness or distance, separateness or similarity, became part of the process of working out perceptual differentiation as well as separation-individuation problems. Thus, based on the premise that the therapy session is a work of art, then affect, imagery, perception, and cognition from both patient and therapist must be unified into a whole. This shift in figure-ground relationships will be connected to the transference/countertransference relationship.

In stage one field, my experience of being an appendage needed some reconciliation with my own self and object representations that demanded recognition and praise from my mother. My own struggle with these externalized identifications ultimately gave me the permission to hear her imagery communication and employ it as a course of action for treatment. As an act of my own therapeutic struggle, I finally heard her wish to be in complete charge of our relationship. This permitted the field to change, and thus led into a new set of interpersonal and intrapsychic forces. My own mother made contact with the dirty lost child in both of us. We avoided gratification of our mutual needs and slowly worked through a new field by allowing our communications and efforts to focus upon her son. She sought guidance and direction, and received clarification and understanding of the lost child that was being expressed through the problems of her son. Finally, in stage three, our field becomes libidinized with anal-sadistic components. I wrestle with my own disguised wishes to symbiotically fuse on a sexual level with my mother. Both of us are now ready to face her ultimate rage regarding the whole series of narcissistic injuries. Our mutual imageries were both interpersonally and intrapsychically based. This was equally true for the multiple valences of hostile and libidinal forces. The constant challenge was to hear the image that would offer clues as to how our emerging field could change.

Thus, the therapy field is often characterized by stability or fluidity, direction, and intensity and our creativity will be challenged to facilitate a change in the quality of this field (Combs, 1959). Field theory may also offer a connecting link to neurophysiology: an electrochemical field, neurologically, bears striking resemblance to the valences of our psychic space. Thus we see as a goal of treatment a greater differentiation of the complex network of perceptual-affective communications. Neurologically, the more complex and differentiated the neuroconnections, the greater the ability for organismic self-regulation. We will devote considerable time in future chapters to describing the neurological research in right and left hemisphere cognitive styles (Ornstein, 1972) and extending these notions to primary and secondary process thinking.

THE CONTRIBUTION OF VERBAL THERAPIES TO EXPRESSIVE THERAPY

Double-bind theory also utilizes the field theory of communications. In double-bind theory the terms *digital* and *analogical communication* are used, digital for the logical order of words and analogical for their contiguous or concrete likeness. Communications theory offers the expressive therapist a new language to understand the subtle mixture of double-binding affects that are contained in words as well as actions. This mixture is often built into the therapy situation, and may in fact be a way for both therapist and patient to struggle and reorder their field. Thus a therapeutic intervention that accepts contradictory forces within the same metaphor reduces the patient's built-in resistance to change. Finding creative ways to see the productive expression of pathology can often change defeat into victory. The use of paradox that seems to contain bipolar discrepancies in attitudes and feelings fits very well into a framework of verbal and nonverbal therapy. Berger (1978) speaks of analogical communication as a defense against directness and clarity used by the schizophrenic.

There are many schools of therapy that utilize imagery as central to their therapeutic work. Implosive therapy utilizes imaginative work within a directive relationship; through imaginative trial adaptation the patient is encouraged to find new solutions to old problems (Stampfl, 1967). In behavior therapy, desensitization often takes place through the vehicle of imagery exercises (Wolpe, 1958).

Working creatively is certainly not restricted to the psychoanalytic therapist. Zinker, in his text *Creative Process in Gestalt Therapy* (1977), works within a gestalt framework, applying many of the theories of creative development to gestalt therapy. Character resistances are confronted through creative exercises. However, the slow and systematic building of transference and the very delicate process of externalization of introjects and reintrojection of healthy internalizations do not seem to receive the emphasis in the gestalt theory of treatment. In expressive therapy we try to maintain a delicate balance of theoretical complexity, avoiding a mind-body dualism in approach to patients, as is also the case in experiential therapy.

All the above-mentioned therapies can include an expressive and creative framework. Although transference may not be part of other therapeutic orientations, we find that difficult to comprehend, because transference exists in all relationships, in treatment or otherwise. Different theoretical models undoubtedly attract different therapeutic personalities. The notion of creativity and expression, and the elaboration of an underlying theory or orientation will also make a statement as to the personality of the therapist and the kind of transference that will be evoked in his work. To the degree that a therapist can use his theoretical model as a fulcrum for creative discovery, rather than as a straightjacket that causes perceptual premature closure, we believe that all creative therapists share the same values and philosophy of following a patient to his deepest level of self-exploration.

THE CONTRIBUTIONS OF NONVERBAL THERAPIES TO EXPRESSIVE THERAPY

The nonverbal therapies of art, dance, and music have made significant contributions to the field of expressive therapy. In *Art Therapy in a Children's Community* (1972), Edith Kramer utilizes a psychoanalytic notion of sublimation as applied to art activities, using creative expression to give patients a firmer grip on ego mastery functions. Art therapy within this context is a separate discipline from psychotherapy, a discipline that minimizes insight and interpretation and does not have as a goal modification of personality structure. Naumberg (1966), on the other hand, applies depth-oriented psychoanalytic insight interpretations to patients' art productions. Her frame of reference, however, is more in keeping with the earlier psychoanalytic formulations of making the unconscious conscious than with this author's orientation of effecting a congruence of inner and outer realities. Robbins and Sibley (1976) modify this position and apply some of the principles of creativity development to therapeutic expression. Their text is essentially a forerunner of the material in this book.

In the field of music therapy, the supportive and socializing aspects of music have been the major concern for practitioners (Gaston, 1968). P. Nordoff and C. Robbins (1977), however, offer a far more flexible approach to the use of music as play, as they creatively work with pitch and rhythm to frame feelings and expression. In their work, improvisation becomes part of a very creative musical dialogue.

In dance therapy, under the tutelage of Marian Chace (1953) in her work at St. Elizabeth's Hospital, movement becomes a basic tool establishing resonance and communication. Dance therapy, according to Schmais (1977), works on three major assumptions: firstly, that movement reflects personality; secondly, the relationship established between the therapist and patient through movement supports and enables change; and finally, significant changes occur on the movement level that can effect total functioning. A few therapists have moved toward using dance as a primary therapeutic tool within a psychoanalytic context. We will present work illustrating this approach in later chapters. Other dance therapists have developed within a Reichian framework a more bioenergetic approach to movement in which the emphasis has been on the release of muscular tension through active manipulation of the body armor. Birdwhistell (1970), in his research in kinesthetics, which is based on a structural linguistic model, concentrates on looking at the body movements accompanying speech. Judith Kestenberg (1967), working within a depth psychoanalytic framework, formulates an extensive theoretical description of body tension communications that demonstrate a complex mixture of drive, self-object representations, and one's relationship to the outside world.

Movement, music, and art can be placed in a variety of theoretical frameworks. Art can be used as a model of reality in which rational decisions and choices can be made, or imagery and imaginative exercises can be employed for desensitization and fantasy exploration. From a Sullivanian point of view, parataxic distortions are often highlighted through visual play and imagery expression.

THE HUMANISTIC ORIENTATION OF THE EXPRESSIVE THERAPIST

I have described in some detail the rationale and direction as well as some of the underlying theoretical formulations for the expressive therapist. They are in striking accord with a humanistic orientation. Thus, as inner and outer realities find greater concordance, there comes an inherent sense of unity and wholeness very close to what Maslow (1968) described as a peak experience. Thus, we see the characteristics of a peak experience being similar to the orientation and goals of expressive therapy. In accord with Maslow, expressive therapy attempts to effect an integration of polarities and dichotomies. Maslow describes as one of the characteristics of a peak experience a state in which cognition is passive and receptive and there is a disorientation in time and space. In short, intense cognition and an experience of wholeness and self-validating transcendence are goals that belong to all therapies and are found in all good sessions. Yet, such experiences are not always attainable, either in therapy or in art, and much perseverance and hard work must be directed towards arriving at this state.

Psychoanalytic treatment holds as postulate that in order to leave the past we must relive and resolve it in all its complexity of pain, confusion, hate, and love. The creative task of expressive therapy, as with all therapies, is to help patients separate and leave old conflicts so that their world can be met with fresh eyes and new perceptions.

All therapists potentially are expressive therapists. What we have presented is an orientation or an approach to therapy, rather than a series of techniques or tools. Underlying such an approach is a value system that believes in the inherent worth of creative expression and the importance of making the excitement and joy that originates in our innermost symbols find some expression in our outer behavior. Expressive therapy, therefore, is against adjustment or behavior adaptation for the sake of functioning. Yet in this pursuit, both patient and therapist, like the artist, may from time to time suffer the pain of birth, death, and regeneration. But as a patient's creativity is freed so that life may be met with challenge and risk taking, the artist in the patient will be free to experience life in its fullest dimension. We have given you the raw shape of our thesis, now you as reader can join us as we give shape and direction to our material.

REFERENCES

Arieti, S. *Creativity the magic synthesis.* New York: Basic Books, Inc., 1976.

Balint, M. *The basic fear: Therapeutic aspects of regression.* London: Tavistock, 1968.

Berger, M., Ed. *Beyond the double bind.* New York: Brunner/Mazel, 1978.

Birdwhistell, R. L. *Kinesics and context.* Philadelphia: University of Pennsylvania Press, 1970.

Chace, M. Dance as an adjunctive therapy with hospitalized patients. *Bulletin of the Menninger Clinic,* 1953, *17,* 219–255.

Combs, A., Richards, A., & Richards, F. *Perceptual psychology.* New York: Harper & Row, 1959.

Gaston, T. E., ed., *Music in therapy.* New York: Macmillan, 1968.

Gendlin, E. A theory of personality change, in Worchel, P., & Byrne, I. D., Eds., *Personality change.* New York: John Wiley, 1964.

Haley, J. Ideas which handicap therapists, in *Beyond the double bind.* New York: Brunner/Mazel, 1978.

Hartmann, H. *Ego psychology and the problem of adaptations.* New York: International Universities Press, 1958.

Hochheimer, W. *The psychotherapy of C. G. Jung.* New York: G. P. Putnam's Sons, 1969.

Kestenberg, J. S. *Suggestions for diagnostic and therapeutic procedures in movement therapy.* American Dance Therapy Association, Proceedings of the Second Annual Conference. Reprinted in Monograph No. 1, Writings on Body Movement and Communication, Columbia, Md., 1967.

Khan, M. M. *The privacy of the self.* New York: International Universities Press, Inc., 1974.

Kramer, E. *Art as therapy with children.* New York: Schocken Books, 1972.

Kris, E. *Psychoanalytic exploration in art.* New York: International Universities Press, 1952.

Lacan, J. *Fonction et champ au la parole et du langage en psychanalyse in ecrit.* Paris: Du Seuil, 1966.

Langer, S. *Philosophy in a new key.* Cambridge, Mass.: Harvard University Press, (1942) 1951.

Langs, R. Some communication properties of the bipersonal field. *International Journal of Psychoanalytic Psychotherapy,* 1978, *7.*

Maslow, A. *Toward a psychology of being.* New York: D. Van Nostrand Company, 1968.

Milner, M. Aspects of symbolism in comprehension of the non-self. *International Journal of Psychoanalysis,* 1952, *33.*

Milner, M. *The hands of the living god.* New York: International Universities Press, 1969.

Naumberg, M. *Dynamically oriented art therapy: Its principles and practices.* New York: Grune & Stratton, 1966.

Nelson, M., Nelson, B., Sherman, M., & Stream, H. Roles and paradigms. *Psychotherapy,* New York: Grune & Stratton, 1968.

Nordoff, P. & Robbins, C. *Creative music therapy.* New York: The John Day Company, 1977.

Noy, P. The development of music ability. *The Psychoanalytic Study of the Child,* 1968, *23,* 332–342.

Ornstein, R. *The psychology of consciousness.* New York: Penguin Books, 1972.

Racker, H. *The meaning and uses of counter-transference.* New York: International Universities Press, 1957.

Robbins, A. & Sibley, L. *Creative Art Therapy.* New York: Brunner/Mazel, 1976.

Rycroft, C. Beyond the reality principle, in *Imagination and reality.* New York: International Universities Press, 1968.

Schmais, C. Dance therapy in perspective. *Dance Therapy, Focus on Dance VII.* Washington, D.C.: Canper Publications, 1977.

Searles, H. *Collected papers on schizophrenia.* New York: International Universities Press, 1955.

Spitz, R. A. *The first year of life.* New York: International Universities Press, 1965.

Spotnitz, H. *Modern psychoanalysis of the schizophrenic patient.* New York: Grune & Stratton, 1969.

Stamplf, T. G., & Lewis, D. J. Essentials of implosive therapy: A learning theory based on psychodynamic behavioral therapy. *Journal of Abnormal Psychology,* 1967, *72,* 496.

Wolpe, J. *Psychotherapy by reciprocal inhibition.* Palo Alto, California: Stanford University Press, 1958.

Winnicott, D. W. *Playing and reality.* New York: Basic Books, 1971.

Zinker, J. *Creative process in gestalt therapy.* New York: Brunner/Mazel, 1977.

Part I

THEORY AND PRACTICE

Chapter 2

THE CREATIVE ACT AS A MEANS OF OVERCOMING RESISTANCE IN TREATMENT*

Donna Bassin, M.P.S.**
Frances Lyshak, M.P.S.
Arthur Robbins, Ed.D.***

It is the intent of the authors to illuminate the relationship of the creative process to psychic healing and growth, and to describe its use as a method of ego integration. More specifically, we wish to describe the creative act as a means of overcoming resistance in treatment. As a part of this process, the relationship of primary and secondary thinking to metaphorical and imaginative productions will be expanded upon. Finally, we will describe some of the creative uses of a therapist's personal resources that can be mobilized to overcome crucial barriers in the patient-therapist dialogue.

As a specialist in symbolic communication, an expressive therapist requires a theory that relates both to the patient's

*In press, from the *Psychoanalytic Review,* through the courtesy of the editors, National Psychological Association for Psychoanalysis, N.Y., N.Y.

**All authors bear equal responsibility for this chapter and the names are placed in alphabetical order.

***This chapter as well as chapters 4, 5, 6, 8, 11, 17 and 18 have been edited by Naomi Frankel.

symbols in the treatment process and to the developmental meaning of these symbols. Dreams, fantasy, art, and play operate by condensation, displacement, and symbolization, which are the organizing modes of the primary process. These are the tools of the expressive therapist, functioning in the service of ego mastery or self expression.

Noy (1969, p. 169) proposes that during the first years of life condensation, displacement, and symbolization serve to organize experience towards the creation of self-nuclei, the basic components of the self. The primary process is associated with the normal development of the self. It is not an inferior process but an essential, life-giving force that remains with us throughout our entire existence. It acts as an organizing force for experiences about the self and as a source of nurturance to build and expand the self. His main thesis is that "primary processes are used by the ego for all functions aimed at preserving self-continuity and identity and assimilating any new experiences and lines of action into the self-schema. The secondary processes are used for all functions aimed at encountering reality and for any inner integration and mastery which is done in relation to reality" (p. 162). This assimilation enables the self not only to maintain its sameness but to change slowly in terms of reality and to provide the necessary background for the reality adjustment needed for any of the progressive developmental stages (pp. 174–175). Piaget (1969) describes the early symbolic play of childhood in a similar way. It is this area of activity that characterizes expressive therapy and consolidates its many forms in clinical practice: The child "needs a means of self-expression, that is, a system of signifiers constructed by him and capable of being bent to his wishes. Such is the system of symbols characteristic of symbolic play. These symbols are borrowed from imitation as instruments, but not used to accurately picture external reality. Rather, imitation serves as a means of evocation to achieve playful assimilation."

Primary process is viewed in this context as a thought process that not only develops and matures, but is also accessible to the conscious regulation of the ego. An individual's object relations and lack of ego development can serve either to keep primary process disassociated, as with fantasies and daydreams, or to integrate it through art, intuition, play, or other creative communication. With no self-awareness to regulate it, the unconscious contents remain egocentric and narcissistic. The use of expressive modalities is a framework for the enhancement of the self and integration, as well as a symbolic medium for communication. It can be a tool for communication by the patient as well as a vehicle for intervention by the therapist.

Moustakas (1974) states that resistance is "a way for the individual to maintain consistency of self in the light of external pressure. It is an effort by the individual to sustain the integrity of the self." Understanding resistance as a protective response to the impingement of reality, expressive analysis, as related to the primary process, accommodates to the self rather than intrudes. We conceptualize expressive therapy as having its main activity in the process of symbolic assimilation and having its main arena in the "potential space" (Winnicott, 1971) of the patient-therapist dyad. It is in this very redefinition of terms, with its underlying attitudinal ramifications, that we conceive a new way of handling resistance.

Resistance refers to everything in the words and actions of the patient that obstructs gaining access to what is not conscious (Laplanche & Pontalis, 1973). It functions to protect the ego through the manipulation and control of consciousness. In the therapeutic situation, it is ultimately the lack of contact that stands between the patient and psychological health. It is the patient's resistance to contact, in light of the therapist's comprehension of intrapsychic life, that undergoes transformation with the help of the treatment tools of psychotherapy.

Deep interpretation or reality confrontation can demolish defenses and drive a person to assume more pathological forms of self-protection. Paradoxically, a resistance may be joined for the express purpose of helping a patient give it up. "Joining" is distinguished by taking pressure off the ego, effected by focusing on the object or concentrating on external reality (Spotnitz, 1969). Resistance may also be the activities of the archaic nuclear self, which does not want to reexpose itself to the devastating narcissistic injury of finding one's basic mirroring and idealizing needs unmet. These resistances are motivated by disintegrating anxiety designed to preserve the self, as differentiated from the schizophrenic defense designed to protect the object. The "mirror" response enhances cohesion and produces a stage of understanding based on an accurate, sensitive recognition and communication of the patient's affect. However, in the face of characterological or acting-out defenses (Reich, 1972, and Masterson, 1976), the bulk of treatment is devoted to thawing out the frozen conflict between instinct and defense so that, in place of automatic ways of acting, a conflict is once again experienced (Fenichel, 1941, p. 40). "Confrontation" isolates the defensive maneuver for the inspection of the observing ego and, if it is ego-syntonic, makes it ego-dystonic. Finally, a resistance can be clarified in the transference by splitting the ego into a reasonable judging portion and an experiencing portion. This is done through using the positive transference and transitory identification with the therapist, which is available in the treatment of neurosis (Fenichel, 1941, p. 53).

How to interpret a resistance, by joining, mirroring, confrontation, or clarification, is determined by the transference relationship and level of ego development. In addition to these forms of intervention, the authors pose the creative act, which combines many qualities of these modes, as an additional intervention in response to resistance to change in therapy. By the creative act we mean communication that unifies one's personal existence, the integration of disparate elements and polarities, which defies and reorders one's personal assumptions accrued out of learned behavior.

The creative process as defined and elaborated by Wallas (1926), Patrick (1935, 1937, 1938), Vinacke (1952), and Osborn (1953) is conceptualized in a manner akin to the patient's experience of working through resistance. Initially perceptions and sensations are gathered and investigated. A period of incubation occurs until the psychic material emerges above the threshold of consciousness. This sudden illumination in the creative process and the "aha" of the therapeutic insight represent the climax of a process where energy is withdrawn from a restrictive barrier and added to the speed or intensity in which the new gestalt is formed.

Resistance or opposition from an object in the environment enables the self to know itself. The encounter with the object in the creative act provides a structure for the struggle for form. The analyst in the treatment relationship and concrete materials in the creation of art are the media by which energy can be converted into expression. Creativity and growth require both limitations and possibilities. Within this context we explore the nature and form of an encounter that can release the vitality in the therapeutic relationship. The manner of handling a resistance is determined by assessing the balance between each patient's personal reservoir of images and symbols, and the demands of reality that require secondary process thinking. Thus each patient-therapist dyad is viewed as an electrical-chemical field that has its own inner integrity. The creative therapeutic act is seen as a restructuring of this field so energy may flow between patient and therapist and thus allow for the nourishment of the patient's self. This process requires both a discovery of the affective energy that is associated with a particular patient's symbol formation and the production of the appropriate conductor for this flow of energized communication.

For some patients who are overcharged with unneutralized affective imagery, the therapist must lay back and not burden the patient with his or her own images. Paradoxically, the therapist must also transcend the limits of his or her own personal boundaries in order to resonate with the patient's primary self, enabling a bridge to be built towards secondary process communication. Such therapy requires that the therapist work on a multitude of levels in order to transform communication into the very orbit of the creative act.

The creative act, in the therapeutic encounter, can encompass a variety of psychic stimuli and responses. For instance, the metaphor is used to overcome the barriers of verbalization where direct confrontation would create more resistance. The visual image, which is the language of the primary process, can be created by the evocative use of words and can stimulate a process that Kris refers to as "a regression in the service of the ego." In Noy's schema, this regression is redefined as a shift from primary to secondary process (1937). This process appears to operate in love, creativity, and play. By playing with language, we can say something about ourselves while avoiding the pain of looking too frontally. One is reminded of Hammer's comment to a masochistic patient, "How nice to get a wound you can lick" (1968, p. 149).

The symbolic communications in expressive modalities have qualities distinctive to themselves that meet particular patient needs; that is, they are preverbal, affectively charged, spacious, and tangible. Kubie (1958) states that "thinking back verbally is a smoke-screen for that true remembering which is affectively charged reliving." The higher energy of the primary process symbol has powerful ramifications in the treatment of disorders where a defense against affect is the main block. Expressive modalities are both more threatening and have more impact if anxiety can be tolerated. Where verbal analytic work may fall flat and fail to develop an energetic engagement, symbols stimulate, having the advantage of density of affect. Hammer sees that "images have as their objective the production of an effect through multi-layered communication." The experience of such an intervention is "not in the nature of something inferred but something experienced . . . not merely cognitive but affective . . .. The thought and the affect merge in the symbol rather than staying apart" (1968, p. 150).

The psychic container in which the patient can experience the empathic understanding of the therapist can expand through the inherent ambiguity of the metaphoric statement. The outer defensive but protective image of the patient can be maintained until the inner image is strengthened and anchored by elaboration of reality testing, formulation, and synthesis. The limitations of unilinear language can deprive an individual of the uniqueness of his or her felt personal experience, while metaphor can provide for many planes of experience. The inspirations for a poet's work are often metaphors of intrapsychic conflict. The metaphor is in part defensive in that it binds diffuse anxiety, but at the same time it stimulates a discharge. It is an adaptive disguise in the form of a valued product, invoking new perceptions of experience.

Concretization, giving a substance and a name to fears and affects through the creation of a tangible image, is ego-building. The process of ego development is stimulated by inner and outer conflicts. The inevitable opposition to treatment can at times be displaced to the opposition of a hard piece of stone to be sculptured. One has to harness, mediate, and synthesize energies into something comprehensible and communicable. The symbol must be seen in order for it to be altered. The creative act, under the guidance of the therapist, can allow for a slow and tolerable energy release. The pace and rhythm of discharge can be varied by the art medium chosen. Potential chaos is solidified and provided with an organizing structure, which can be presented to the outer world.

Balint (1968) raises the problem of what the analyst is to do when issues concerning body representations and experiences based on sensory communications from preverbal relationships arise in treatment. The actual creation of a visual image allows the patient to hold and make real a nameless, formless experience in the same way a mother makes her infant real. This process can enable the patient to find and recall a memory unit or impulse that has no words.

At times it is important for the patient and analyst to mutually observe a third object. The patient's use of a concrete object to examine his or her self helps diminish the wish for and consequent fear of symbiosis, since the therapist is responding to the expressive act and not to the patient's mind. The product may be used to underline the patient's resistance when both parties of the therapeutic dyad have equal opportunity to inspect, respond, and relate to its meaning. Because the act is "art," it also has a limitation, a frame. There is an intrinsic permission in this format that invites free and unqualified responses within its borders, as opposed to acting out in the transference relationship. In all, the expressive modality functions as a safety valve because it is bound and inanimate; yet it is plastic and real and therefore a confrontation with reality.

Through the symbol created without conscious control, one can see what one cannot verbalize. Patients who function at an early primary process level often fuse self and object. Consequently, they do not have the verbal facility or secondary process to clarify what their problems are about. However, with the symbol, metaphor, or concrete object to play with, they can reach a part of themselves that could not be comprehended through words. A clinical example highlighting this point is that of a young, borderline woman who was struggling to define her feelings regarding her mother. Words were not forthcoming. When encouraged to draw a picture of herself, and then afterward her mother, her dilemma was clarified. Spontaneously she drew herself inside the body of her mother—and this act of creation became the first step of a long trip towards self and object differentiation.

The nonverbal quality of the interchange can have the ingredients of an early primary relationship. It solidifies the encounter by making minimal verbal demands, which is especially important in working with a depressive patient. Eventually the patient's symbol provides a mirror of his or her self-reality. According to Winnicott (1971), such a reverberation "brings the individual together as a unit, not as a defense, but as an expression of 'I am.' If the therapist's intervention is a reflection of the patient's self, then it becomes part of the organized individual personality, to be found and to postulate an existence on the self." It is the perception of such imagery, facilitated by the creative act, that is functional in therapy, rather than the use of deep interpretation.

Expression, speaking through the symbol, is facilitated and determined by inherent qualities of the creative process. What are the conditions that enhance this process and the use of creative metaphoric engagements? Of importance is the suspension of judgmental, moral attitudes of both parties. Secondly, a sense of play and illusion can be introduced, which encourages a switching back and forth of a variety of ego states within both members of the therapeutic dyad. Thirdly, there must be an unvarying respect for the patient's potential to surpass the limits of his or her defensive barriers and fears in order to encourage an underlying wish for growth.

The expressive analyst may, so to speak, lend his or her creative strengths to the patient in therapy. According to Beres (1957): "What the artist can do with his own creative genius, the analysand can accomplish only with the help of the analyst in the mutual communicative experience." The artist-as-therapist enters the field ideally with an agility and maturity in the areas of aesthetic response, "controlled illusion" and sublimation. Aesthetic distance and controlled illusion allow the therapist to let go of the past experience of the patient, or to hold it in suspension, in order to look at each moment with fresh perspective so that new gestalts based on mobile field independence can be created. Nietzsche wrote of treating oneself as a work of art, which is suggestive of this aspect of the expressive therapy interchange. Rosen (1964) says that the cognitive style of the artist "permits the handling of perceptual ambiguity from an optimal distance and with the necessary flexibility that is demanded by the process of controlled illusion" (p. 4). Controlled illusion is an "implied agreement on the part of both artist and audience to abandon the axioms of logic, particularly the exclusion of contradiction, and to treat the creative product as simultaneously fantastic and real" (p. 3). In superego functioning "the discrete cognitive interpretation of conventional mores and systems is exchanged for an ambiguous treatment of them" (p. 14). Ideally both the patient and the therapist can have an aesthetic response to what the other communicates— like finding oneself in a great work of art or a novel.

Fenichel (1945) spoke of sublimation in a way that is much in keeping with the capacity of the symbol to join and transform the resistance, thereby deferring it. He said that "the defense forces of the ego do not oppose the original impulse head on, as in the case of countercathexis, but impinge at an angle, producing a resultant, which unifies instinctual and defensive energy and is free to proceed." Such an interplay involves no countercathexis or resistance to the aims of the patient; rather, as in judo, one uses the opponent's thrust, changing its aim or objective without blocking an adequate discharge of energy (Watzlawick, 1974). First there must be a lifting of inhibition and then a symbolization of unbound energy before the process of assimilation can occur. Resistance in treatment may indicate that any of these steps have been bypassed.

According to Kris, the creative process includes a period in which there is a hypercathexis of preconscious activity with some quantity of energy withdrawn from the object world. However, if the resultant raw energy is too strong and the ego too weak, there is an estrangement of ego and drives. Pine (1959) states that: "An early developed need to defend against drive content in thought may spread to a generalized tendency to limit thinking; dynamically, anxiety over an encounter with drive material when thought is given free rein may underly unreceptivity to experience from within or without." If secondary process, such as intellectualization with the obsessive compulsive, functions as a defense against the emergence of the self, then expressive therapy, utilizing primary processes, bypasses the defense by this shift from the secondary mode to primary. If primary process functions as a defense against reality, as in psychosis, then secondary process, reality-oriented interventions, intensifies the stress on the ego and compounds the resistance. Expressive therapy, through the use of mental representations of the primary process, allows the gradual assimilation of reality to the self, speaking the patient's own preverbal language. As emphasis is shifted from objective reality to the experience of self, then the value of the primary processes is simultaneously elevated and a bridge can be made to repair the social feedback system.

The psychotic whose investment in the outside world becomes threatened organizes a narcissistic perceptual system to secure self-affirmation or self-actualization. By contrast, imagination may be used as a constructive force to maintain contact with the outside and facilitate a flow of energy from the inner world to the outside. In pathological disturbance, the primary process symbols remain hypercathected with libidinal energy as the individual relies on an autistic self-reinforcing system to ward off a very threatening outside world. The implications of this distinction have important meaning to therapists. Primary process can either be used to reinforce a pathological process or to aid and facilitate the development of the self that is based in and gets fed by reality.

In many instances, the therapist-patient relationship is relatively neutral or bland. In these instances there may be a lack of creative interchange between patient and therapist. According to Avstreih and Brown, expressive therapy "allows the expression of primitive affects, so often only experienced on a sensory level, to be experienced in symbolic form" and thereby "is instrumental in gaining a sense of ego mastery over them." By going through the creative process with the patient, the therapist encounters the energy the patient is trying to expunge as it is reexperienced in the expressive act. Thus the energy is experienced at first in the patient's body. Then the therapist engages and captures the psychic life of the patient and externalizes it through a deep sense of relatedness and empathy, not to be confused with a fusion based on countertransference. In this way the patient ultimately gets a second chance to have a dialogue with the introject. What occurs, therefore, in the therapeutic process is an induction of affects from patient to therapist. The latter, receptive to the induction, is neither rigidly encased by this induction nor out of control. The therapy room soon becomes alive with libidinal affects that both parties experience. Therapy occurs when the therapist gives the patient an opportunity to dialogue by this role induction.

Occasionally, the therapist may be too protective or frightened to really experience the patient's primary process. This inability may interfere with the process and fantasies that are stimulated during the therapeutic encounter. Ideally, the therapist should have a capacity to move towards a passive-receptive position, where images and feelings can literally inundate the therapist's ego. The sensitive integration of the therapist's affect, perception, and imagery, as well as the skill that lies within his or her secondary process, make therapeutic communication an integrated act that harnesses energies, unifies polarities, and enhances the patient's sense of being understood and respected. This is the very essence of therapeutic love.

Thus, we see that the symbol can function as the medium for objectification, which both binds and discharges primary drives in order that they can become available for the autonomous ego functions. However, the creative process of symbol-formation requires a dissociative function that cannot proceed without the patient-artist's ego strength or the auxiliary ego of the expressive therapist.

The artist-therapist working with people who are highly narcissistic can use art materials that reflect their inner world. Essentially the therapist can use the material to make a statement that says in so many words, "I know how you feel, I accept how you feel, and I will reflect how you feel." At the same time there can be a sense of irony that one has to play with when working with resistance; the bittersweet confrontation with reality, spiced with empathy and surprise, speaks on many levels. The expressive therapist who is "dead serious" is locked away from assertion in this primary process mode. The use of tongue-in-cheek humor involves an integration of primary process, which has the potential to bypass defenses and produce pleasure. The pleasure response produces an energy discharge that disrupts the defense economy and lifts the inhibition.

We have presented a definition of resistance as well as explored some of the dimensions of expressive therapy. In what direction do we take these concepts, in view of the real patient who stands before us? Our goal in treatment is toward the integration of the primary and secondary process. Ornstein (1972) provides evidence of these two functions in human anatomy based on neurological and physiological research, which indicates that there are different functions for the right and left brain hemispheres. The right hemisphere, more dominant with nonverbal, spatial material, the night part of the person, is very basic to the way we operate and function in life. To have as our goal in therapy the conversion of all material to secondary process thinking is to ignore the great importance of primary process life and its relationship to self-development and creative expression. It is up to the therapist to work with and relate to both cognitive modes of operation. We see spatially what we cannot say verbally and analytically. Before we can find words, we must perceive experiences that give substance to our words. As therapists, we go from self, which has to do with right hemisphere thinking, to the functions of ego mastery, which have to do with left hemisphere thinking, and hopefully we learn to integrate both.

In light of all the preceding, the primary responsibility for the unworkable resistance must be to a large extent shifted to the treatment modality and, for the maintenance of resistance, to the lack of personal resources of the therapist. The patient can be resisting expressive modalities due to a fear of loss of control, as in the case of an obsessive patient, or resisting verbal analysis when the intrusion of reality onto a most fragile self is intolerable, as in the case of a highly narcissistic patient. The therapist, too, might be resisting, using primary or secondary process interventions to protect his or herself from the patient who induces intolerable anxieties.

The expressive therapist's abilities and awareness highlight the nonverbal interchange. His or her role requires unusual strength and skill in the realm of the primary process and in the areas of humor, play, and spontaneity. Creativity uses energy in the service of the self. By and large, with patients, the question becomes one of how to develop the primary symbolism so it can be made available to the self for this function. Energy is locked in the character structure. Primitive energy is hard to release and puts a tremendous strain on the ego. The expressive therapist, by relating particularly to the self, creates a new energy field, which acts to unlock and enliven the distorted rhythms of tension and discharge, disassociation and reintegration. Hopefully, the expressive therapist will have a highly integrated primary and secondary process facility that is articulate as well as spontaneous.

Thus the therapist's creativity is called to task as he follows the patient's lead, shedding expectations and mobilizing his or her primary and secondary process thinking, which are no longer experienced as discrete and separate functions. Indeed, we soon discover our mutual craziness can contain the logic of self-survival, while reason can often harbor the seeds of madness. Without a clear synthesis of these two basic styles of being and perceiving, any real integration of self and reality is at best a spurious one. We as therapists are constantly challenged to unite these worlds into an ever expanding field of knowledge. By attempting the impossible, we join many artists who must take their grandiosity with a grain of salt.

We have described the artistic process of treatment in scientific terms. Hopefully, neither the artist nor scientist has been lost in the process, as we need all our skill and acumen to move self into reality and reality into a form of self-affirmation.

REFERENCES

Avstreih, A. & Brown, J. Some aspects of movement and art therapy as related to the analytic situation. Pending publication in *The Psychoanalytic Review.*

Balint, M. *The basic fault: Therapeutic aspects of regression.* London: Tavistock Publications, 1968.

Beres, D. Communication in psychoanalysis and in the creative process: A parallel. *Journal of Psychoanalysis,* 1957, *5,* 408–423.

Fenichel, O. *Psychoanalytic theory of neurosis.* New York: W. W. Norton & Co., 1945.

Fenichel, O. *Problems of psychoanalytic technique.* Albany, N.Y.: The Psychoanalytic Quarterly, Inc., 1941.

Hammer, E., Ed. *Use of interpretation in treatment.* New York: Grune & Stratton, 1968.

Kohut, H. *The restoration of the self.* New York: International Universities Press, 1977.

Kris, E. *Psychoanalytic explorations in art.* New York: Schocken Books, 1952.

Kubie, L. *Neurotic distortions of the creative process.* Kansas: University of Kansas Press, 1958.

Laplanche, J. & Pontalis, J. B. *The language of psychoanalysis.* London: Hogarth Press, 1973.

Masterson, J. F. *Psychology of the borderline adult.* New York: Brunner/Mazel, 1976.

Moustakas, C. E., Ed. *The self: Explorations in personal growth.* New York: Harper & Row, 1974.

Noy, P. A revision of the psychoanalytic theory of the primary process. *The International Journal of Psychoanalysis,* 1969, *50,* Pt. 2, 162, 165, 169, 174–175.

Ornstein, R. *The psychology of consciousness.* New York: Penguin Books, Inc., 1972.

Osborn, A. *Applied imagination.* New York: Scribner's, 1953.

Patrick, C. Creative thought in poets. *Archives of Psychology,* 1935, *26,* 1–74.

Patrick, C. Creative thought in artists. *Journal of Psychology,* 1937, No. 4, 35–73.

Patrick, C. Scientific thought. *Journal of Psychology,* 1938, No. 5, 55–83.

Piaget, J. & Inhelder, B. *The psychology of the child.* New York: Basic Books, Inc., 1969.

Pine, F. Thematic drive content and creativity. *Journal of Personality,* 1959, *27,* No. 2, 136–151.

Reich, W. *Character analysis.* New York: Simon & Schuster, 1972.

Rosen, V. Some effects of artistic talent on character style. *Psychoanalytic Quarterly,* 1964, *33,* 3, 4, 14.

Spotnitz, H. *Modern psychoanalysis of the schizophrenic patient.* New York: Grune & Stratton, 1969.

Vinacke, E. E. *The psychology of thinking.* New York: McGraw-Hill, 1952.

Wallas, G. *The art of thought.* New York: Harcourt Brace Jovanovich, 1926.

Watzlawick, P., Weakland, & Fisch. *Change: Principles of problem formation and problem solution.* New York: W. W. Norton & Co., Inc., 1974.

Winnicott, D. W. *Playing and reality.* New York: Basic Books, Inc., 1971.

Chapter 3

CREATIVE EXPLORATION OF COUNTERTRANSFERENCE EXPERIENCES

Marilyn LaMonica
Arthur Robbins

In relationships with people in our professional as well as our personal lives, there is a certain subtlety to understanding that occurs. This way of "knowing the other" takes many forms—sometimes bursting through as a blinding insight, sometimes emerging as a rumbling that takes days or weeks to come into awareness, sometimes arising in the form of images and associations—but the common thread of this understanding is that it is rarely arrived at by a logical, step-by-step, linear process of thinking about someone. Rather, these insights emerge as a result of the impact of the other person on us, as though we, as therapist or friend, act as a filter. To carry the analogy further, as a filter we are not an empty sieve, but filled with our own substance, and it is through this substance, specifically our emotions and thoughts, that the other is filtered and discovered.

A good therapeutic session is like a work of art. Two people touch one another on a multiplicity of levels, imbued with a force that makes the communication dynamic. As with a work of art, patient and therapist reach a level of understanding that goes beyond words. In this manner, the expressive therapist, whose investment is in the creative as well as the therapeutic process, attempts to mobilize all of his/her personal resources in the service of making therapy both an artistic and healing experience. To accomplish this, the expressive therapist calls upon the clinical experience of psychoanalysis, as well as the artist's sensitivity to poetry, literature, music, and art.

The purpose of this chapter is to explore the creative use of the countertransference experience. First, we will focus on an historical survey of the concept of countertransference as it appears in the literature. From this summary, we will attempt to arrive at a working definition of countertransference and its use in arriving at a fuller understanding of the patient.

Countertransference has captured the imagination of the psychoanalytic community. This growing interest is indicative of the shift in psychoanalytic thinking from the classical school's emphasis on libidinal drives and analysis of the content of the unconscious to the ego psychological school's emphasis on object relations, ego defenses and character analysis (Wolstein, 1959). As psychoanalytic theory has shifted, for some at least, so has its therapeutic technique. The therapist's use of self has evolved from one in which he/she acted as a "mirror" excluding him/her self as much as possible from the interaction, to one in which the analyst's personality and attributes have become central to the therapeutic process (Sandler, Holder, & Dare, 1970).

The concept of countertransference has come to be used in a general sense to describe the whole of the therapist's feelings and attitudes towards the patient. This general use of the term is very different from what was originally intended. As a consequence, confusion has arisen about its precise meaning (Sandler, et al. 1970). Countertransference, as first used by Freud, referred to that which arises in the therapist as a result of the patient's influence on his/her unconscious feelings. It was assumed that it was necessary for the therapist to recognize the countertransference and overcome it. Thus, countertransference was first seen as a manifestation of the therapist's neurotic conflicts and as an obstacle to the therapist's understanding of the patient.

Countertransference has, however, been progressively re-evaluated and redefined in ways that are strikingly similar to the transformations that occurred in the psychoanalytic understanding of transference. Transference was initially viewed by Freud as an obstacle to uncovering the repressed unconscious. He initially considered it a disadvantage and an impediment. Later, he suggested that every conflict of the patient must be fought out in the transference situation (Greenson, 1967). With the emphasis on the ego and its defenses, transference came to be seen as an important vehicle of therapeutic investigation. A similar shift is currently taking place in the view of counter-transference.

Baum (1969–70) describes the rift in psychoanalysis as it concerns the concept of countertransference. The classical analytic school is represented by the work of such authors as Fleiss, Glover, and Reich. This group views countertransference, in the purist sense, as the analyst's transference to the patient based on the analyst's own past. This school of thought regards countertransference as a distortion, as unconscious, and as a resistance to the work of therapy.

In contrast, theorists such as Heimann, Racker, Searles, and Kernberg hold to a broader, all-encompassing definition of countertransference as the total emotional reaction of the therapist to the patient. According to these authors, countertransference includes the therapist's "conscious and unconscious reactions to the patient's reality as well as his transference." According to Kernberg (1965), this definition implies that the emotional reactions of the therapist to the patient are fused, and that, although countertransference must be reckoned with, it is useful in gaining more understanding of the patient.

Kernberg further adds that this totalistic concept "does justice to the conception of the analytic situation as an interaction process in which past and present of both participants, as well as their mutual reactions to their past and present, fuse into a unique emotional position involving both of them."

Most of those theorists who hold to the classical position, account for nonresistive emotional reactions to the patient through such concepts as empathy, transient trial identifications, and intuition. But their unwillingness to group all such processes under the concept of countertransference is more than semantic fastidiousness. As Baum (1969–70) points out, these therapists are concerned with analyzing libidinal strivings and working in alliance with an already developed ego, with the role of the therapist as a neutral screen onto which the patient can project fantasies, which will then be interpreted.

Many of those who hold to the totalistic concept of countertransference are therapists who tend to work psychoanalytically with more disturbed patients. Roland (1977) suggests that in working with such patients issues of the self and of early internalization processes predominate and, consequently, there are far greater frequency and intensity of the therapist's emotional reactions and attitudes. Baum (1969–70) also points out that "where there is more regression, fuzzier ego boundaries, more denial and projection ... the analyst's psyche is bombarded more intensely so that more regressive influences are also exerted on him, and therefore more intense transference and countertransference responses occur." These analysts have developed a revised theoretical framework to take into account their emotional experiences in relation to these patients.

In summary, we see two schools of thought regarding the place of countertransference reactions within a psychoanalytic model. Essentially, the classical approach views countertransference as an obstacle that interferes with the therapist's effectiveness. The latter group, described here as the totalistic school, views countertransference as a vehicle that can facilitate understanding the patient's dynamics.

Kernberg (1965) presents a survey of the literature on the topic of countertransference as well as a thorough treatment and defense of countertransference viewed as the total emotional reaction of the therapist to the patient. As he describes it, the totalistic school of thought believes that the analyst's conscious and unconscious reactions to the patient in the treatment situation are reactions to the patient's reality and transference, as well as to the analyst's own realistic and neurotic needs. "Further, this approach uses a broader definition of countertransference and advocates a more active technical use of it."

Kernberg makes distinctions between reality-based reactions, neurotic reactions, and characterological reactions on the part of the therapist. Within all three of these categories, he makes use of the notion of induced countertransference reactions, although he does not use the precise term.

Kernberg's view of characterological reactions is particularly interesting in that he takes exception to the idea that these reactions can only be considered obstacles to therapeutic understanding. "Even countertransference reactions which reflect predominantely unresolved character problems of the therapist are intimately connected with the analytic interaction with the patient." Kernberg recommends exploring the specific way in which the patient provokes a reaction in the therapist in order for the therapist to better understand the patient's unconscious behavior.

Kernberg further makes a distinction between unconscious and conscious reactions on the part of the therapist. Often, he points out, the problem is not discovering reactions that are repressed, but rather dealing with very strong emotional reactions that the therapist experiences and that influence treatment. The implication is that the therapist may come to an understanding of the function of his/her countertransference reaction, as it is relevant to the ongoing treatment, without understanding the roots of this reaction in his/her past.

The crux of Kernberg's attitude toward countertransference is that all emotional reactions of the therapist are grist for the mill of observing and analyzing the special interlocking of patient and therapist. Emphasis is placed on discovering through this process important diagnostic information, specifically, "the degree of regression of the patient and the predominant emotional position of the patient toward the therapist and the changes occurring in this position."

In an attempt to explain the process by which a therapist becomes affected by the patient's unconscious, Kernberg turns to the concept of identification, particularly, projective identification. Especially in working with borderline and severely regressed patients, the therapist experiences "intensive emotional reactions having more to do with the patient's premature intense and chaotic transference, and with the therapist's capacity to withstand psychological stress and anxiety, than with any particular, specific problem of the therapist's past."

Through the process of projective identification, the therapist becomes involved in a process of "empathetic regression in order to continue his emotional contact with the patient." Projective identification, as defined by Kernberg, is a precursor to, or earlier defensive operation than, projection. Included in this defensive process, is a lack of differentiation between the self and the object, which makes for a chaotic fusion.

What all of this means in terms of countertransference is that the therapist's own early identifications may become reactivated as he/she is inundated by the patient's primitive projections. Kernberg goes on to describe the dangers that the therapist is now open to experiencing: (1) the reemergence of anxiety connected with the early impulses, which may be directed at the patient; (2) a loss of ego boundaries in relation to that patient; and (3) the urge to control his patient who may now represent an early object of the therapist's past. Even under these circumstances, when the possibility is so strong that the therapist's actual intervention with the patient may become contaminated, Kernberg feels that the emotional experience of the therapist *can* be useful, because it may indicate the kind of fear the patient is undergoing and the fantasies connected with it.

Preceding Kernberg's work chronologically, is Racker's

contribution to the theory of countertransference. Of particular interest is his understanding of the dynamic interplay between therapist and patient, which he defines as concordant and complimentary identifications.

Relying heavily on the influence of the English school, with its emphasis on early internalization processes and self and object representations, Racker evolved a theory for understanding the process by which a therapist's thoughts and feelings were affected by his patient. Hunt and Issacharoff (1977) state that Racker's central thesis is that "there is no 'normal' emotional state for the therapist, but that the therapist's inner state is continuously, profoundly, and in certain precise and defineable ways, responsive to the patient. . . . " Racker (1957) classifies the therapist's responses into two categories—concordant and complimentary identifications. The concordant identifications are equivalent to empathetic identifications.

Racker's unique contribution is his concept of complementary identifications, which "are produced by the fact that the patient treats the analyst as an internal (projected) object, and in consequence the analyst . . . identifies himself with this object." Racker goes on further to state that "every transference situation provokes a countertransference situation, which arises out of the analyst's identification of himself with the analysand's (internal) objects." Racker suggests that these countertransference situations may be repressed or emotionally blocked, but "should not be avoided if full understanding is to be achieved."

Moeller (1977) adds to the understanding of countertransference reactions by taking them out of the sphere of normal vs. neurotic, and reactive vs. general, and placing them in a self and object representation paradigm. In agreement with Racker, he views countertransference as having two dimensions. In the first, we perceive our patients' actualized self-representation described by the formula: "I feel (myself) what the patient is like, or I feel as the patient does." In the second, we perceive our patients' actualized object representations described in the formula "I feel (myself) what the patient is making out of me, or I feel as the father (mother) of the patient felt." What Moeller is describing here is, of course, directly analogous to Racker's concepts of concordant and complementary identifications. Moeller's unique contribution to understanding this process is his concept of the relationship-representation, which is experienced by the therapist in the countertransference.

According to Moeller, self and object occur in the patient's intrapsychic experience "in a specific, meaningful relationship, e.g., a helpless, angry, infantile self with a powerful, threatening object." What is experienced then in the countertransference is "an actualized, early object representation with the relevant infantile self-representation in a specific, conflict-laden relationship . . . This relationship is communicated as a whole to the analyst. He can feel the tensions and conflicts of this relationship between subject and object in himself, and must be in a position to grasp this interaction and to conceptualize it in his working model." He further adds that the psychical material of the countertransference and the transference is primarily the relationship between self and object.

Because these self-object relationships have their origins in a preverbal stage of development, and because what must be experienced and then conceptualized by the therapist is itself a process, an expressive therapy technique to explore the countertransference-transference interlocking can be especially valuable. The experience of one of the authors with a 20-year-old female patient will be described to illustrate this point:

> Maria came into treatment because she was depressed, and as a result, had dropped out of college and quit her part-time job. She attributed her depression to a peculiar obsessive symptom: she had persistent thoughts of David Berkowitz (the Son of Sam mass-murderer) whenever she was in the company of her boyfriend, which interfered with her relationship with him and her ability to concentrate. An adopted child, she lived with her parents and maintained "special child" status within her family. In her first session, she presented her symptoms, history and

problems in an intellectualized and isolated manner. Her language was stilted and her thoughts compartmentalized. In that first session, I sensed that Maria was presenting herself as a jigsaw puzzle, and subtly, but demandingly, challenging me to put the pieces into place. The playfulness of this puzzle image belied the seriousness and unrealistic, infantile quality of the demand being placed on me.

Maria's sessions took on a distinctive pattern. In one, she was productive and talked freely; in the next, she was constrained and inarticulate. These sessions left me feeling frustrated and incompetent. The productive sessions left me feeling blissful and gratified. My struggle to understand the significance of Maria's two alternating modes of relating and the intensity of my emotional reaction to her, led me to work on a piece of pottery to represent her.

What evolved was a large platter with bottle necks symbolizing her compartmentalization. In considering the shape, glaze and texture I would choose to depict this young woman, I began to think of the round shape as representing her ego, and suddenly it occurred to me to rip open the form and place a menacing monster in the crevice. It was only after I decided to violently destroy the perfect circular shape that I realized the intensity of my anger. My rage went far beyond what I usually experienced in response to a withholding patient, accounting for my need to defend against it, and I began to seek out clues in Maria's symptoms and dynamics that would explain this reaction.

Gradually I perceived that I had partially identified with Maria's early self-representation of a frustrated, alienated child who experienced her anger as frightening and monstrous. Through the transference, Maria was playing out an early object-representation of a mother who oscillated in her inconsistencies, alternatively withholding and giving, disconnecting and connecting, and presenting a frustrating image of relatedness. Through the countertransference, I defended against, but then gradually made contact with her primitive rage; and Maria, as a child, with her undeveloped ego, had had to split off these affects, which then were never integrated into her self experience. At this point, both therapist and patient were fully engaged in the early family drama.

This is an example, in Racker's framework, of the therapist's concordant identification with the patient's early self-representation. Thus, an understanding of the counter-transference aided in unraveling and understanding the transference, which had come to interfere with the progress of treatment.

We have thus far arrived at a working definition of countertransference as including all the therapist's emotional reactions to the patient. We also have concluded that these reactions yield valuable information about the patient's transference, and with Racker's theoretical formulation of self-object representations in mind, have arrived at a dynamic understanding of how these reactions are induced in the therapist.

A method we have used to discover unconscious reactions to a patient as well as clarify conscious reactions, is to create an artistic representation of the patient. First we start with a conceptualized idea, some way of representing the patient. As the work proceeds there are usually many changes in the art piece that were not originally intended. These changes are not accidental, but rather indicative of something about the patient's reality or transference, about the therapist, and/or the relationship. The work of teasing apart these factors takes place during the contemplative time of actually creating the piece. The very process of creating provides a relaxed, almost meditative atmosphere during which free associations are possible. Thus what is experienced is a subtle interplay of the art process, the art product, and a free associational response to the patient in absentia. There is a subtle oscillation between experiencing and observing ego states where the spatial and intuitive become interwoven with the logical and linear part of the therapist.

The art product becomes the vehicle that integrates a number of different processes so that transference and countertransference meet. The synthetic function of the therapist's ego can then put together alternating ego states and a multiplicity of psychic levels. By way of the creative act, the merger of primary and secondary process thinking facilitates an understanding of the transference-countertransference interlocking and lends a rich dimension to the therapeutic process.

Implicit in the expressive therapy process is that creative productions express preconscious and unconscious material. Often the creative process reveals that which is hidden by offering a vehicle to externalize the inexpressible. In the context of discussing the irrational aspect of human experience, Robbins and Sibley (1976) point out that "artistic creation gives the individual the opportunity to harness the energies and images into a concrete manifestation."

What we are proposing is an approach rather than a technique. Techniques will follow, but more importantly, there is a particular way of approaching the treatment process that facilitates an accessibility to imagery, fantasies, and early parent-child dyads. The therapist's emotional posture is one of passive receptivity. He/she does not resist stimuli either from his own unconscious processes or from his patient, and does not attempt to put things in order, or work on a logical, linear level. There is a concentration of energy in this relationship so that nothing outside of it seems to exist, yet there is an awareness of another self that is observing this process.

When the therapist is fully enmeshed in this state, he/she becomes aware of early sensory tactile impressions. In effect, this approach opens the door to a preverbal world that was experienced through images and sensations rather than any direct verbal communications. The therapist can more easily discover this door through employing an expressive modality that gives a frame to this amorphous process. This modality may be art, but it may also be poetry, fables, songs, or movement.

The process of creating a wheel-thrown clay sculpture, made to represent a depressed hospitalized patient, and its potential for uncovering transference-countertransference dynamics is described by one of the authors in the following vignette.

> I originally conceived the sculpture to represent a split in this patient between a well-controlled, soft-spoken part that she pre-

sented to the world, and a raging, fearful part that emerged during her psychotic episodes. It is a vessel and the head and neck form a stopper. I intended to glaze the piece, but then grew fond of the texture of the clay, and decided against it.

It was not until the sculpture was finished that I realized that even though I had made a vessel, it was incapable of holding water because it was unglazed. Any liquid poured into it would gradually ooze out. This led me to realize my feelings of hopelessness about this patient which were dissociated from awareness.

My associations to the porous vessel were that no amount of feeding could fill up the patient's child-self. Her impact on me had churned up my own unsatisfied dependency needs which I experienced as a bottomless pit, and therefore had to defend against. With this perception, a slow disengagement emerged between my own rageful, hungry child self-representation and that of the patient.

Through the art, the creative act of viewing the multiplicity of levels that can evolve in therapy was clarified. The transference-countertransference was perceived, clarified, and disentangled. The creative process on the one hand creates distance via externalization. Subsequently the therapist's defensiveness is lowered and a greater capacity to understand the relationship results.

The creative act illustrates the paradoxical nature of bringing polarities into play. At one and the same time the therapist takes distance from the therapeutic entanglement and by the very nature of this externalization becomes more emotionally related to the true nature of the transference-countertransference relationship.

The expressive technique, be it through dance, music, or art, gives both parties an opportunity to meet each other through imagery play. The participants are then able to have a far more resonant, nonverbal interchange, where a structure is afforded for neutralization of energy through symbolic experience. Concurrently, the quality of the mother-child dyad becomes reexperienced through this same nonverbal dialogue.

And in this resonance, both parties rediscover the texture of an early preverbal relationship that has no words but only archaic symbols that lend definition to a felt experience.

If we are to recapture this very early process where the essence of self and object are formed through sensory impressions and affect states, we must utilize a process within ourselves as therapists that is receptive and available to this early primary experience. The creative process taps the resource of our early internalizations and, within the context of this paper, makes a bridge between the dyad of the therapist's mother-child with that of the patient's.

Further clinical illustrations will now be offered to highlight the various nuances of the use of the creative process within the countertransference-transference relationship. As seen in the following example by one of the authors, the therapist does not necessarily have to become involved with his own creative productions in order to become more in tune with the induced countertransference. Often it is the patient's artwork that facilitates a greater receptivity to the countertransference.

> A 26-year-old male patient, whose idealization of the transference hides an underlying hostility, came into my office raging at himself and his inadequacy at being unable to pass an exam. He drew the exam and went through crossing out line after line. This exam paper soon became an externalization of the patient's bad self. As the patient released the hostility toward the exam (and his bad self), he also started to direct his anger at me for my lack of sensitivity and understanding of his pain. His pain, however, was full of maudlin self-pity. Previous to this I was basking in the patient's projective identification of being the omnipotent ideal. Now for the first time, I was able to experience the patient's negative introject. Feelings of contempt and cold removal came into my awareness. Far from being sympathetic, there was an uncomfortable feeling of scorn felt towards the patient as he seemed to wallow in his plight.
>
> Gradually the patient's father entered into the therapeutic relationship through this induction: an insensitive, cut-off man, unrelated and scornful of his son. The patient and I were no

longer on the rational level of verbal dialogue. We had found a
transitional space where a more profound reexperiencing of the
transference-countertransference could proceed.

This transitional space came through some form of externalization process. Now, however, the externalization was initiated by the patient, which served to facilitate a greater
relatedness on the part of the therapist to the patient's internal
self and object representations.

The brief clinical example suggests that there is more than
just empathetic resonance that is required for a good therapeutic experience. The relationship must be charged with the energy coming from the therapist's own past, which can either
ignite, underscore, or discover an appropriate responsiveness
that fits with the patient's role induction.

Parenthetically, if the cumulative energy is too charged via
the transference-countertranference, therapy can become explosive and difficult to manage. On the other hand, when the
transference-countertransference is devoid of libidinal and aggressive energy, treatment evolves into a flat and sterile affair.

In summary, we have attempted to demonstrate the subtle
and complex interrelationships of the verbal and nonverbal
medium that inevitably highlight the transference-countertransference relationship. Countertransference reactions are often the vital diagnostic tools that are keys to facilitating the
treatment process. Based on the inductions and images that are
stimulated in treatment, a therapeutic decision can be made as
to a particular stance or intervention. Without this material, we
believe that the raw guts of the treatment process are missing.
Thus, as an artist and a clinician, the expressive therapist moves
from one psychic level to another. At one and the same moment, he/she is with the patient, experiences the early preverbal
introjects and object representations and still has sufficient ego
organization so that he/she is neither captured nor fused by his
identifications but indeed finds knowledge, insight, and some
answers that will move the therapeutic dialogue forward.

REFERENCES

Baum, O. E. Countertransference. *Psychoanalytic Quarterly,* 1969–1970, 621–637.

Fleiss, R. Countertransference and counteridentification. *Journal of American Psychoanalytic Association,* 1953, 268–284.

Freud, S. The future prospects of psychoanalytic psychotherapy, in *Standard edition,* Vol. 11, 1910. London: Hogarth Press, 1962.

Freud, S. The dynamics of transference, in *Standard edition,* Vol. 12, 1912. London: Hogarth Press, 1962.

Freud, S. *Collected papers,* Vol. 1. London: Hogarth Press, 1953.

Glover, E. *The technique of psychoanalysis.* New York: International Universities Press, 1955.

Greenson, R. *The technique and practice of psychoanalysis.* New York: International Universities Press, 1967.

Heimann, P. On countertransference. *International Journal of Psychoanalysis,* 1950, *31,* 81–84.

Hunt & Issacharoff. Heinrich Racker and countertransference theory. *Journal of American Academy of Psychoanalysis,* 1977, *5*(1), 95–105.

Kernberg, O. Notes on countertransference. *Journal of American Psychoanalytic Association,* 1965, *13.*

Moeller, M. L. Self and object in countertransference. *International Journal of Psychoanalysis,* 1977, *58,* 365–374.

Racker, H. The meaning and uses of countertransference. *Psychoanalytic Quarterly,* 1957, *26,* 303–357.

Reich, A. *Annie Reich: Psychoanalytic contributions.* New York: International Universities Press, 1973.

Robbins, A. & Sibley, L. *Creative art therapy.* New York: Brunner/Mazel, 1976.

Roland, A. *Induced emotional reactions and attitudes as transference in actuality.* Unpublished manuscript, 1977.

Sandler, J., Holder, A., & Dare, C. Basic psychoanalytic concepts: IV. Countertransference. *British Journal of Psychiatry,* July 1970, *117,* 83–88.

Searles, H. *Collected papers in schizophrenia and other related subjects.* New York: International Universities Press, 1968.

Wolstein, B. *Countertransference.* New York: Grune & Stratton, 1959.

Chapter 4

OBJECT RELATIONS AND EXPRESSIVE SYMBOLISM
Some Structures and Functions of Expressive Therapy*

Michael Eigen
Arthur Robbins

In human life, object[1] relationships are as ubiquitous and necessary to psychological birth and growth as air is for breathing.
This seems a truism, yet it is only fairly recently in human
history, even on the late side in the evolution of psychoanalysis,
that the effects of object relations on the development of the
human self have been brought into focus for systematic study.
On the other hand, the history of art is nothing if not the study
of relations between objects. It charts, in part, the adventures
of expressive awareness, the changing colors and forms of the
human self as it creates and is created by worlds within worlds.
The impact of art and therapy on one another is in its infancy.
Each involves powerful forces concerned with what is most

*Dr. Eigen is responsible for the first three sections; Dr. Robbins, for the
final section.
[1]The term "object" is a carryover from philosophy. Psychoanalysts usually mean by it the subject's experience of "otherness," the psychological
other.

alive in the feeling life of our times. To bring these forces within the same discipline inevitably opens an uncharted field for exploration in both directions, expressive work and healing. In this chapter, we will try to discern some possible implications of their coupling, if only tentatively.

An exhaustive account of psychological-psychoanalytic object relations theory is beyond the scope of the present work. However, the first section offers an orienting sketch, some background for the study that follows. The second section presents major criticisms of typical starting points for object relations theory and tries to clear the way for a sound and healthy view of early development. The third section explores core meanings of symbolic expression in terms of object relations and vice versa. The final section studies expressive action and object relations in such therapeutic processes as "reliving," "working through," and "new beginnings."

OBJECT RELATIONS THEORY: A BROAD OVERVIEW

In recent years psychoanalysis has been struggling to evolve an object relations viewpoint or, at least, to acknowledge this viewpoint as part of its basic theoretical-clinical concerns. In fact an object relations perspective has always been an intrinsic part of psychoanalysis, although the latter's style of thinking and talking about objects has undergone (and continues to undergo) quantum leaps (e.g., Guntrip, 1971; Grotstein, 1978a, 1978b; Meltzer, 1978; Stolorow & Atwood, 1978; Eigen, 1980a, 1980b).

In Freud's formal theory, objects or fantasies of objects most basically subserve the personality's drive reduction or, more generally, drive regulation needs. However, Freud's more informal clinical examples abound in richly varied self and object dramas. He often links symptom formation with the ego's sensitivity to emotional injury, particularly slights and failings (real or imaginary) by others. Words, deeds, or gestures, he suggested, may be experienced as a "slap in the face" or "stab in the heart" (Breuer & Freud, 1893–1895, p. 181); felt wounds, which tempt the ego to hide and reroute its reactive feelings, a pattern that feeds the vicious spiral of character deformations and symptoms. Again, he often stresses the ego-supportive and, especially, the inspiring-stimulating (ego ideal) aspects of others (e.g., Eigen, 1979c). Even so, the overall thrust of his writings does tend to relate others to their anxiety producing-reducing dimensions, particularly with reference to unconscious drive-oriented desires.

Melanie Klein (Klein, 1948; Segal, 1964; Meltzer, 1978; and Eigen, 1974) more systematically focused on the ego's dramas with objects, especially inner objects. She described in great detail possible ways the ego splits itself and its objects, and the ways the ego projects out or takes in bits and pieces of itself and others, and variously combines aspects of self and others in complex defensive patterns. She particularly stressed the ubiquitous importance of unconscious fantasy, a subjective world, in an important part, fueled by the ego's seemingly limitless capacity to create and mix inner-outer identifications. Such considerations make it possible to chart, for example, some ego aspect's identification with an internal object, itself possibly identified with another object (or ego aspect). One's internal divisions and cross identifications can complexly multiply. A quote from Grotstein (1978c, p. 56) conveys some flavor of this proliferating internal world.

> We can envision narcissism . . . as an inner galactic condition in which orbiting caretaking objects are constellating around a nuclear self which contains identificatory (internal) objects . . . Object love, on the other hand, could be pictured as the reverse, i.e., self representation(s) orbiting around the object . . . In all probability it is more complicated. It requires a dimensional concept beyond the third to contemplate the simultaneity of the self with its orbiting objects itself orbiting around the object, where the object thus has two separate relationships to the self, stationary and orbiting.

Klein was especially concerned with the early ego's fantasies about the insides of mother's body. She traced the baby's possible preoccupations with the rivals, goods or spoiled-spoiling elements it might put or find there (or which might get put into it). Of special importance in the present context is the detoxifying function the fantasy mother's insides must perform. For example, if the infant evacuates painful "shit" feelings into mother's "toilet" breast, the latter ideally must find a way to convert them into pleasurable "milk" feelings, which the baby can usefully take in. If the breast fails in its reprocessing function, the infant is left in the position of having to take in what he is trying to get rid of. In such a state of affairs the infant's own self-feeling is in danger of becoming spoiled or poisoned. Bion (1977) has generalized the transforming function of the breast in his container-contained model. Almost any psychological function within or between personalities can act as container or contained for any other one (see also Grotstein, 1979).

Klein assumes that some modicum of reality perception must begin very early in infancy if the infant's fantasy life is to have material to assimilate and build on. The unconscious baby-mind in all of us continues throughout our lifetime to make use of reality perceptions-cognitions as raw material for hidden symbolic processes, which refer, in the first instance, to our own and mother's bodies. The symbolic world elucidated by Klein is as narrow as it is important. She is, in essence, a specialist in unconscious fantasies revolving around mother envy, especially envy (with consequent fear-guilt-reparation dramas) of mother's power, whether creative or merely physical.

Fairbairn (1954) utilized the inroads Klein made into the territory of ego/object splitting but attempted to move beyond her epistemological flaws. He saw the fallacy involved in starting an account of ego-object development with part-object perception. Klein's uncritical thinking on this point is a throwback to the "sensationalist" error: one cannot derive "wholes" from "parts" anymore than a summation of sensations leads to ideas. The reverse seems more structurally sound: the differentiation of parts requires some sense of the whole. Therefore, argued Fairbairn, the baby's primary object is the mother, not simply the breast. The ego seeks emotional contact or connectedness with the other, not merely food or drive reduction. Addiction to tension reduction as a way of life may result, insofar as the primary need for emotional relatedness meets with failure. The subject may then resort to the use of part-objects (e.g., breast or penis, the other as body) to reduce tension as a substitute for fuller self-object contact. From this vantage point, Freudian-Kleinian part-object tension-reduction mechanisms outline a defensive mode of being. They tend to depict desperate measures a degraded self will resort to in order to maintain some sense of cohesion.

Even the part-objects described by Fairbairn refer to psychological rather than physical qualities of mother. For example, he suggests that the exciting and rejecting aspects of mother may provoke unmanageable anxiety, which the baby tries to master by complex ego-object splitting and internalization processes. In brief, split off aspects of the self become addicted to internal models of mother's exciting-rejecting aspects, which are projectively played out in future relationships (for details see Fairbairn, 1954; Guntrip, 1969; Eigen, 1973). The personality's primary, undefensive drive toward wholeness persists and the goal of therapy is to help heal splits.

Some aspects of Winnicott's contributions were described in an earlier chapter (Robbins, Chapter 1). Here we wish to emphasize the double directionality of Winnicott's descriptions of transitional experience, a theme that will be built upon later. For Winnicott (1971, Chapter 1), the transitional object carries the meaning of that which is and yet is not the other, and that which is and is not self. It, like the other, mirrors the self and, like the self, mirrors the other, yet cannot be reduced to either.

Winnicott associates the inherent ambiguity of transitional space with creativity. For Winnicott, creativity characterizes healthy development and pathology is creativity gone wrong. He thus situates creative action at the heart of human development. This, strictly speaking, sharply contrasts with Freud's view of creativity as a special capacity reserved for the very few ("sublimation"). For Freud, normal development unfolds via tension-reduction mechanisms. The contradiction that emerges is at the core of the long-standing split between psychoanalytic theory and practice. The practical psychoanalyst soon learns that he is caught between a theory that excludes creativity for most people and the need to heal, which involves addressing oneself to the creativity at the heart of every person. Winnicott attempts to heal the gap between theory and practice by locating the phenomenon of creativity at the center of both. It is, in part, the increasingly felt need to give creativity in everyday life its due that has motivated successive revisions in both theory and practice.

Bion's (1977) work is at present the most detailed attempt to study the vicissitudes of creative thinking in the analytic situation. He utilizes but goes beyond Klein's discoveries in trying to apprehend the modes of experiencing which permit or block creative personal development. In particular, he moves toward a rigorous psychoanalytic phenomenology of attention, an open-ended state of mind which permits evolution of thoughts and feelings. He pays special attention to the kinds of thought processes that pervert the attentional capacity and interfere with genuine psychic movement.

Bion attempts to rectify critical epistemological flaws in Freud and Klein by assuming that part-object/whole-object perception and primary process/secondary process thinking arise together and require each other. When functioning properly the human personality utilizes part-object/whole-object perception and primary process/secondary process thinking to create and undergo meaningful experiences. In pathology the subject's drive to utilize all of his resources in the creation of meaning is subverted. One becomes dedicated, instead, to variously attacking or dismantling one's meaning, creating capacity and putting true possibility out of play.

Bion believes that the drive to meaningful emotional

knowledge, the need to know the truth about oneself and others, is as primary a motivating force as love or hate. Freud and Klein, to be sure, placed great store on the wish to know (Klein's "epistemophilic instinct") but in their formal theories knowing (learning, the creation of meaning) played a basically defensive role, a problem that furthered the gap between theory and practice. In Bion's view, psychic life requires truth linked with felt meaning for its development, as much as well-dosed emotional factors such as love and frustration. Bion moves forward in healing the gap between thinking-feeling (theory-practice) by viewing the thirst for truth as a principle of emotional growth, not merely a derivative or superordinate function.

Kohut (1971, 1977) grounds creativity in an original empathic oneness of self and other, which undergoes maturation. He links the development of an adequate sense of self to successful mirroring and idealizing processes. He, for example, points to the "gleam in the mother's eye" as opposed to the emptiness that follows when such empathic responsiveness is missing. In this process, syntonic otherness adds to and actually becomes part of a cohesive self-feeling. The mother's expressive gestures, particularly facial and vocal, coupled with the quality of her touch and more obvious action patterns, may enrich or wound the infant's emerging self-feeling. Kohut coins the term *self-object* in order to express the depths of this self-other interweaving (at its best, Balint's, 1968, "harmonious interpenetrating mix-up").

Kohut's forte is in describing narcissistic transference states, which involve mirroring and idealizing processes supposedly related to early developmental phases. He emphasizes the importance of allowing the patient (and therapist) to tolerate the tension of idealized self ("grandiose self") and object experiences ("I am god-you are god), with all its oscillations and mixtures. He feels that the sense of vitality and expansiveness generated in such states frequently leads, as development proceeds, to creative work. Once in contact with this realm, the subject potentially has available a seemingly limitless source of inspiration.

A SEARCH FOR A STARTING POINT: THE BASIC NATURE OF THE SELF

When describing the early self, psychoanalysts tend to swing back and forth between emphasizing an early autism, merger, or simply lack of differentiation between self and object. Mahler (1968), for example, believes the early self arises with no sense of otherness ("autism") and moves to a state of fusion with the other who was not yet here ("symbiosis"), in effect postulating a merger of beings who do not yet psychologically exist. Winnicott (1971, Chapter 1) also begins his account with "primary omnipotence" (also, "absolute dependence") before passing to his structurally more viable transitional phase (Eigen, 1979a, 1979d). At some point prior to transitional experience, the baby seems a kind of God creator for whom "otherness" is an irrelevant or unaskable question.

In most psychoanalytic authors, some notion of original "undifferentiation" or "omnipotence" commingle. These and similar concepts are rooted in (or in reaction to) Freud's view of the early self as a self-contained pleasure ego, a kind of "egg" or "psychical system shut off from the stimuli of the external world . . . able to satisfy its nutritional requirements autistically." (Freud, 1911, p. 219). Freud theorized that knowledge of the external world is coincident with hatred of it: "Hate as a relation to objects is older than love" (Freud, 1915, p. 139). "Others" are either experienced as part of the self or as painful stimuli. If it were up to this infantile ego, there would be no otherness at all.

It has become increasingly clear that Freud's epistemological premises are doubtful, and there is much experimental evidence that points in another direction (viz., Peterfreund, 1978; Grotstein, 1978a, 1978b; Eigen, 1979a, 1979b). There is no substantial evidence that early object perception is necessarily hate-motivated or that awareness of self and other may arise independently of each other. Logically and experientially awareness of self and other are conditions for one another; each makes the other possible. In reality, pure cases of fusion or self-sufficiency do not present themselves. One finds various amalgams with characteristic emphases. Pure union and distinction are abstract concepts that do not characterize living experience. Since in reality there are always varying degrees and qualities of separation and union, there is no reason to conceptualize the original self in terms of one pole without the other. It seems fairer to say that a basic ambiguity—a simultaneity of areas of distinction and union—represents an essential structure of human subjectivity, whatever developmental level. If one tries to push beyond these poles, the sense of self must disappear: to be undifferentiated and to exist is not possible.

Human existence is always basically transitional. The feeling of wholeness may initially be rooted in the implicit awareness of self and other giving rise to one another, permeating, yet transcending one another—a primary creative act repeated anew at every developmental juncture. Personal being is here felt to be distinct, yet to exist fully and mysteriously in a state of union, each pole made possible by the other. Insofar as the infant lives in this subject-subject psychical reality, expressive meanings, moods, intentions, and attitudes appear to be experienced with direct, immediate transparency.

In light of the above considerations, the infant's most basic reaction to the world need not be paranoid. Otherness may be experienced as syntonic or dystonic depending on a variety of conditions. The ego may have a mixture of paranoid and nonparanoid foundational experiences, the particular balance in important part dependent on the overall quality of responsiveness by the parental milieu.

Fairbairn's (1954) starting point attempts to do justice to the nonparanoid intrinsic relatedness of the human ego to its world. However, he seems to stress the *separate* ego's inherent need and wish to make contact and to connect with the other. Identificatory processes, which lead to internalization, are viewed by him as strictly pathological. In his viewpoint, internalization (presumably, also identification) would be unnecessary if we lived in a perfect world, one that supported our simple relatedness. The present view differs from Fairbairn in placing equal emphasis on both separation and union dimensions in the constitution of the self. The human self is an identificatory self. It, in part, thrives and grows through its capacity to identify. It is the capacity to identify that links the human race and links humankind with the cosmos. It may be shown that the phenomenological structure of the capacity to identify contains both distance and union elements, neither possible without the other. A certain structural "dual unity" characterizes human experience, both in the realms of self-other and mind-body relations. It characterizes our relation to creative symbols in general.

OBJECT RELATIONS AND SYMBOLIC EXPRESSION

For the human self, object relations are symbolically mediated. Symbols and object relations necessarily reflect, reinforce, stimulate, and extend each other. Creative acts of symbolic expression may summarize, distill, or carry the quality of object relations forward and vice versa. They are mutually dependent, copenetrating aspects of the psychological field.

Both creative work and object relations participate in the essential "dual-unity" structure (see preceding section) which characterizes human consciousness in general. The work reflects self but not only self. It has its own often unforeseen requirements, temperament and directional swings. It may even seem strange as it stands over and above the self, a stimulus for new intuitions and realizations. The work is mirror yet other.

The compressed, focused, and relatively bounded nature of the work enables it to heighten and reflect paradoxical structures (e.g., closeness-distance, presence-absence, concealed-revealed, immediacy-delay), which characterize object relations in general. The symbolic work acts as a condensed and highly charged organizer of the fluctuating affinities and oppositions that make relationships possible. Symbols function as transistors to facilitate or redirect the flow of polydimensional meanings, a veritable multiple-circuitry of meanings. The symbolic work is often a point of intersection for the pressing diversity of concerns and tensions, which, in part, make the subject who he or she is.

In the course of therapy, creative work by the subject may mirror aspects of therapy, its blocks and possibilities. The work may offer hints about who the therapist is and how the latter's personality inevitably contributes, consciously or unconsciously, to the possible forms treatment can take. It often leads to learnings about other important relationships in the subject's life, past or present.

Further, the subject may use his own creative work as an aid to begin to understand and respond to the very structures that constitute object relations as such. The repeated fits and starts, impasses and passages that belong to creative struggle act as a microcosm, a circumscribed analogue of life, which refers back to life and spreads into it. In spite of his immersion in his work, the subject comes to see at a glance a certain rhythmic flow in mood, the up's and down's, high-lows related to different phases of his efforts. His awareness deepens of transcendence and immersion, with all their pulls, frictions, and mutual enhancement. He learns to expect polar oscillations of all sorts, which he comes to value as raw material, not only of his work but of his self. He gains a certain distance from the transverse trajectories of inner-outer movements without losing contact with their felt meanings and impulsive force.

When the subject creates a symbol during the course of therapy, its suggestive vectors can coax or propel him into more intense and meaningful contact with both himself and the world. The symbolic work simultaneously points to the subjective processes that gave rise to it, and to its own existence as a mysterious sign of quiddity or "isness" as such. On the side of the object, the creative work focuses awareness of possibility, of being itself. It gives rise to ontological wonder. As an energetic *"art-e-fact,"* whether as movement, line, or succession of words, it carries life forward. The work comes into existence under one's questioning gaze. In its very advent, it frames existence, a sign of all existence. Its force as a message makes one more sensitive to hints of meaning everywhere.

The work also refers back to the subject. As a presence, it thematizes creativity as such. It points to its own birth and the processes that made it possible. It thus stands as a sign of subjectivity, the invisible. It is charged with the atmosphere of interiority, the inside become outside. It evokes an awareness of the self who helped it, of the self who hindered it, and possibly also of the hidden, anonymous workings of psychic life, which the self tries to run from or claim.

The work as meditative object has inestimable value. In therapy, the creator reads his creations, which play back to him what they will. He must learn to pay attention to what he produces, give it its due, allow it to work on him. The subject undergoes transformation not only in the creating but in the aftermath, the receiving. He becomes gradually more attuned to the ways self and work affect each other at various phases of their journey together, such as the beginning, working out, and reading of the accomplished gesture. The reverberations of the work, however raw or simple, themselves require creative responses. The work shoots through the subject and when it returns it is not the same. Self and work create and transform each other. While they are alive to one another they live in permanent symbiosis. They form something of an analogue for self and other relations in general. For self and other simultaneously giving rise to one another must surely be the most creative act of humankind.

The subject's attempt to express and read back felt meanings in the work is necessarily fragmentary. Expressive activity gives practice in tolerating ambiguity and incompleteness. The subject meets the work at the edges of intelligibility. A sensitive groping or cultivation of mute knowing gains dignity as a method. In both the creating and reading back the subject increasingly grows able not merely to tolerate but also to expect and look forward to something more. Creative gestures in therapy bear witness to and enrich the sense that further development is possible.

As the individual's sensitivity to moment to moment nuances and possibilities of his work quickens, he becomes more committed to a lifestyle aware of dangers inherent in premature closure operations. He learns not only to expect the unexpected but to rely on what the unforeseen must teach him. This leads to better use of one's incessant stream of silent questioning. As the subject becomes more finely attuned to shifts of form and meaning in his specific objects and objects in general, he may also grow in ability to make use of questions concerning the nature of form and meaning as such. Through repeated contact with one's expressive work the very sense of what an object is or can be enters new dimensions. One's attitude toward what an object is, what is possible for an object, itself becomes a source and means of wonder.

The creation and transformation of expressive objects leads not only to a fresh sense of what an object can be but radicalizes our awareness of what it means to be a subject. One tastes the seemingly unending depths and expanses which sustain the work's birth, the invisible threads through which the work shapes itself. In repeated contact with his expressive acts the person becomes more thoroughly identified with an underlying sense of generativity and renewal. He lives more and more in the rebirth experience. His time becomes the time of creativity, of absorption: a primordial or natural time with its own rhythms, turnings, juttings, caesuras, curves. Although the subject may lose himself in his work, he is questioned by it. The work asks the subject what kind of being emits live symbols and is recreated by them.

Attention to the work leads one closer to one's center, past representational barriers. In creative action, one is more than the sum of one's representations. A work may reflect one's character and strivings, one's place in time. But it is not identical with them. A symbol may evoke more meanings than a subject can exhaust. Symbolic expression always contains an element of transcendence. Creative immersion provides an experiential reference point outside or other than one's pathology. In the moment of creative action the subject undercuts or goes deeper than his pathology. The creative subject moves in gaps and interstices, in moments of linking and remodeling, as well as through the hearts of objects. The encounter with the creative subject in oneself is the disclosure of "another me," bound by the unknown, the universal, someone for whom no language is foreign. In creative moments, one claims one's share of primordial awareness, a precious, if sobering, intimacy with the same processes that create stars and living bodies: words, movements, lines, and colors spontaneously distribute themselves in analogy with the energic fluidity of subatomic or cellular processes. Partnership or disaster. One builds core aspects of one's identity on generativity as such.

Where or what is the body during creative work? A detailed discussion of this question cannot be undertaken here, but some remarks seem pertinent. Classical psychoanalysis, rightly or wrongly, believed our body to be the first object. The Kleinians took parts of mother's body, especially mother's insides, to be the first object. Adrian Stokes, a "Kleinian" painter, saw the formal properties of space and objects as expressive signs of mother's body life. Marion Milner's (1950) concern with the body in creativity is still broader. She speaks of "the other body," the "imaginary body," a body sense that can empathically project itself into objects, feel them, as it were, from the inside. The "imaginary body" is feeling-oriented mind. It overlaps with Polanyi's (1958) "tacit knowing" and Merleau-Ponty's (1962) "body subject." Here the literal, blindly grasping body gives way to mind-full body. Still further on is St.

Paul's descriptions of transcendent immersion states. When in grace, St. Paul remarks he can't tell whether or not he has a body, the question becomes irrelevant. There is simply joyous radiance, wholeness. However, before and after take-off, he speaks of human beings, all of us, linked as parts of one (spiritual) body. He was trying to speak with precision.

Creative work, in part, functions as "another body" or, more precisely, a sign of the body (Paz, 1974). In the work of art the expressive function of language is center stage. To be sure, each medium presents itself in another language, human experience in another key. Dance is not the same as poetry is not the same as music is not the same as drawing, and so on. They may at times overlap or even be explored in terms of like values (e.g., Ellsworth Kelly's artwork). But after all these years of art criticism we have not exhausted, possibly scarcely penetrated, their interrelationships and meanings (the same may be said for the various senses, seeing, hearing, etc.). Still, whatever the medium at hand, the very fact of any artwork brings into focal awareness a dimension of experience that runs through human existence. Art by its very appearance bears witness to "another me," the "other body," "another world." The area of "illusion" it marks off at times lays claims to penetrating deeply into the Real. It rushes like water downhill toward a "truer" self. At times it claims to create a new reality, a new self. It listens. It provokes.

EXPRESSIVE THERAPY: RELIVING, WORKING THROUGH, NEW BEGINNINGS

During the first months of life, mother and child reclaim the rhythm and resonance of a sublime and/or demonic state of unity. This state is explored through mutual touching, holding, and caressing, as well as through smiling, cooing, and singing. In the most ideal of circumstances, both participants move in and out of states of separateness and union. Each discovers the me and the not me, the part of me that is you, and the part of me that is not you. The quality of this exploration lends an indelible stamp to our relationships and finds particular expression through creative outlets, which bind, frame, and contain the inexplicable but not insensate traces of our early childhood.

Much of this early experience is nonverbal and diffuse. Nonetheless, its reverberations are very much felt by both patient and therapist. The task for expressive therapy is to make explicit memories that have defied words, but continue to crave definition. Through play[2], or in working toward play, patient and therapist relate on a multifaceted level of psychic existence, which is reminiscent of the communication within the early mother/child dyad. Here patient and therapist shift ego states and come to know one another's rhythm and energy, yet protective barriers are recognized and respected. Throughout, each participant seeks to release and redefine self and object through the discovery and mastery of developmental tasks. For instance, analogues of peek-a-boo and hide-and-seek are played out within this very intimate and finely attuned relationship. Thus, through this process, the forces of union and individuation, which are bound by the sensory motor experience[3], become reordered in a more self-regulatory manner.

As therapy proceeds, both patient and therapist work toward perceiving, feeling, and sensing their experiences, which in turn facilitates the creation of mutual imagery. These communications now become part of a transitional space that permits the process of discovery, recognition, and understanding to continue. Words are attached to images and sensations, which increase communication between the inner and outer worlds, and, as a result, the patient's vague boundaries of self

[2] I refer here to Winnicott's "transitional space" as discussed in Chapter 1.

[3] I refer here to the total context of cues that are communicated between mother and child through the sensorium and perceptual apparatus.

and object become more clearly perceived. To move in this direction, the expressive therapist is consistently alert to invent or employ a medium that will transcend the indefinable and move the noncognitive—sensation, perception, and imagery—into the cognitive—words and reality.

In the struggle toward profound relatedness, the past can be reexperienced, reconstructed, and reparations made. Transferences of primitive love and hate move toward emotional reintegration. This process is everchanging and has its inevitable progressions and regressions. Through creative expression these movements are recorded and may become historical and biographical documents of the attempt to change and to grow. Visual work particularly has the paradoxical effect of recording movement for perspective and review without interfering with the process of change.

Within the parameters of therapy, the safety of a "good enough mothering" environment unfolds and creative expression allows the patient to rediscover a bodily stage of separateness and fusion while taking tentative steps toward individuation. As expressive therapists, we make our inevitable mistakes and occasionally contribute to the recreation of past traumas and painful defeats. Only this time, hopefully, we can allow our patients to have a second chance to communicate their rage, indignation, and pain.

Thus, expressive therapy offers the patient many of the ingredients of the early mother/child relationship. It permits distance with resonance, symbolic holding and releasing, binding yet remaining open; but it is not the gratification of infantile needs that repair old wounds. Rather, the patient is allowed to reexperience his loss and loneliness within a relationship that is sensitively attuned to his early symbiosis. His grief becomes felt and known and he is helped to give words and meaning to these experiences. Within this space, the therapist, while fully separate, is also very much available to the patient, offering a unique emotional relatedness that permits the development of trust and the discovery of autonomy.

Disturbances in patients' object relations create chaotic and catastrophic levels of anxiety; the patient doesn't face mere danger but is overwhelmed by fantasies of annihilation and doom. Early losses or fear of penetration cause massive primitive defenses as well as formidable protective narcissistic layering. This makes the development of a working therapeutic alliance a most difficult challenge. For many patients these disturbances in object relations are of such a profound nature that the protective distance of creative work may be required to ground the terrors of unmet needs and lost battles. Creative work then becomes a transitional object offering the patient space, distance, and control. Within this safety, the patient can find a midpoint between me and not me and express the message that is shared between the self and the other. Under these conditions, the patient must be offered the experience of being heard without being intruded upon.

As noted above, projected, introjected, split, or part-objects can produce terrifying fantasies. Within the safety of the expressive therapy relationship, these terrors can be explored and expressed and part-objects can become externalized and find definition. Swooping witches and frightening teeth are released from the darkness of being unknown and unnamed. Slowly through the structure and concretization that comes with communication and understanding, primitive introjects find compassion and become more fully human. The transitional space then becomes a playground, although at times it is a very frightening one indeed. Here images loaded with enormous libidinal energies of love and hate can be faced and the patient's vague, fluid boundaries become clearer and more apprehendable. Cognitive generalizations, over-concretizations, and massive abstractions become better integrated. Reality testing and some objectification become possible through taking distance and viewing one's creative productions. The disappointments of object losses and their attendant rage now become apprehendable as splits of good and bad, love and hate. Slowly, the expressive therapist brings these parts together by offering a frame to contain contradictory affects.

As the underlying quest for wholeness is explored, trial adaptations take place in which the patient and therapist see and play with the polarities that have accrued from massive splitting. The veils of denial and compartmentalization are slowly lifted, and as the good and bad part-objects become multidimensional, they take on their own particular spatial and temporal characteristics. The patient moves in and out of alternate cognitive states as he experiences first one and then the other aspect of his part-objects. His feelings of love and hate are played out, both within the relationship and through creative expressions. As the patient's own externalizations are more clearly experienced as self and object, reality and fantasy, an integrated picture can slowly arise.

The therapeutic and developmental task of mirroring goes on throughout this process both within the relationship and through the creative act. Reflections then serve to repair the deficient internalization process that has been rediscovered in treatment. Expressive therapy facilitates the use of spatial and multileveled communication, which enhance the process. The richness of movement, music, or visual perceptions closely replicates the wide range of primitive affective and sensory motor communications intrinsic to the early mother/child dyad. Now, however, perceptions can be far more objectified and attain a greater degree of specificity. Patients learn about their predilections to make massive perceptual generalizations and broad cognitive sweeps that are based on part-object representations. Concurrently, they have the opportunity to see, feel, and hear the reverberations of a more fully dimensional and complete mirroring relationship.

Along with mirroring, the defensive grandiosity and idealizations, which protect patients from pain and rage, are concretized and confronted. Concurrently, through the open and reparative agent of communication, the magic and fear of primitive wishes become more human and more sane. Using his own artistry in depth communication, the expressive therapist helps his patient to laugh and accept his own frailties and deprivations. Ultimately the patient is able to make peace with his early maternal environment and with his own humanity. Gradually, his/her search for omnipotent ideals subsides.

As therapist and patient, we work through hate and love, and, ultimately, face our early losses; but pain cannot always be directly faced. Creative expression offers the patient the option of taking in or simply being. Verbal demands can be minimal and consequently the material stimulates a state of being quite by oneself, and yet not feeling alone. The quality of intense but quiet creative expression recaptures the rhythm and sense of wholeness of one's primitive past. Here one can experience feeling healed. Slowly the creative work also makes a statement that "I am"; the expression of grief and pain then can become a form of self-affirmation. Creativity becomes an avenue for identity formation with all the underlying and transitory stages of exhibitionism, self-revelation, and ego mastery. Yet we cannot shortcut the difficult route of working through material within the transference relationship. Creative work must also occur within the context of affective transference communication so that one's introjects can be finally neutralized of their primitive terror. For a while, however, creative work can allow time for both patient and therapist to reinforce their egos in preparation for the explosive communications that are associated with primitive transference reactions.

A therapist's receptivity to sensory cues can facilitate the emergence of transference material of a preverbal nature. The characteristic touch, vision, or sound of a patient has often a magnetic quality that captures the essence of a deeper identification and/or a nameless terror. Here, within this preverbal matrix, our attunements to the particular sensory receptivity of our patients are refined. The melodies or visions of past experiences take shape and are formed in images, bound by sensation, and sometimes distorted by either inadequate cognitive abilities, or warped by restricted or limited reality testing. What words fail to clarify, the expressive therapist picks up on a bodily communication level through a heightened sensitivity to movements or sounds. Within this field, the spatial, temporal, or sequential characteristic, of a very complex experience is organized within the therapist's image. Thus, the undifferentiated or intangible quality of early experiences gains a moment of apprehension as we move in and out of altered perceptual states. The expressive therapist, therefore, does not limit himself to the confines of direct linear communication, but travels to the genesis of one's early imprinting experiences so that he relives, in part, the development and struggles of introjective phenomena. Here lies the real strength of the expressive therapist who will ultimately reach out for words to give specificity and clarity to his therapeutic experiences.

REFERENCES

Balint, M. *The basic fault.* London: Tavistock, 1968.

Bion, W. R. *Seven Servants.* New York: Jason Aronson, 1977.

Breuer, S. & Freud, S. 1893–95. *Studies on hysteria.* Standard Edition, vol. 2. London: Hogarth Press.

Eigen, M. Abstinence and the schizoid ego. *International Journal of Psychoanalysis,* 1973, *54,* 493–498.

Eigen, M. On pre-Oedipal castration anxiety. *International Review of Psychoanalysis,* 1974, *1,* 489–498.

Eigen, M. On the significance of the face. *Psychoanalytic Review,* to be published, 1980.(a)

Eigen, M. *Guntrip's analysis with Winnicott: A critique of Glatzer and Evans.* Unpublished paper, 1980.(b)

Eigen, M. Creativity, instinctual fantasy and ideal images. *Psychoanalytic Review,* to be published, 1980.(c)

Eigen, M. On the structure of the self. Unpublished paper, 1980.(d)

Fairbairn, W. R. D. An object relations theory of personality. New York: Basic Books, 1954.

Freud, S. 1958. *Formulations on the two principles of mental functioning.* Standard Edition, vol. 12, pp. 218–26. London: Hogarth Press.

Freud, S. 1957. *Instincts and their vicissitudes.* Standard Edition, vol. 14, pp. 117–40. London: Hogarth Press.

Grotstein, J. S. The psychoanalytic concept of schizophrenia: I. The dilemma. *International Journal of Psychoanalysis, 58,* 403–425, 1978.(a)

Grotstein, J. S. The psychoanalytic concept of schizophrenia: II. Reconciliation. *International Journal of Psychoanalysis, 58,* 427–452, 1978.(b)

Grotstein, J. S. Inner space: Its dimensions and its coordinates. *International Journal of Psychoanalysis, 58,* 55–61, 1978.(c)

Grotstein, J. S. Who is the dreamer who dreams the dream and who is the dreamer who understands it. *Contemporary psychoanalysis,* 1979, *15,* 110–169.

Guntrip, H. *Schizoid phenomena, object relations and the self.* New York: International Universities Press, 1969.

Guntrip, H. *Psychoanalytic theory, therapy and the self.* New York: Basic Books, 1971.

Klein, M. *Contributions to psychoanalysis: 1921–1945.* London: Hogarth Press, 1948.

Kohut, H. *The analysis of the self.* New York: International Universities Press, 1971.

Kohut, H. *The restoration of the self.* New York: International Universities Press, 1977.

Mahler, M. 1968. *Infantile psychosis.* On Human Symbiosis and the Vicissitudes of Individuation, vol. 1. New York: International Universities Press.

Meltzer, D. *The Kleinian development.* Perthshire: Clunie Press, 1978.

Merleau-Ponty, M. *Phenomonology of perception.* London: Routledge & Kegan Publishers, 1962.

Milner, M. *On not being able to paint.* New York: International Universities Press, 1950.

Paz, O. *Conjunctions and disjunctions.* New York: Viking Press, 1974.

Peterfreund, E. Some critical comments on psychoanalytic conceptualizations of infancy. *International Journal of Psychoanalysis,* 1978, *59,* 427–441.

Polanyi, M. *Personal knowledge.* Chicago: University of Chicago Press, 1958.

Segal, H. *Introduction to the work of Melanie Klein.* New York: Basic Books, 1964.

Stolorow, R. & Atwood, G. *Faces in a cloud,* New York: Jason Aronson, 1978.

Winnicott, D. W. *Playing and reality.* New York: Basic Books, 1971.

Chapter 5

IMAGERY IN THEORY AND PRACTICE

Carmela Luongo, M.P.S.
Arthur Robbins, Ed.D.

As specialists in the expression of creative potential, we need to familiarize ourselves with the literature related to the imaginary life of the individual, and the purpose of utilizing these findings in our therapeutic practice. Our task is to prepare a path of knowledge and, ultimately, to transcend the self as "a mode of being which is more meaningful, more whole" (Corsini, 1973). Our vehicle in treatment is the creative use of imagery, which may well be our profession's genius.

Creativity is an illusive phenomenon whose definition has been a source of disagreement and semantic difficulty. Through usage, we have come to associate it with mental and behavioral functionings, positioning it along a cognitive-emotive continuum. Creativity may be defined quite simply as the ability to bring something new into existence. Because, as human beings, we are not able to make something out of nothing, the human act of creation involves a reshaping of given materials, whether physical or mental. This something new, then, is a form made by rearrangement, integration, or juxtaposition of continuous and discontinuous elements hidden in mind and matter. The creative act is the constitution, regeneration, and transformation of what already exists.

The desire to create, no matter how strong, would be unexpressed without imagination. Originality becomes creative when the inner life of the creator becomes an intrinsic part of this process. William Blake views imagination as "some form of spiritual energy"; Arieti, as "the precursor of creativity"; while Webster defines it as "the formation of mental images of objects not present to the senses." In addition to these, the creative analyst views imagination as an affirmation of positive self-esteem. The expression of imagery in one's life facilitates an integration of inner and outer reality that makes the creative act synonymous with the experience of self-affirmation.

Imago, the Latin word for image, means likeness, picture, or idea of something not present in the sensory field. Like the images in a kaleidoscope, these ideas and pictures constantly dissolve and change, only to begin again. They go on and on and flit and pass like shadows on the ceiling, grouped and parting like loosened pollen on the wind.

In its most basic sense, imagery is charged with all the emotions, complexes, inhibitions, and mysteries surrounding our deepest biological, psychological, and spiritual urges. The image, then, is not an isolated element in a synthetic process. It is a spontaneous, creative, imaginative act, inclusive of signs, thoughts, feelings and sensations. It is our power and our distinction.

In spite of the lack of adequate statistical studies, psychological investigation testifies to the fact that we live, awake or dreaming, against a shifting background of imagery. On a personal level, the fact that imagery exists, is an experiential one for most of us that needs no further validation; on a broader level, testimony exists throughout the history of civilizations in which imagery has been relegated to a place of importance, and its use continues to be manifested in philosophical, mythical, religious, and artistic themes.

The questions, however, remain: Where does imagery come from? How does it develop and in what context does the image move within the therapeutic encounter?

Of imagery, Don Juan says, "It is where power hovers; it is the only part of us that can create. . . ." and ". . . . the part of us with which we do not deal with at all" (Castaneda, 1974). Its foundation is the perception of internal and external stimuli, coded, translated and stored in memory. Gowan (1978) states that all imagery is "post-perceptual, after- imagery, or a kind of eidetic imagery consequent on the sensorium." Physiological and neurological research has demonstrated that imagery is always present and manifests itself in the cognitive style of the brain's right hemisphere, which is imaginative, analogical, and nonverbal. It contains the richness of our primal and creative energies whose uniqueness and expression are seen in the context of one's life experiences. According to Jung, images are the product of a collective unconscious, expressions of archetypal material or universal themes stored in a shared unconscious memory. Once emerged, they carry the quality of inner convictions.

Images then, are a subjective personal creation, which are present in many minor acts at many different levels of intelligence. This is witnessed in the five-year-old who gives us an image of the world, littered with square horses and peopled with neckless parents. Probably, the experiences of most people consist of some sort of imagery; memory images of things once seen, as well as imagined images of things never visually, kinesthetically, or auditorially experienced.

The earliest concept of the role of images in thought was a philosophical one, the Aristotelian view. Here, "images are basic elements of thought which have the power to motivate a person to emotion and efforts" (Horowitz, 1978). Psychologists who supported this view, formulated the "law of association," which, in general, claimed that thought proceeded by selecting the images in a hierarchy of activation. The early controversial issues between the "associationists" and the advocates of "imageless thought," as well as later researchers, led to several important formulations: thought is an unlimited construct, and multiple thoughts may be experienced simultaneously, with ideas and feelings taking the form of representation or not. Persons differ in the vividness of their imagery and in perceptual capacity, excelling in one or more sensory mode over another. Even at this, most individuals are mixed types and rarely think in one exclusive sensory mode, while others seldom form representations in any sense mode (Horowitz, 1978). The reasons for this are hypothesized and range from constitutional factors, environmental, and perceptual stimulation and cultural experience. Out of these early theories evolved the role of memory, perception, and thought in imagery and the motivational aspects of image formation.

Psychodynamically and cognitively, image formation is viewed as a symbolic acquisition, which grows from the simplest to more complex patterns in a process of gradual differentiation.

Piaget, for example, places the development of symbolic representation within the framework of mental operations. In Piaget's schema, creativity development is the evolution of increasingly complex mental representations. The child at first compensates for the lost object through symbolic play. Eventually, the child internalizes the object sufficiently to reconstruct it verbally. Rosen (1960) postulates that the first stage described by Piaget as the "objective" one is the cessation, by the child, of relating everything to his state or actions. This stage is the precursor of the capacity for image formation. Movement into the second stage of permanent objectification includes the active search for an object after its disappearance, which presupposes a primitive capacity to retain an image of the vanished object. The final state of representation not only indicates the child's capacity to retain images but to recreate the image of the absent object.

Freud perceived the child's behavior toward vanished objects as the building blocks for the eventual maturity of the ego's synthetic capacities. His example of the child mastering separation anxiety in his mother's absence by means of a game with an object on a string is the symbolic recreation of the child's separation from mother. Inherent in this symbolic act is the motive force for the creation of an inner world and its imagery correlates. The interconnectedness between symbol and object symbolized is the child's magical wish for mastery, continuity, and control in a situation that imposes ambiguous representations, threat of object loss, and delay on his instinctual demands for gratification. It involves a satisfaction in abstraction, as in dreaming by imagining the achievement of what he wants. Although, not conscious, this substitute means of problem solving presupposes an identification process modeled after imitation. While imitation is never an end in itself, it is a developmental necessity acting as a continuation of understanding and assimilation and recognition of differentiation with respect to new models. According to Rosen (1960), we see here the underpinnings for "later complex imaginistive processes, such as the syntheses of new ideas," which is the organism's passive capacity to receive, examine, and reorganize raw material with an inner active power to elaborate, regenerate, and transform what already exists. According to Piaget (1968), "This initial absence of a substantive object, followed by the construction of permanent and constant objects, is the first transitional phase from total egocentricity to the final elaboration of an external universe." Fantasy, imitation, play, and imagination are outgrowths of this early symbolic state. It comprises the first attempts to know, cope, and master percepts; to assimilate ongoing stimuli within the self-system and accommodate that self to the world of external reality.

Creative imaginative play and identity formation have their genesis at the very origins of existence. Mother and child first meet through the act of creation, bringing their own inner world of symbols and imagery to form a magical synthesis. In this receptive fusion by parent and child, there emerges a playful and imaginative space. According to Winnicott (1971), it is this transition, that is neither inside nor outside, but somewhere in-between, that marks the origins of a creative integration of man and his symbols with the outside world. Through play, mother and child find the level of a coesthetic existence that contains a sensory coloration and texture, be it a mixture of auditory, tactile, and visual stimulation. The image originating from this matrix, gives shape, form, and meaning to their experience. Imagination, with its emphasis on imagery, begins with a statement of one's experience in this transitional space that emerges into an identity affirmation that is ever changing and moving between self, object, and the outside world.

A healthy portion of delay and frustration, as well as need satisfaction, enhance the formation and quality of imagery and invigorate secondary process thinking. The potential space between frustration and satisfaction is one of hopeful expectation evolving out of the images of remembered experiences of an average expectable, constant environment. Herein, is contained the underpinnings for the development of imaginary ways of achieving one's goal: daydreaming, remembering, reflecting, thinking, and reasoning as substitutes for immediate action when the reality of immediacy, must be held in abeyance. The formation, then, and richness of a personal imagery life, the images of self, our bodies, and our social roles, as well as the selves, bodies, and social roles of others, have their genesis in the early phases of development.

As the ego matures and develops in complexity and richness, more abstract and logical representations adhere to the original images. As Freud insisted upon and Piaget rediscovered, old infantile ways of perceiving, remembering and conceiving do not disappear. "They continue," as Freud said, "like the remains of an ancient civilization under successive layers of later civilizations, but with all of them, to some extent, alive and active" (Cameron, 1963), and will be reactivated in adulthood. In a healthy, awake individual, these early reverberations enhance a sense of identity and continuity and add warmth, color, dimension, and playfulness to actions. In sleep and dreaming, these unrealistic symbols and conflicts coalesce with yesterday's and today's experiences and find satisfaction and release of drive cathexis in a manifest dream. In the psychotic, neurotic, and character disorders, these memory images give us the developmental clues of inadequate or confused internalized object of one's past experience. It is for these reasons that any discussion of imagery, with the hope of effective therapeutic intervention in mind, must be approached from a developmental framework. To move within the imagistic life of an individual is to encounter the intimate self.

Given this general prevalence of imagery and its development, it is the authors' intent to now explore the use of imagery within the context of the therapeutic environment. Our frame of reference is derived from the foregoing theoretical formulations, which build on one another and afford us a holistic view of the personality.

Imagery, for the creative analyst, is a theory of personality, a diagnostic tool, and a vehicle for communication on many levels. Klee states that an "image which possesses simultaneously a number of dimensions, cannot be reduced to the linear dimensions of the spoken word" (Naumberg, 1950). The expressive therapy encounter, then, is fertile ground for symbolic imagery dialogues. Patients choose many symbolic forms to show us their conflicts, their confusions, and their fantasies. We have witnessed anger clarified by the jagged teeth and bulging lines of a monster face. Its evolution was from a tiny dot and timid spiral followed by brusque, hard, angular lines of devouring teeth and lashing mouth. Loneliness and alienation were demonstrated by the motion of the hand as it directed the lines of the drawing toward the self. It ended in a reduction of the area of the paper, as the patient shut out more and more of the world around him until he stood in the center of an enclosed line. Patients tell it all in the images of the searching movement, the hopeless hunting, the scenes of desolation, the eyes of fear, and the abrupt erasures of confusion.

Generally, images are a response, "a bi-polar action of

outer situations and inner stress systems. They are powered by a fusion of inner and outer drives; stimuli from the real world culture of moving people and things integrated with stimuli from the inner flux of remembered images, motor tendencies and unconsciously produced metaphor images, symbols and concepts" (Rugg, 1963). Expressive therapy conceives the image to be the medium of potential transformation of the personality, a means of reconciling opposites in the conscious and unconscious. With this vehicle in treatment, expressive therapy is a reaching-out receiving-in process with the patient/therapist dyad as the playground for exercising freedom, spontaneity, and creative exchange. Play, as the characterizing feature of the therapeutic relationship, "is a journey of progress toward experiencing" (Winnicott, 1971) from the purely subjective to objectivity.

Imagery, as a primary process activity and as a theory of play, forms a gestalt of many meanings through the playful disguises of condensation, displacement, and symbolization. It serves to code relevant issues and affords distance from painful emotions associated with unassimilated material. Free from the constraints of logical thought and the controls of the environment, the image, associated with these painful conflicts, seeks discharge through repetition, as an attempt at mastering the material and as a rehearsal for later integration.

In the free, structured environment of the therapeutic relationship, the use of imagery functions as a safety valve through which reality can be "assimilated to the whims of the ego" (Piaget, 1962). The graphic expression adapts itself to unconscious strivings that are unacceptable to the ego, and at the same time binds id cathexis by channeling and taming primitive drives into a neutralized zone.

However, before the raw and primitive can be transformed into the service of a self, patient and therapist must traverse through a number of stages. A clinical example comes to mind of a patient who literally enmeshes himself in clay. The patient feels the texture, gets lost in its undulations, and regresses to a level that comes near a smearing defiance of the world. Without condemnation or criticism, the therapist receptively receives these messages. In time, images emerge from the fecal mass that reach out to a higher level of communication. From fecal mass to flowers, vases and houses, from formlessness to form, from instinct to object related, the energy and anxiety that was previously repressed now finds freedom and communication within the ego. The image joins and transforms the conflict toward assimilation and primary/secondary process integration.

There are vast areas of experience that can never be adequately verbalized. Experiences of pain, alienation, closeness, fear, as well as intense joy, the reaches of mystic heights and homecomings, cannot be formulated through the use of language. Words cannot totally express a statement of "I am," since perception and language do not always speak the words of a unit-system. Where interior thought lacks precision, and verbal thought is vague and inadequate, the use of imagery concretizes, animates, and activates a sharing through vicarious communication. The metaphorical image, as symbol, formulates an expression of the wordless. It functions as a vehicle for reality testing and focuses on differentiating between fantasy and imagination, drive derivatives, and satisfaction, and between the experienced memory images of childhood and the needs that reactivate them. Its implications for therapy can be seen in the clinical pictures of the schizophrenic or borderline personality whose energies are bound up in a defensive disavowal or painful perceptions substituted by a world of omnipotent wishes. Due to early object deprivations, the immature ego organization lacks adequate synthetic capacities. The journey in treatment, within the context of a dependable, stable environment, is a phase or juxtaposition rather than integration, with a goal toward intellectual realism and insights of proximity, separations, and enclosures. The following clinical case is cited as an illustration of this process.

A young woman sits terrorized in the analyst's office. Unable to verbalize a nameless terror that pervades the room, she looks helplessly frozen. She responds to the therapist's invitation to draw, with jagged black and red lines. The therapist joins by sharing with his own imagery that is soft, round, and circular. The patient endows the jagged lines with life through verbal expression of fear: "They are chasing me . . . they want to take my life. . . ." Unable to identify who "they" are, she repeats ambiguously, "They." As the therapist gently prods with "Who?" the patient associates the jagged lines with her father, whom she experienced as sadistic and rageful and contemptuous of her mother's helplessness. As the discontinuous threads become connected through a therapeutic dialogue, the patient slowly takes distance from the merger of her helpless mother.

In this illustration, the missing polar image of roundness and softness that is supplied by the therapist forms a beginning synthesis for the patient. The images, however, contain a primary and secondary process communication, which converts the material into a meaningful statement of the patient's existence. The father imago becomes more complete in dimension and scope. He is no longer a red, jagged line. With the externalization, both therapist and patient now build on this image. The patient dialogues with this image and is able to approach, avoid, control, and to some extent, rotate this menacing figure. With each dialogue, primitive affects are released and the image loses some of its early menacing power and becomes more integrated within the self. Concurrently, a similar process will someday go on with the mother imago. In each instance, the nature and quality of the imagery expression makes a screaming statement of the diagnostic and therapeutic level of this patient's self and object relations. They are highly symbolic, condensed, lacking in synthesis with secondary process, and are fragmented. The therapist meets this patient on this imagery level and together they reconstruct and build towards a more stable and clear representation that will be the cornerstone of a potentially healthy ego. Thus, the slow building of external imagery through graphic expressions serves to facilitate the process of differentiation. The patient, as described above, vaguely sees the father and mother. The image and the association begin a slow separation from a noxious symbiosis.

Man's adaptive capacity, his sense of reality and reality-testing, involves the capacity to think and, to an extent, is a reflection of the interactive quality and use of external objects. Our reference here to thinking is in relation to verbal language but is applicable to the metaphoric image as well. The schizophrenic regressive mode of psychological functioning is comparable to that of a young child who is unable to differentiate the concrete from the symbolic or metaphorical forms of thinking. In severe language disorders, the schizophrenic patient may reach a level of using verbal metaphors as a communicational device. Thus, the communication, under the auspices of primary process condensation, is the patient's need to "refind" the early symbiotic relation. The creative analyst must be able to abandon secondary process thinking and rely on creative intuition, recognizing in the metaphor, complimentary elements. By withholding interpretation, s/he explores previous unsuspected connections and in confrontation, s/he also uses the metaphor as a convicting device, skirting a specific problem and talking about a general issue. This allows the patient to reexamine his ideas with a sense of attachment and distance. The process involves a constant interplay between creation and criticism, functional regression and control; the alternation between artist/therapist working on her piece and then stepping back in order to observe the effects more closely. This is the paradoxical situation in art as it is in therapy. The work of preparation for the therapist is to abstract from the more logical, literal features of the patient's perceptual and conceptual mental world, the analogical and metaphorical penumbras, in order to integrate the goal of treatment. A reach for the patient's bipolar image can be employed for creatively assessing the extent of the repression, the manner of handling drives and the intensity of the anxiety. In this context, the therapist decides to what extent the image will be used for problem solving, by moving the patient away from the goal, in order to ultimately reach it. The treatment goal is to provide an atmosphere that persuades "a shift in a psychic level" (Kris, 1976). The therapeutic environment, then, can be used as an effective playground for surprises so that the doctrine of abandonment may emerge in place of anxious self-security. An integrated sense of self requires not only a sense of purpose but a sense of humor.

The expressive therapist needs to differentiate empty fantasy with imaginative expression. Fantasies of omnipotence of a narcissistic embodiment are frequently defensive operations that prevent the person from any real form of self-discovery. The daydreams of power or stardom that can be endlessly repetitious do not lead to an unfolding of the self. They are the sterile barriers that keep the person out of touch with his preconscious imagery. Material, therefore, that is repetitious and sterile should not be seen as the rich resource of self-development and can be treated as a resistance. Along the same lines, autistic and hallucinatory imagery, often expressed in schizophrenic states, has the same purpose. It serves as a hiding place rather than a means of expression between the patient and the outside world.

The question of working with schizophrenic primary process imagery has been an area of controversy for the expressive therapist. Some therapists are concerned that any concentration on imagery play can lead patients away from reality. Paradoxically, unless we enter the patient's world, we cannot lead him out of his refuge. The preoccupation of directing the entire treatment emphasis upon the ego may well be a necessity in short term contracts. Yet, in some treatment situations, one even wonders if there is any recognition that a psychotic has a self to be attended. Much of the emphasis seems to be on behavioral reinforcement and ego-functioning. However, imagery play with psychotics can lay the foundation for the expansion of ego-functioning. Symbolic expression can be ultimately moved in a direction of making trial communications about the patient's relationship with the outside world. Indeed, if the outside is experienced as threatening and menacing, there will be a need for protection through distant and disguised symbolism. The therapist's job, in part, is one of entering into these disguised communications and slowly bringing the patient, through imagery play, back to reality so that the threatening object can someday be confronted. The patient who plays cops and robbers in a desperate game of survival and chase, needs to be met and participated with on the level of play. The task for the therapist is to help the patient test out these imaginative but real conflicts, which will ultimately lead toward an experiential understanding of father, mother, and lover as well as employer, therapist, and friend.

At this point, it is necessary to retrace our steps and review our main thesis. Imagery play must be viewed within a developmental context of self and object representation. Within this framework, the therapist offers reparative responses that facilitate a process of differentiation of meaningful symbols within the patient's ego. By this we mean imagery becomes more fluid and less bound to the past, more complex and integrated, rather than split and compartmentalized and fragmented. Consequently, as a corollary of mental health, we are proposing that richness and accessibility to a meaningful and fluid set of images and symbols facilitates decision making, mastery, and a dynamic growth of identity formation. The following illustration will attempt to highlight this interconnectedness.

History

A 38 year old married man now in his second year of treatment has spent the major portion of his life being pseudo-self-sufficient. Essentially removed, and contemptuous to the world, his marriage was one of convenience, while most of his energy was invested in casual homosexual love affairs. Life was a big game where one kept constantly on the move with little time for self-reflection or insight. His family background, stark and empty, was reflected in his current relationships with people. His parents, owners of a candy store, spent most of their time involved with the transactions of their business. Consequently, they provided little parenting and left the young child to develop through his own devices. When present, however, their impact was a negative one. They were invariably controlling and constrictive with their child.

TREATMENT COURSE

Verbalizing was a problem for the patient, indicating the deprivation of his colorless childhood. His surface reason for treatment was in an attempt to persuade his wife of his interests in preserving their marriage. On a deeper level, however, he seemed to be reaching out for "something" outside of his empty existence. During therapy, he was often overcome with feelings of discomfort and sadness and expressed a desire to flee from the room. The patient's inner world was devoid of imagery and his orientation was one of action and movement.

In one of these sessions where intense feelings of emptiness and sadness pervaded the room, the therapist asked him to describe the color of his feelings. The patient compared them to a "big, black mass without shape." Since any kind of graphic play was frightening and alien, the therapist requested that he merely focus on the black mass until it took on form or shape. What eventually emerged were "huge buttocks—fat and ugly." Certain only of their repulsion, the patient was unable to identify their origin or to form associations. To encourage the emergence of identification and associations, the therapist introduced a field of imagery; a book of classical paintings. As the patient leafed through the book, he was suddenly faced with the repulsive buttocks in the works of Rubens. The therapist and patient proceeded to dialogue on the art forms and the sensory experience. Encouraged and stimulated, a thread of

connections erupted. The patient associated the grotesque buttocks to his fat, repulsive grandmother who cared for him in his
parents' habitual absence. This was the first time he was able
to identify the connecting link between his emotional blackness
and sadness and some of its genesis.

The grandmother, a tyrant, reentered his awareness for the
first time in our relationship. She demanded order and conform-
ity and the patient suspected that she was directly involved in
his toilet training, for she was, in fact, the mother-surrogate
during the long absences of his parents. Now the patient enters
the world of the dark, ugly self. The patient relates to the
therapist, the heavy-handed impact of his grandmother. He
even begins to approach his inner fear and repulsion but has a
long road to travel toward wholeness and integration.

The introduction of visual stimulation through the vehicle
of a picture book becomes a means of a disruptive symbiosis.
The blackness, badness, and anality are all fused into a highly
symbolic and charged symbolization. Slowly, the patient will
have to discover the good as well as the bad, the sensuousness
that is hidden within the revulsion, and his own power that is
lost within the oppression of the grandmother introject. At least
some beginning is made towards bringing fragments of the past
into a more cohesive sense of continuity. We see here the emergence of primary process imagery that is given words and direction so that a long, unattended self is heard, mirrored, and
responded. In short, an expressive therapist discovered ways of
introducing imagery that responded to problems in self and
object representation development. Frequently, our imagery
will stimulate connections to the past, while on other occasions,
fragmented images can be externalized and coalesced. Often,
images that are part of projective identifications can be reintrojected. In other words, the expressive therapist, with his/her
own imagery, mirrors, responds or confronts, depending on the
developmental and diagnostic state of the patient. Narcissistic,
borderline, and psychotics often need their imagery to be externalized and mirrored. Borderlines in particular, need their split

images reintegrated. In more neurotic constellations, the family drama around sexual identification can be explored through metaphorical image communication that goes on between patient and therapist. Character problems require action images to capture motor expressions so that impulse can be converted to ideation and symbol. Thus, as we translate the patient's image communication within a developmental context, we soon discover the remedial treatment plan that repairs old wounds and losses.

As it has been presented in this paper, one's personal resource of imagery and the capacity for imaginative, creative living, is dependent on the experiences with object constancy and the quality of personal object relationships. For the expressive analyst, the creative act is one of discovering lost images of the past so that new meanings are apprehended in the conception of self and reality.

The therapeutic encounter, then, with a dynamic use of imagery, is the therapist's/patient's canvas and dance of life. Here, many minor forms and general schemas of movement are established and abandoned, are rearranged, juxtaposed, and integrated. The creative encounter is a reach for the fullness of self-realization, not as an abstract schema but as an inviting possibility in the midst of concrete situations. It is the "potential space" where therapist/artist and patient/artist exercise the freedom to play in a new world of inner space and outer reality.

REFERENCES

Arieti, S. *Creativity: The magic synthesis.* New York: Basic Books, 1976.
Arnheim, R. *Visual thinking.* Los Angeles, Calif.: University of California Press, 1969.
Beard, R. M. *Piaget's developmental psychology.* U. S.: New American Library, 1969.
Blanck, G. & Rubin. *Ego psychology: Theory and practice.* New York: Columbia University Press, 1974.
Cameron, N. *Personality development and psychopathology.* Boston: Houghton Mifflin Co., 1963.

Castaneda, C. *Tales of power.* New York: Simon & Schuster, 1974.

Corsini, R. *Current psychotherapies.* Illinois: Peacock Publishers Inc., 1973.

Gowan, J. C. Incubation, imagery and creativity. *Journal of Mental Imagery,* 1978, *2.*

Hartman. *Ego psychology and the problem of adaptation.* New York: International Universities Press, 1958.

Horowitz, M. *Image formation and cognition.* New York: Appleton-Century-Crofts, 1978.

Kris, E. On preconscious mental processes. Reprinted by Rothenberg, A. & Hausman, C., in *The creativity question.* North Carolina: Duke University Press, 1976.

Kris, E. *Psychoanalytic explorations in art.* London: George Allen & Unwin Ltd., 1953.

Mahler, M. S. *On human symbiosis and the vicissitudes of individuation.* New York: International Universities Press, 1968.

Modell, A. *Object love and reality.* New York: International Universities Press, 1977.

Naumberg, M. *Schizophrenic art: Its meaning in psychotherapy.* New York: Grune & Stratton, Inc., 1950.

Neuman, E. *Art and the creative unconscious.* New Jersey: Princeton University Press, 1959.

Noy, P. A revision of the psychoanalytic theory of the primary process. *The International Journal of Psychoanalysis,* 1969, *50* Pt. 2.

Ornstein, R. E. *The psychology of consciousness.* New York: Harcourt Brace Jovanovich, Inc., 1977.

Piaget, J. & Inhelder, B. *The psychology of the child.* New York: Basic Books, Inc., 1969.

Piaget, J. & Inhelder, B. *Mental imagery in the child.* New York: Basic Books, Inc., 1971.

Piaget, J. *Play, dreams and imitation and childhood.* New York: W. W. Norton & Co., Inc. 1962.

Piaget, J. *Six psychological studies.* New York: Vintage Books, 1968.

Rosen, V. H. Some aspects of the role of imagination in the analytic process. *Journal of American Psychoanalysis,* 1960, 8.

Rugg, H. *Imagination.* New York: Harper & Row, 1963.

Winnicott, D. W. *Playing and reality.* New York: Basic Books, Inc., 1971.

Chapter 6

NEUROPHYSIOLOGICAL AND PSYCHOANALYTICAL PARALLELS TO EXPRESSIVE THERAPY*

Margaret Wilson, Mary DeVincentis, Katherine Irish, Maureen Renehan, Arthur Robbins, Althea Rose

As a treatment modality, expressive therapy is still in its formative, developmental stages as to its theoretical identity. This chapter will explore expressive therapy in light of its traditional psychoanalytic roots and will attempt to draw parallels from field theory and neurophysiological research. The purpose of this chapter is not to describe the intricacies and complexities of neuroanatomy, but to point out the important significance of neurophysiological processes to various treatment approaches. We will explore the relationship between expressive analysis and recent neurophysiological findings in order to provide a more holistic approach to working with both normal and disturbed individuals.

There seems to be a growing movement in this culture toward bridging the gaps between fields such as sciences, religion, philosophy, psychology and the humanities, which have

*We are grateful to Sandra Leftoff for her critical review of this chapter.

long been inimical. Historically, there has been a split in the field of psychology, dichotomized by the behaviorists/associationists versus the gestaltists/cognitive theorists. As with the general, parental field of psychology, the field of expressive therapy experiences a similar split into two distinct psychological traditions and positions. Jerome Bruner, in his work *On Knowing,* defines this kind of rift as an inability to integrate our conception of ourselves as human and animal, primitive and civilized, rational and irrational, sane and insane, conscious and unconscious. Bruner feels that the first successful attempts to establish some sense of continuity between the varied conceptions of man were by Darwin and Freud in the nineteenth century. Darwin's theory of evolution humbled man by reminding him of his commonality with all other living creatures in the shared instinct toward biological survival. Freud pointed out man's unending struggle with his unreason, his impulses, and his primitive origins. He showed us evidence of the relationship between dreaming and waking life, of the continuous scale rather than sharp division between mental health and illness, and of the universality of the unconscious (Bruner, 1966, pp. 150–158).

In particular, the divergent disciplines of science, art and psychology have begun to converge in one specific area of study. Each discipline attempts, through widely varied methods, to understand the development and functioning of the whole human being through an inquiry into the nature and workings of human consciousness.

The concept of a "third force" psychology is experiencing a new fervor in trying to bridge the traditional chasm in the field. It is most commonly associated with "humanistic" psychology (Maslow, Rogers) based on priciples of motivation and growth needs in contrast to the principles of the unconscious emphasized in psychoanalysis or the principles of reinforcement in behavior-oriented therapies. In a recent article, Michael Mahoney (1977) cites a contemporary trend of this "third perspective," which he sees as an integration of behavioral techniques and cognitive and affective intrapersonal processes. This trend emphasizes the intercausal and interactive workings between the organism (internal, self) and the environment (external, other).

The interdisciplinary concept we are proposing in this paper involves a basic correlation between neurophysiology and behavior. In this approach, the internal psychic factors are considered as well as the individual's physiology and biochemistry. These factors are integrated to assess the functioning of the total organism. Therefore, one's neurophysiological makeup seems to be a sound basis for understanding one's behavior. The physiological basis for integrative functioning and human consciousness will now be explored briefly.

The central nervous system is the central filter that processes information necessary for the organism's successful adaptation. The functional and integrating unit of the nervous system is the neuron. It is the neuronal system that reacts and conveys information to the central nervous system about the organism's internal or external environments. The nervous system receives, identifies, and organizes this information. The brain is a living circuitry of electrical energy and firing nerve cells.

The cerebrum, one section of the brain, is the seat of our voluntary or higher mental faculties, as well as various autonomic reactions. The cerebrum is composed of the two cerebral hemispheres. These two 'thinking caps' are located atop the brain stem, which is connected to the spinal cord: the basis of the nervous system. The right and left cerebral hemispheres are connected by a bundle of nerve fibers called the corpus callosum. The function of the corpus callosum has been indicated in various split-brain studies. Its role is not only to exchange information between the two hemispheres but to synchronize the cortical activity between the two spheres.

Neurological research during the past fifteen years has attempted to prove that each side of the cerebrum has a particular specialization. Research on split-brain patients (Sperry, Bogen, Gazzaniga) demonstrates that the right and left hemispheres of the brain function in two distinctly different styles, encompassing distinct modes of perception and sensation and perhaps even conceptualization. Each hemisphere can function independently, although, in the normal person, the two hemispheres are assumed to cooperate and to possess the capacity to work in an integrated fashion. Studies by Robert Ornstein and David Galin suggest that, ideally, usage flows freely from hemisphere to hemisphere depending upon the task.

However, to characterize the hemispheres in strict terms of sensory modality or function (for example, to say that the left hemisphere is the language hemisphere) is incorrect. The hemispheric functions are not that strictly delineated. Most functions are represented in both hemispheres, as in comprehension of written and spoken language. But a clear relation between handedness and cerebral dominance has been established (Peele, p. 531). Linguistic functions reside within the dominant hemisphere, although some individuals have the capacity for linguistic expression within both cerebral spheres.

For methodological purposes, the way that the right and left hemispheres characteristically process the same information distinguishes one from the other. The two different cognitive styles of the right and left hemisphere can be simplistically contrasted with adjectives; the right being imagistic, nonverbal, alogical, spatial, global, intuitive, circular, holistic, while the left can be described as analytic, verbal, rational, direct, mathematical, systematic, linear, sequential. The left hemispheric mode is one of building systematically and methodically, in contrast to the right mode, which is one of intuitively assembling mental images into a whole.

The left hemisphere can be seen as housing the operations of ego functioning: planning, structuring, tasks of mastery, reality-oriented behavior, decision-making, perception, musculature control, and defensive functions. Right hemisphere operations, on the other hand, can be seen as involved with the symbolic development of the self: abstractions, symbolisms, imagery, and play. We refer to ego as a series of psychic operations that facilitate adaption; by self we mean mental representations that make up a person's identity and connect his/her experiences from the past to the present.

We have seen that both neurophysiological and psychological experimentation support a theoretical distinction between right and left modes of functioning. As expressive therapists, this research leads us to an investigation of how the two hemispheres may be encouraged to cooperate more fully and work in a fluid, balanced fashion to facilitate a more total integration or reintegration of the personality, which is the major goal of therapy. One possible outcome of this scientific research might be that the right hemisphere imagistic "gestalt" mode of functioning (which until now has been underrated and underestimated in both scientific and psychoanalytic theories, and overestimated in early theories of art and creativity) may begin to command a proper measure of respect and contribute significantly to a theory of expressive therapy.

At this point, an important notion to include is that of hemispheric dominance. A particular hemispheric dominance occurs through an excessive reliance on a certain cognitive and perceptual style. For example, there is a strong emphasis on the verbal or correlated left brain mode of functioning. In turn, a suppression of the other mode—nonverbal, visual, or correlated right brain functioning—occurs. The specialty that the expressive therapist brings to the arena of treatment is the awakening of the suppressed mode of functioning, which is usually an unsettling of the left brain dominance. Expressive therapy does not compartmentalize the two cognitive and perceptual styles, but strives to facilitate the release of energy in the neural structures through both verbal and nonverbal means. If a fluidity is reached between the two cognitive styles, the self can be used more completely and creatively.

In addition to the above research, another area of neurophysiological study that supports the theory of bihemispheric modes of functioning is that of measurement of the brain's electrical activity in different states of consciousness. Electroencephalography (EEG) is the graphic recording of the electrical activity of the cerebral cortex. Different types of electrical waves or rhythms are produced during different states. The wave we are most concerned with is the alpha. The alpha wave is the rhythm from the adult cerebral cortex in a rest state; thus, it is an indicator of a mental state in which there is an absence of visual imagery or activity. Alpha discharges tend to disappear when the subject concentrates. When alpha waves appear, it means the diminution of information processing over the particular cerebral hemisphere that is involved.

As we have already discussed, different tasks will stimulate one hemisphere or the other, predominantly. An example is the task of arranging blocks. Since this is basically a right hemisphere problem in spatial abstraction, the alpha waves, indicating a rest state, are located in the left hemisphere (Ornstein, 1978).

When the alpha is "on" in both, a subject reports that he/she is relaxed and not experiencing any visual imagery. Subjects who have experienced long periods of alpha activity report it to be very pleasant (Stoyva & Kamiya, 1968). The meaning of alpha waves as related psychodynamics has to do with altered states of awareness and, more specifically, to organismic self-regulation. Aside from rest, alpha activity is connected with particular types of task involvement, activities, or states of being, implying that certain kinds of psychological work may involve an alpha type of operation. In studies, it has been shown that as long as the individual tries to control his behavior or makes a conscious mental exertion, the alpha wave is not present. Therefore, the achievement of an alpha state involves the ability to let one's own organismic processes flow, to spontaneously self-regulate instead of acting in a deliberate, controlled fashion. It requires a certain level of risk-taking, akin to the fluidity of the creative state and parallel to the free associative state in psychoanalysis. Stoyva and Kamiya have shown a correlation between the private experience reported by the subjects and the recorded physiological event. They have also demonstrated that the subjects were able to achieve some level of control over that mental experience and concurrent physiological event.

Research at Rutgers Medical School is revealing the correlation between sexual and creative or problem-solving energies. Researchers have reported that during orgasm and creative states a shift in brain wave activity dominates on the right side while an increase in the alpha waves is found on the left side of the brain. This corresponds very closely to the psychoanalytic theory of creativity development that views a creative state as being the sublimation of libidinal drive into a socially useful act.

This same type of alpha shift and brain wave activity is experienced in meditational states. In the effort to induce a relaxed state and to reduce inner tensions, alpha wave EEG biofeedback techniques have been used. Within the central nervous system, the electrophysiological pheomena that accompanies the meditational process is this augmentation of alpha density. It has even been demonstrated that subjects can learn to self-regulate the production of alpha waves.

Besides the increase of alpha wave production, another effect of the meditational state is the high percentage of alpha and theta synchrony in the temporal and cortical areas. This synchronization is characteristic of the relaxation effect produced by a meditational state.

> More recent evaluations of EEG records in patients and subjects using these relaxation techniques reveal remarkable periods of intrahemispheric alpha and theta synchrony at times, even for inexperienced subjects (Glueck & Stroebel, 1977).

These observations have been confirmed in the studies of intrahemispheric and interhemispheric synchrony in experienced meditators.

In addition to the neurophysiological effects of the meditational process, another influence of the process seems to be the release of repressed memories. Within reports by subjects, this release has been described as a flood of intense affects and ideation (Whitman, Kramer, Ornstein, & Baldridge, 1967, p. 290). This appears to be a release of unconscious processes, which may well have a high content of nonverbal characteristics. There is no doubt that the therapeutic process could be hastened by the use of meditational techniques, which release previously repressed material.

These ordinarily repressed ideas, which surface during the meditational state, have been found to contain highly libidinal and aggressive ideations. This brings us to recent dream research, which in neurophysiological terms provides reason to reexamine original Freudian id/instinctual theory. The same limbic-midbrain circuits that regulate REM sleep are involved in sexual, oral, and aggressive behavior (Whitman, et al., 1967, p. 11).

The electrical activity that occurs in the dreaming state varies according to the stage of sleep. During the dreaming state (REM sleep) the EEG waves are similar to those produced at the initial transition from waking to sleep. The dreaming state has been described as a right hemisphere way of processing information (Cherry, 1977). One of the theories about the dream state is that during the period of time when the limbic system acquiesces, there is increased access to the nondominant hemisphere. Since this is usually the right hemisphere, sleep is often called the province of that hemisphere. The metaphorical activity and upsurge of repressed memories that occur in the dream state may be produced in altered states of consciousness, meditational states, and the free associative state in psychoanalytic therapy.

In REM deprivation studies, an interesting correlation between dreaming, access to fantasy material, and the psychological type of field independence has been proposed. Field independence is the quality of being able to hold onto one's perceptions within a changing environment. The field independent individual relies more on one's own internal cues, in contrast to the field dependent individual, who relies much more on external stimuli (from the "field") in making perceptual judgments. Of the three responses to REM deprivation, one pattern noticed in some individuals was the ability to compensate by "tapping the dream stream." It was generally found that these individuals possessed the ability to gain access to fantasy under all conditions. This was "associated with good control, high perceptual field independence and tolerance for delayed fantasy gratification" (Jones, 1970).

In addition to the research already mentioned, another theoretical position that deserves consideration is gestalt field theory. Field theory is an attempt to structurally organize data through an analogy with physics: fields of force (manifestation of energy), vectors, valences, charges. Metaphorically, the physics terminology is applied to human relationships and the inherent tensions therein. Specifically, within the therapy situation, the therapist must develop the particular charge or valence that will 'hook in' to the patient and his/her field in order to charge and ultimately change the relationship. In this usage, valence is used to describe positive and negative space, dependence and independence, submission and dominance.

The field is defined as the totality of coexisting, behavior-determining influences, which are conceived as being mutually interdependent. The individual is conceived as being a complex energy system. Psychical energy is released when the psychic system attempts to return to equilibrium after it has been thrown into a state of disequilibrium produced by an unequal, unbalanced tension within the system. Both organismic self-regulation and cognitive growth depend upon the balance and exchange between the psychic, interpersonal field space and the neurological, intrapersonal field space. Essentially, this movement involves establishing pathways from internal to external spaces.

Field theory and neurophysiological theory are chemical, electrical formulations. Both involve the concept of developing optimal charges and the concept of differentiation. What differentiation means, essentially, is that the perceptual field becomes more interconnected and consequently more complex so that we see a process of differentiation in motion. The premise of connecting field theory and neurology is that, with both, a psychic and hemispheric differentiation (highly developed, specified functions and abilities) is necessary in order for an individual to be able to move between hemispheres and the hemispheric thinking styles freely. This facile movement between spheres is similar to the ability to move freely between internal and external space. Furthermore, as the individual is able to avail him/herself of both modes of cognitive styles, his/her approach to the world is potentially more creative and differentiated. On a neurological level, there is equally a parallel in terms of neurological connections and complexity of neural transmissions.

The more cognitively mature an individual, the more differentiated his life space will be. An individual equally right and left sphere differentiated and field independent conceivably will be better able to move from inner to outer space. This would result in making one's own boundaries more permeable and in establishing flexibility and fluidity, which would increase one's ability to interact with others and the total environment.

The boundaries between the organism and the psychological environment (the individual's life space and the physical world) are permeable and mutually influencing; therefore, if an individual is field independent, he is able to move back and forth between those boundaries and adjust to the changes in his own inner life space and the outer environment. Conceivably, this individual may be more capable of creative problem-solving and greater integration of self, as opposed to the individual who is more fixed or rigid and therefore, less able to transcend or permeate his boundaries in interaction.

When greater specialization and differentiation are achieved in right and left hemispheres, greater integration and autonomy in the psychological life space should ensue. As of yet, differentiation remains a hypothetical construct, since it is not directly observable or measurable. At this point, differentiation within the physical substrata is not detectable or quantifiable. Among neuroanatomists, this type of theory remains mostly on the theoretical plane, since neuroanatomists are still debating the definition of consciousness.

As mentioned previously, the purpose of this paper has not been to describe the complexities of neuroanatomy but to point out the important significance of neurophysiologic process to various treatment approaches. One of the first simple implications for clinical treatment is the awareness that neural events are implicit in change; there is an interdependence between neurodynamics or physical structure and psychodynamics or mental structure.

The recording of EEG alpha waves has been useful in establishing the concept of interhemispheric exchange and synchrony as related to corresponding psychological states. The EEG evidence that information processing between cerebral hemispheres can be self-regulated in order to produce desired states can be applied to therapeutic endeavors, in an effort to achieve a greater synchrony within the self.

The implications of Kamiya's studies, dream research, meditationally related EEG research, and biofeedback techniques are that individuals can control neurophysiological events and the associated mental state or affect. This has also been demonstrated in the work of the Simontons with cancer patients at the Cancer Counseling and Research Center, Fort Worth, Texas. In addressing the emotional aspects of the cancer patient, they report a considerable effect on the patient's prognosis and the cancer remission (Simonton & Matthews-Simonton). By learning to control one's own internal environment, the chances for survival are greater. This control is achieved through mastery techniques such as visual imagery and relaxation-meditation.

This view of organismic control and self-regulation is contrary to early Freudian, deterministic beliefs. With the concept of controlling or changing stimulus situations in order to modify one's own internal environment follows the underlying assumption that maladaptive patterns are psychologically reversible. Establishing more adaptive patterns of behavior involves the rerouting of energy in the circuitous process of the nervous system to produce situations or relationships in which the individual can experience himself in different, positive, adaptive ways. This also involves connecting this new emotional state or experience with an interneuronal reorganization as expressed in the more adaptive behavior.

Spotnitz conceptualizes the analytic task in neurodynamic terms as

> ... one of shifting roundabout to more efficient interneuronic pathways, of deactivating pathways that drain off interneurons required for personality growth, or of increasing the neuron reserve (Spotnitz, 1969, p. 59).

Movement and change have to do with accepting polarities and making one's psychological life space boundaries more fluid and permeable. Neurodynamically, this involves a greater differentiation of neuronic organizations in order to allow a freeing and recircuiting of neuronic pathways.

It is notable that the present intense interest and investigation of cerebral hemispheric differences is an experience of cyclical revival. Historically speaking, the beginning connections of psychological implication to neurological study were founded in the late nineteenth century when concentrated attention was paid to cerebral splits in the study of aphasia. Before Freud committed himself almost totally to psychological investigation, he wrote on the subject of the split brain in his last neurological essay, *On Aphasia* (1891). Thus, he laid the foundation for the neurological implications in psychological treatment.

Our discussion of psychoanalysis and its theoretical correlations to neurophysiological research will be broadened more generally to the topic of psychotherapy and treatment. One of the techniques of classical psychoanalysis, free association, has specific reference to our discussion. The free associative state has been briefly mentioned in relation to meditational and alpha states. Paralleling the effect that the meditational state has of releasing repressed memories and affects, the free associative state is effective in reaching deeper psychical levels. Free association has to do with tracing a symbol backwards, with the eventual ultimate being to reach the symbol's primary energy source. There is a progressive peeling off or spiraling down to the more core issue and essential energy. Attainment of this state involves an "allowing" of organismic energy and attitudes in contrast to a concentrated "doing" effort. This state also involves a certain amount of risk taking to be able to lose control in order to engender the creative part of one's self. This "allowance" is similar to the alpha state of spontaneous self-regulation. In neurodynamic terms, the neuronic pathways are opened up for the easier facilitation of the discharge of feelings. There is an unlocking of energy in the neural structures, which ordinarily inhibit communicative discharge. This release of neuronic pathways not only creates an available neuron reserve, but allows for change, in that neuronic pathways are freed for the necessary reorganization involved in learning. "An excessive tie-up of neurons in fixed and pathological patterns is generally associated with mental illness" (Spotnitz, 1969, p. 56). One of the tasks of therapy is to facilitate the activation, organization, and release of this energy through verbal and nonverbal means.

In addition to the technique of free association, another concept from the psychoanalytic tradition that relates to our discussion is the postulation of primary and secondary process. This theory of the psyche has many parallels in the scientific findings concerning bilateral cerebral cortex structure and functioning. It is striking that the right hemisphere, which has strong similarities to the primary process, is essentially nonverbal and does not appear to communicate with the socially oriented methods of verbalization and logical thought, but which nonetheless contains a full range of emotion, memories, images, and unique areas of specialization. Like the right cerebral hemi-sphere, primary process working is one of association rather than syllogistic logic. Secondary processes easily correspond to the rational, linear, and verbal modes of the left hemisphere. It is concerned with analytically and causally oriented relations.

The need for the integration of both verbal and nonverbal qualities can be illustrated more generally in the two current divergent trends in the field of art therapy: that of Edith Kramer, espousing art as therapy in a sublimating, Apollonian, left hemispheric sense, and that of Margaret Naumberg, espousing art as a tool for verbal psychotherapy in a spontaneous, insight, Dionysian, right hemispheric mode. The integration of verbal and nonverbal therapies is the acknowledgment in a third alter-native trend, creative expressive analysis, that one cannot deal in imagery without words, and reversibly, in words without imagery.

Therapy is the activity of achieving synchrony within the self; synchrony in the conceptual as well as hemispheric sense. Metaphorically, the attitude and discipline of therapy can be viewed as the true integration of right and left hemispheric functioning. Effective psychotherapy involves the discipline of analysis combined with the flexibility of receptivity; analytic and playful skills coalesce to integrate content and feeling in treatment. Therapy is a reeducative process, which involves learning and defining one's needs. It is analogous to education in that one learns the art of problem solving and the art of self-expression; ultimately, it is all about change.

Truly oversimplified, therapy aims for striking balances and setting seemingly diverse dichotomies into equilibrium. It also involves reconnecting to lost parts and experiencing an openness within one's self to different thinking styles. Expres-sive analysis involves connecting the verbal and nonverbal parts of ourselves.

> Expressive analysis attempts to bring about an integration of the spatial, intuitive and nonverbal modes of interaction with the ego mastery skills that are so necessary to function in today's society.

> Expressive analysis combines right and left brain oriented thera-
> pies to help the client achieve body-mind integration . . . The
> expressive analyst works within a framework of ego development
> where goals are self-actualization and the mobilization of cre-
> ative energies (From a brochure produced by the Institute for
> Expressive Analysis, New York, New York).

Effective therapy, then, is a two-step process entailing the primary ventilation, expression, or catharsis followed by the development of alternative methods of coping, which involves a
more secondary type of process of mastery and integration. The
insight or expression does not acquire its full meaning unless
cathected to the secondary process sphere in verbalization.

The act of integrating verbal and nonverbal, primary and
secondary, left and right hemispheric modes of being involves
a certain level of creativity. In this light, creative living (along
Maslowian concepts of creativity as a lifestyle) means constant
change and movement. It is seen as a state of being: spontaneous, fluid, divergent, and a supreme state of emotional health.
One of the key elements in creativity is the ability to take a risk,
to effect a change, and to give up the known. In the therapeutic
situation, the creative process can serve as an agent to foster
investment in an experience or image. This absorption or investment in image or experience allows transcendence of it, bringing new creative elements to the therapeutic vista. This notion
is surprisingly similar to the previously mentioned neurodynamic states experienced in the alpha and interhemispheric
synchronization: both involve a state of spontaneous absorption, which allows transcendence through integration.

The creative process could be compared to a Piagetian
stage of development, the preoperative stage, when intuitive
thinking frees the child to fantasy, free association, and ani-
mism. It is exactly this childlike naivete and openness to experience that in an adult is manifested by heightened sense of
awareness and absorption. In other terms, this creative state of
metaphoric thinking can be viewed as an openness to primary
process in psychoanalytic terms, or in a neurophysiological

phrase, an openness to the less dominant mode of operation, usually the right hemispheric mode.

Creativity involves the vacillation between two different ego states of inner fantasy and outer reality, analogous to the two different cognitive-perceptual styles related to right and left brain functioning. Creativity is not correlated to one style, but to the ability to travel fluidly between the two. Bringing the different processing of the two hemispheres together can result in the most creative solutions to problems. Therefore, the creative individual has a greater integrative capacity. One measure of both creativity and emotional health is flexibility and the ability to creatively change, while illness or emotional distress leads to a "freezing of behavior into unalterable and unsatiable patterns" (Kubie, 1958, p. 20). In neurophysiological terms, this would be demonstrated in a greater synchronization and integration of the right and left hemispheric operations. Psychodynamically, in psychoanalytic terms, the creative individual would be one who integrates primary and secondary process. Within a Jungian frame of reference, this same individual would have a greater capacity to integrate polar opposites. While in gestalt terminology, creativity would involve integrating differentiated parts within the totality of the life space. Essentially, the creative individual is able to strike a delicate balance between his inner (fantasy) and outer (reality) perceptions of the world.

Among the many tasks facing the therapist, one of the first is recognizing energy balances within relationships. There is a particular beat, rhythm, and charge to therapy. Every client has a different electrical charge, and the therapist's countercharge in balance makes for an optimal, electrical field. The therapist must learn to break through defenses and resistances creatively, establishing the proper valence.

One may conceptualize the expressive therapist's job as helping to facilitate the creative and therapeutic process, via different approaches, techniques, and materials. The expressive therapist offers a different cognitive style, akin to a nonverbal, right brain functioning, ultimately working with both cognitive styles to organismic integration. The expressive therapist needs to assess for each client how he or she utilizes the two hemispheric modes of operation, which is dominant and when, where the two conflict, in what situations or activities they are most cooperative or most at odds, and when one mode is used habitually or defensively. Resistance in an area may be seen as a fear of change reflecting a lifelong pattern of dominance or conflict and as a major impediment to creative growth.

After a study of neurophysiological research, it is quite possible to see how these points may be related to the use of expressive therapy in many varying situations. Mindful of establishing the appropriate charge within the relationship, the expressive therapist chooses the prescriptive expressive treatment experience: mirroring, playful, meditative, mastery, expressive, ventilative. If the expressive therapist is highly conscious of evidences in the client's behavior that indicate either a right or left cerebral specialization, they can thereby identify an individual's dominant mode of operation. After establishing an individual's cognitive style and manner of perceiving the world, the therapist is better able to locate the source of the client's strengths and energy.

Apart from verbalization, a separate, symbolic process exists as is manifested in right hemispheric, spatial thinking. The implication being, that in working with a certain psychic structure, the therapist must develop commensurate techniques to deal with those particular hemispheric functions and their styles. Most of this paper is a presentation of philosophic ideation and premise, not a directive set for treatment. The ultimate goal of this exploration of correlates is to develop a system of personality structure and specific therapeutic techniques that have a neurological basis. Creativity diagnostics or assessments considering particular hemispheric thinking modes would be used as prescriptions for treatment in the expressive therapies.

The latter portion of this text will deal with several clinical examples to illustrate the use of expressive therapies in light of neurodynamic considerations. Hopefully, these specifics can be generalizable to many populations. One type of client who would especially benefit from this approach would be the aphasic, who is able cognitively to understand language but whose verbal ability to communicate is impaired. Through art or expressive therapy, the aphasic would be able to develop this nonverbal and basically imagistic means of communication. This therapeutic approach would call for a holistic, right hemispheric style on the part of the therapist in order to foster and to establish new patterns of understandable communication. In work with a child whose right cerebral hemisphere had been damaged in an automobile accident, the interworking between the two cerebral types of expression was actualized.

In light of his brain damage, the factors of short-term memory deficits, fatigue, and spatial orientation problems had to be taken into consideration. The neurological deficiency leads to an ego deficiency, causing a tremendous sense of inadequacy and perplexity within the child. Expressive therapy with this child, as with other brain-damaged individuals, calls for a controlled and structured means of expression that will foster mastery and competence without being a disorganizing experience. Initially, the child expressed a set pattern of images, which he was allowed and encouraged to repeatedly depict pictorially. After several months, with each session he would add a new element to his imagery repertoire. With this slow expansion of his nonverbal, right-hemispheric-like vocabulary, there was a concurrent increase in his verbalization and left-hemispheric-like productions. Conceivably, the development of holistic right hemispheric modes of cognition and perception could stimulate the left hemispheric workings.

With another patient population, such as the schizophrenic, different approaches in treatment will be taken. The schizophrenic patient may need the therapist to help ground the fantasy in reality and to aid the client in slowly replacing its defensive function with a more communicative one. Schizophrenic imagery may be used defensively; and in such a case, art is not just for imagery but is used in the service of developing ego skills as well. The schizophrenic remains locked into his private fantasy world of imagery, and one task is to help the client permeate his boundaries in order to move between his inner life space and the psychological field of his outer world. Similar to the young child's experience of the world, the schizophrenic state is one of undifferentiation between self and world. Through a process of differentiation, the individual becomes less perceptually and stimulus bound by the immediate situation. The aim of the creative aspect of the treatment, which aids in this type of differentiation, is to center, contain, and direct the energy in a more secondary, left hemispheric type of operation. This focusing and integration of symbolism is done in an ego enhancing way, aiding differentiation. The nonverbal activity acts to structure the flowing imagery and to provide a channel for the discharge of energy. In this instance, expressive therapy is used as a meditative process using the two elements of focusing and repetition in the pursuit of task mastery.

In a specific case of schizophrenia, the technique of mirroring is used. This nonverbal approach is reminiscent of early mother-child mutual cueing in an attempt to restore some early sense of self. In more traditional modes of psychotherapy, verbal reflections would be used to feed back what the individual was experiencing. With expressive therapy modalities, this mirroring occurs on a nonverbal level, where the sensory experience (basically right hemisphere) is related to the verbal experience (basically left hemisphere). Reciprocal movement reinforces the recognition of the self and others and also provides physical stimulation. The mirroring or imitation will lead out of itself with an increasing differentiation between self and the nonself. It is also a means to enter the client's world using his language, acknowledging that he/she is safe to be as he/she is.

Working with such a client who is experiencing a severe disturbance of body image and ego functioning, the therapist uses early forms of the symbolic process in order to recreate and reintegrate very primary sensory and concrete self and object representations. Early preverbal memories may be accessible through movement and more holistic, imagistic methods. After tapping into these spatial representations, they can later be linked to secondary processes and translated into verbal concepts.

With neurotic life styles, the treatment approach within the expressive therapeutic modalities will differ. A neurotic personality with obsessive-compulsive features may indeed have symbolic material accessible, but may need help in connecting those symbols to meaningful affects rather than words alone. The activation of expression and resolution of conflicts takes place within a more spontaneous, loosening up experience. Here the therapist might introduce gestalt techniques of becoming one's images to tap into the feeling tone.

Deikman suggests a relationship between the defense systems of the obsessive-compulsive and hysterical personalities with left and right hemispheric thinking. The obsessive-compulsive is involved with analytically focused thought processes. With an emphasis on left-hemispheric-like thinking, this type of client is adept at heady intellectualization, cutting off somatic experiences involved in emotion and imagination. Expressive techniques to creatively deal with these types of defenses have been briefly mentioned. In contrast to the obsessive-compulsive personality, the hysterical personality as described by Deikman is dominated by the qualities of the right hemisphere. This type of client lacks focus in letting sensory, imaginative, and emotional experiences take control. The task of expressive therapy is to provide a focusing experience where the rational, logical parts of the client can be experienced and internalized within the framework of the nonverbal realm.

Much of the therapist's work with many clients has to do with awakening their sense of play. With appropriate clients, loosening ego controls helps to further the development of the permeability between the parts of the psychological life space. Not only does this help to reach deeper psychical levels, but by aiding in the individual's recognition and integration of the two modes of hemispheric operation, it helps to stimulate interhemispheric synchronization. Through play, imagery places the sensory experience into a sort of framework. The process of play is not self-contained, for in connecting the affects to words, unneutralized energy is transformed into neutralized, reality-oriented secondary process.

Another type of client, who due to faulty or inadequate internalization lacks imagination, may need help in creating his own symbols through art, dreamwork, fantasy, or by the verbal and nonverbal interaction with the "symbol" of the therapist. This is especially true of the depressed client. Characterized by physiological and mental changes, depression is often also marked by sleep disturbances. Not only is there a loss of Stage IV sleep, the deepest and most restful sleep stage, but "brain wave studies of depressed patients have indicated nervous circuits operating inefficiently" (Scarf). The loss of Stage IV sleep and the central processing problem both indicate that the depressed organism's system is unable to restore itself in a self-balancing fashion. Deprived of deep sleep and its right hemispheric work of night organization, the implications for treatment might include those approaches of a restorative nature. The therapist might help the client gain access to the deprived mode through nonverbal modalities and symbolic play in order to restore a semblance of metaphoric activity and a right hemispheric cognitive style, which is at once divergent and connective.

In summary, through an exploration of cerebral hemispheric differences, this paper has attempted to investigate some of the neurological components that may be involved in psychotherapeutic treatment with a special emphasis on the creative aspect, or the integration of different cognitive-perceptual styles. The possibilities in light of this approach seem infinite, yet there remain many unanswered questions, and much more specific research is needed on the different developmental levels of the symbolic process and the bilateral workings of the psyche, in order to fully understand how the expressive therapist can work most effectively with creative and therapeutic process.

In utilizing a neurophysiological framework, some of the implications for treatment are briefly as follows. Treatment should assess an individual's psychic life space and should effect a greater balance of neurological and psychic space. This is based on the premise that by increasing neurophysiological electrical connections, psychological interconnectedness will occur. One of the functions of the therapist would be to assess the polarization of the psychological space in order to make it broader and more permeable with increasing stages of differentiation. The postulation being that regardless of which hemisphere is dominant, if both cerebral spheres are in greater balance there is a greater ability to augment an autonomous, creative state of flexibility.

This type of vital balance of opposites is necessitated by a certain degree of flexibility. This is achieved and promoted in creative states. Expressive analysis can be viewed as a most synthesizing activity, which provides the individual with the opportunity to experience his/her personal creative style or being. Flexibility, as embodied in truly creative work and living, is an essential element of effectiveness and change.

The basic premise of expressive therapy is that the creative state is a healthy state. Expressive therapy is particularly effective in facilitating the state of balance, heightened awareness and flexibility needed to achieve the integration of the two parts of ourselves as symbolized by the two cerebral hemispheric modes. This involves an awakening of the less dominant parts of ourselves (usually right hemisphere operations) and total self-integration. Any type of learning or acquisition of new skills involves reorganization and specialization. This concept of learning as a reorganization of perceptions is a gestalt notion. Ultimately, therapy involves the learning of more adaptive ways of being in the world. Neurophysically, this could involve brain recircuiting and reorganization of neuronal contacts. The implications are that one can manipulate both the inner and the outer environment, rather than passively responding. This manipulation can provide a better understanding of the options for alternative thinking and life change.

In analytic terms, learning to become more open to one's primary process can provide the means to explore self-imagery, which, in turn, leads to knowledge of one's life space. By connecting to parts in images within the field or self, the whole self expands in differentiated function.

Expressive therapy is related to the process of exchange and integration, metaphorically and neurophysiologically. The treatment techniques of expressive therapy and expressive analysis mediate between psychological and neurophysiological space: between right and left modes of operation; verbal and nonverbal modes of communication; ego and self.

REFERENCES

Bogen, J., & Bogen, G. The other side of the brain II: An appositional mind. *Bulletin of the Los Angeles Neurological Societies,* July 1969, *34.*

Bogen, J. The other side of the brain III: The corpus callosum and creativity. *Bulletin of the Los Angeles Neurological Societies,* October 1969, *34.*

Bruner, J. *On knowing: Essays for the left hand.* Cambridge, Mass.: Harvard University Press, 1966.

Cherry, L. A new vision of dreams. *New York Times Magazine,* July 3, 1977, p. 13.

Deikman, A. J. Bimodal consciousness. *Archives of General Psychology,* 1971, *45:* 481–489.

Galaburda, A. M.; LeMay, M.; Kemper, T. L.; & Geschwind, N. Right-left assymetries in the brain. *Science,* February 24, 1978; *199,* 852–856.

Galin, D. Implications of psychiatry of left and right cerebral specialization. *Archives of General Psychiatry,* October 1974; *31,* 572–575.

Gazzaniga, M. *The split brain.* American History Lecture Series.

Glueck, B. C., & Stroebel, C. F. Psychophysiological Correlates of Relaxation. In Sugarman, A. A., & Tarter, R. E., *Expanding dimensions of consciousness.* New York: Springer Publishing Co., Inc., 1977.

Jaynes, J. *The origin of consciousness in the breakdown of bicameral mind.* Boston: Houghton Mifflin Co., 1976.

Jones, R. M. *The new psychology of dreaming.* New York: The Viking Press, 1970.

Kety, S. S. A biologist examines the mind and behavior. *Science,* December 23, 1960, *132,* 1861–70.

Kubie, L. S. *Neurotic distortion of the creative process.* Toronto: Noonday Press, 1958.

Lee, D. Lineal and nonlineal codifications of reality. *Psychosomatic Medicine,* March-April, 1950, *12.*

Lewin, K. *A dynamic theory of personality: Selected papers.* New York: McGraw-Hill Co., 1935.

Lobell, J. Eureka! I'm coming. *Playboy,* December 1977, pp. 137–138.

Lowenfeld, V., & Brittain, W. L. *Creative and mental growth.* New York: Macmillan Publishing Co., 1957.

Luria, A. R. *The working brain: An introduction to neuropsychology.* New York: Basic Books, Inc., 1973.

Mahoney, M. Reflections on the cognitive-learning trend in psychotherapy. *American Psychologist,* January, 1977, *5,* 5–13.

Ornstein, R. E., Ed. *The nature of human consciousness.* San Francisco: W. H. Freeman and Co., 1973.

Ornstein, R. *The psychology of consciousness.* New York: Harcourt Brace Jovanovich, 1977.

Ornstein, R. The split and whole brain. *Human Nature,* May 1978, pp. 76–83.

Peele, T. L. *The neuroanatomic basis for clinical neurology.* New York: McGraw Hill, 1977, p. 531.

Scarf, M. From joy to depression. In Parr, L., Ed. *Science of the Times,* New York: New York Times Books, 1978, p. 119.

Simonton, O. C. & Matthews-Simonton. S. *Stress, psychological factors and cancer.* (Sound recording). Saratoga. Ca: Cognetics. 1974–76, 6 cassettes.

Sperry, R. W. Apparent doubling of consciousness in each hemisphere. *American Psychologist,* October 1968, *23.*

Sperry, R. W. Cerebral organization and behavior. *Science,* 1961, *133,* 1749–1757.

Sperry, R. W. The great cerebral commissure. *Scientific American,* January 1964, pp. 42–52; August, 1967, pp. 24–29.

Spotnitz, H. *Modern psychoanalysis of the schizophrenic patient.* New York: Grune & Stratton, 1969.

Stoyva, J., & Kamiya, J. Electrophysiological studies of dreaming as the prototype of a new strategy in the study of consciousness. *Psychological Review,* 1968; *75,* 195–205.

Von Bonin, G. Anatomical assymetries of the cerebral hemispheres. In Mountcastle, V. B., Ed., *Interhemispheric relations and cerebral dominance.* Baltimore: Johns Hopkins University Press, 1962, pp. 1–6.

Wallace, R. K. Physiological effects of transcendental meditation. *Science,* 1970; *167,* 1751–1754.

Whitman, R. M., Kramer, M., Ornstein, P. H., & Baldridge, B. J. The physiology, psychology, and utilization of dreams. *American Journal of Psychiatry,* September 1967; *124,* 287–302.

Chapter 7

DEVELOPMENTAL ISSUES FROM ACADEMIC CHILD PSYCHOLOGY FOR THE EXPRESSIVE THERAPIST

Floyd D. Turner, Ph.D.
Ann Winn-Mueller, M.S.W.

INTRODUCTION

The goal of this chapter is to introduce the expressive therapist to themes and issues from academic psychology that may be useful in clarifying both treatment and theoretical issues. Since much of expressive therapy involves the use of treatment approaches that are either nonverbal or preverbal in their impact, the focus of this presentation will be on those aspects of early growth and maturation that emphasize this side of the person. Recently, much valuable work has been done by academic child psychologists, and the work seems to point psychology back in the direction of exploring the inner world of the person as well as the stimulus-response (S-R) world of the person.

Learning theory has seemed to be incompatible with much of psychoanalytic and psychodynamic therapies. Academic psychologists are learning that the simple S-R models of the forties, fifties, and sixties cannot account for enough of the human experience to be satisfactory methods of discovery. Research and theory-building by Piaget and Chomsky have accelerated the shift to other models of discovery, and some of these findings should be of great value to the expressive therapist.

It should be noted, however, that this chapter is a sampling of the research, since the limitations of space that are necessarily imposed preclude a full exposition of the field. It is hoped that the reader will pursue the broader issues raised here.

GENETICS

The role of genetics has not been fully acknowledged in the practice of expressive therapy, because one's genetic endowment is not subject to change. It is, however, this very immutability that should prompt the attention of expressive therapists, since heredity can affect not only such characteristics as eye color, sex, and height, but also those properties of a person that are actively utilized in the therapeutic process. Genetic contributions to the development of such traits as intelligence, activity level, disposition, and affect, must be taken into consideration by the expressive therapist who sets out to examine a patient's developmental patterns. Genetically-based discrepancies in, for example, temperament between parent and child may lead during infancy to difficulties in the formation of a symbiotic bond between the two: a mother who is by and large passive, quiet, and good-natured may find herself unable to form an attachment to an active and demanding infant who appears to kick and scream incessantly.

A child who thus does not conform to parents' expectations, whether it be in regard to temperament, activity level, affect, intelligence, or some other characteristic with at least a partially genetic basis, is often in danger of being labeled "bad" and "abnormal." Expressive therapists who are cognizant of constitutional differences among children—even among those belonging to the same family—are less apt to perpetuate the labeling mistakes of parents or to attribute the child's problems wholly to deficits in parenting. Furthermore, such therapists may be able to avoid recreating in therapy the original failure to form a symbiotic attachment, or at least to recognize the difficulty of forming such a bond.

Schizophrenia is perhaps the most salient among disorders in which biochemical imbalance may well play a major role. "Twin studies" conducted with schizophrenics have thus far formed the primary source of data regarding the role of genetic factors in mental illness (Gottesman & Shields, 1972). Greater concordance of traits (symptoms) has been found between identical twins (i.e., the same genotype) than between either fraternal twins (with different genetic endowments but the same family environment) or nontwin siblings. Furthermore, studies investigating the symptom concordance rates among siblings reared apart have yielded results indicating that such rates for schizophrenia are higher among identical twins than they are for either fraternal twins or nontwin siblings. Such findings support the notion that genetic factors are preeminent in the later development of schizophrenia (see Gottesman & Shields, 1972, for an extensive review of this literature).

Caution must be taken, however, to avoid the opposite extreme, i.e., attributing dysfunction, even among schizophrenics, solely to genetic makeup. A number of problems have been noted with regard to the aforementioned twin studies, the most severe of which is the fact that the concordance measure of schizophrenia for identical twins is higher than the reliability of diagnosing schizophrenia in the population at large. It is probable, therefore, that the results have been contaminated by some experimental artifact. Even were this not the case, it is quite possible that other factors could account for the results obtained in twin studies, e.g., prenatal or neonatal environment, the special character of the relationship between twins, etc. Thus, it is prudent to view the findings of genetic studies with caution.

The notion of a genetic or biochemical contribution to dysfunctionality raises a number of issues of concern to expressive therapists. One major implication pertains to the grandiose view therapists may hold of their own efficacy: there may be limits to the changes that therapy can produce. Therapists who operate on the assumption that they can effect improvement in all areas, even when working with schizophrenic or neurologically impaired patients may well be creating a trap for themselves and rendering themselves less effective in those areas more susceptible to intervention.

In addition, for therapists who, by personal inclination or training, tend to spurn the notion of a chemical contribution to psychiatric problems, it is particularly important to be aware of the possibility that genetic or biological factors may well play a major role. Despite individual preferences for this or that school of thought regarding the origins of psychopathology, the field of psychology is far from being an exact science. Practitioners would thus be well advised to retain an open mind when reviewing new evidence as it emerges.

EARLY DEVELOPMENTAL FACTORS

Since the skills of expressive therapists are particularly well suited for addressing early preverbal experience of the patient, it is important for the therapist to understand the structure of development during the early phase of life, and to understand the impact of developmental limitations on the capacity of the child to interact with the environment. It is particularly noteworthy that some of the developmental difficulties discussed in this and the following sections emerge directly as treatment issues, e.g., the problems of maintaining object constancy.

Research on the early developmental skills of the infant, particularly with respect to evolving perceptual capacities, has demonstrated that most children progress rather consistently through a series of observable changes. While some of these stages seem to be related to neurological maturation, others appear to be related to the infant's experience of interacting with the world.

The rate at which the brain develops postnatally follows a relatively well defined course. The early-to-late order of development of brain functions is as follows: motor area; somesthetic-sensory area; visual area; auditory area; and then other areas (Conel, 1952). The expressive therapist should be sensitive to the different orders of regression which may occur depending on the therapeutic modality being used. For example, the motor area is one of the earliest to develop, and the auditory area one of the latest. Therefore, it might be expected that an auditory therapeutic medium would touch later developmental issues (i.e., those around the sixth month) than would such media as dance therapy and activity therapy; the latter may be more capable of evoking in patients the most primitive types of feelings.

Knowledge of the differential development of brain functions may also be helpful to the expressive therapist in assessing patients' progress. Becoming attuned to the sequence could allow the therapist to determine if the same developmental process occurs with regard to developmental regression of patients in treatment.

In the following sections, development of specific skills and functions will be discussed in greater detail. Of particular importance to the expressive therapist, whose work often entails the recreation of preverbal experiences, is the notion that deficits in early physiological maturation may have a profound impact on the capacity of the infant to form an emotional bond with the parent. This limitation is especially important within the context of Melanie Klein's contention that very early personality development is a function of the quality of parenting. Presumably, therefore, the perceptual and developmental skills of the infant play a major role in shaping the character and structure of early objects, e.g. with regard to the "good breast/good mother" and "bad breast/bad mother" dichotomy. Thus, integration of object "splits," impingement of developmental processes on the emerging sense of ego or self, and the impact of evolving skills on the nature of those objects that the infant is capable of internalizing are all issues that bear on the work of the expressive therapist, not only with those patients who have experienced early deficits, but with all patients.

PRENATAL ENVIRONMENT

Certain aspects of the prenatal environment should be noted by expressive therapists, whose efforts to provide treatment may be either blocked or rendered more effective by the patient's experiences *in utero*. Of particular import in this regard are prenatal environmental features, which may influence subsequent developments but which might in the past have been attributed to genetic factors. A number of chemical substances, for instance, when ingested by the mother, are transmitted directly to the fetus via the umbilical cord. Thus, it is probable that the offspring of mothers who make excessive use of alcohol, nicotine, or caffeine during pregnancy will manifest the effects of such use in both physical stature and emotional lability (Arena, 1964; Baker, 1960; Simpson, 1957). Excessive use of caffeine to combat depression or of alcohol to get to sleep may also produce cyclical patterns of behavior that emerge during the first months of the child's life, either in terms of sleep patterns or in diurnal variations of mood.

Recently, there has been concern regarding the impact on the child's subsequent development of pharmacological agents used at birth to reduce maternal discomfort. Substances given to the mother also affect the infant and may limit the child's capacity to form an emotional attachment with the mother shortly after birth (Arena, 1964). The narcoleptic effect of these substances needs to be understood by the creative therapist.

Other features of the prenatal environment that carry implications for the practice of expressive therapy should be noted. As an example, the womb is an effective sound chamber and transmits muffled sounds to the fetus (Peiper, 1925). Recent research has shown that playing the mother's heartbeat seems to be soothing; the greatest effect is obtained from playing the heartbeat of the infant's own mother. Thus, it appears that the infant has the capacity to recall auditory features from the womb[1] (Mussen, 1970).

The implications of such findings for the expressive therapist are manifold. The use of sound (music) with regressed patients may well recreate aspects of a very early symbiotic, fused relationship with the mother and the primitive structure thereof. Cognizance of this possibility would allow the therapist to recognize any tendency on the patient's part to regress around such issues, as well as to capitalize on the process for therapeutic purposes. Schizophrenic patients may be particularly attracted to music and primitive, heartbeat-like rhythms as a means of easing perceived disruptions in the symbiotic attachment with the mother.

For all patients, early object relations may have an audio as well as a visual component associated with them. The therapist needs to understand the nature of internalized objects from a visual, audio, and tactile standpoint in order to make the most effective use of the various media of expressive therapy.

Finally, the sensual similarity between being immersed in a swimming pool and being surrounded by amniotic fluid in the womb should be taken into consideration by therapists who plan to utilize aquatic therapy. Among severely regressed patients in particular, the experience of water therapy may recreate the prenatal environment; therapists should be sensitive to communications around this issue. Moreover, aquatic therapy may be the arena in which activity-level incompatibility between patient and therapist is limned most starkly. While the therapist may envision aquatic therapy as a means of encouraging more active and assertive behavior on the part of the patient, the soothing, womblike qualities of warm water might

[1]Normal hearing is impaired in the fetus, however, because the Eustachian tube is filled with liquid. When the neonate yawns after birth, the fluid drains (Carmichael, 1970).

well produce the opposite effect in regressed patients, i.e., increased passivity.

Another way in which prenatal environmental factors may play a role in the development of the child is through the intrauterine effects of events in the mother's world. Anxiety-provoking occurrences in the external environment (e.g., an argument) can stimulate the secretion of adrenaline in the mother and accelerate the rate at which her heart beats. The adrenaline is rapidly transmitted to the fetus via the unbilical cord, producing a virtually simultaneous anxiety response in the fetus as well. The co-occurrence of an accelerated heartbeat on the part of the mother and a chemically-induced anxiety response in the child constitutes a direct parallel to the conditioning paradigm response (i.e., anxiety following increased heartrate) that may reappear following birth whenever the infant is in close proximity to another person's heart (e.g. during feeding), expecially that of the mother. Thus, tension experienced by the parent may be mirrored by the child, a notion that could carry grave implications for the formation of a symbiotic attachment. This possibility is one that the expressive therapist should remain alert to not only in terms of exploring the patient's developmental patterns, but in regard as well to the anxiety-producing potential of various musical and rhythmic configurations.

PERCEPTUAL DEVELOPMENT

Auditory

Despite the relatively late development of auditory functions, the infant does have early auditory experiences with the mother that can influence the formation of a symbiotic attachment and the internalization of objects. As noted earlier, the infant is capable of differentiating the sound of the mother's heartbeat from the first day of life. Infants become calmer when placed in a nursery where any mother's heartbeat is played over the sound system; the infant whose mother's heartbeat is played is the most calm. It seems clear, then, that the sound of the mother's heartbeat has been stored in the child's memory, and thus constitutes one of the infant's earliest primary organizing perceptions of the mother.

The infant is able to hear at birth, after the amniotic fluid is cleared from the ears, with apparently the full complement of auditory *mechanisms* developed. The literature is not clear, however, regarding the capacities of children to differentiate sound before six months of age, when the auditory area of the brain is thought to reach maturity. Some studies suggest that there is an almost immediate capacity to orient toward sound, while other studies suggest that this capacity is delayed. The contradictions in the literature seem to be due to differences in measures of the wakefulness of the infant during these earlier months of life. It is clear that a sudden, loud sound does produce a startle response in the first month of life, whether or not the infant is asleep. The lack of specificity in other areas of audition is probably due to the relatively late postnatal development of the auditory area of the brain (Carmichael, 1970).

A number of implications for the practice of expressive therapy can be derived from the aforegoing data. Despite the fact that infants can hear and respond to sound from birth, their ability to process and integrate auditory input is relatively slower in developing. Throughout the maturational process, however, they are subject to auditory experiences, which appear to play a pivotal role in the development of early object relationships. The fact that sound is received by the child, but not adequately processed, leads one to expect that the internal auditory representations of objects thus formulated might well be more distorted and primitive than, for example, visual representations.

One effect of this process might be an inability on the part of the patient to connect a reevocation in therapy of primitive feelings with an actual developmental memory. While patient response to certain rhythms may suggest the reaction of early auditory experiences, and while the patients themselves may recognize and acknowledge the familiarity and primitive quality of the feelings thus evoked, the chances of their being able to link the sensations they are experiencing with actual memories are slight. With regard to auditory experiences in particular, distortions caused by the developmental lag between the capacity to receive input and the capacity to process it is probably too great to allow accurate recall. Furthermore, since almost all such memories are preverbal, they may not easily lend themselves to recall and expression by someone who has long since learned to deal with the world primarily through verbal means. The latter consideration affects not only auditory, but visual, motor, and somesthetic experiences as well.

Given the temporal gap that separates the development of auditory reception capacity and auditory processing capacity, the role of sound may assume particular importance in treatment situations, not only for expressive therapists, but indeed for all therapists. When dealing with the early precognitive auditory experiences of regressed patients, it is likely that tonal patterns, rhythms, and other specific features of sound have greater impact on patients than does the specific content of the sound itself. Similarly, patients may be more keenly attuned to the therapist's tone of voice than to the content of his/her speech. It has been noted frequently that patients who consistently function in a more regressed mode are often extremely sensitive to the mood of the therapist. It is likely that this sensitivity to mood operates through an auditory medium; that is, the patient hears anxiety (or depression or anger) in the tonal quality of the therapist's voice, regardless of the content of the therapist's speech.

Visual

Visual imagery plays an important part in establishing the earliest relationship between self and other and even in the establishment of the earlier body-self. The visual skills of the infant have been extensively studied and the development is characterized by a complex sequence of stages with certain perceptual capacities present at birth and others emerging later. There is evidence that the child possesses most of the essential ocular skills at birth, although the eye itself is not fully developed. Notable exceptions include an inability to focus the eyes closer than eight (8) inches until the age of four to eight weeks, and an apparent lack of color vision until well after birth (Carmichael, 1970).

The infant is able to track movement in the first hours after birth and to distinguish shades and brightness from the first day. The existence of more organized perceptions has been documented in the work of Bower (1966), whose studies indicate that the infant has the capacity to observe objects holistically by the age of three months and to rotate objects by the age of nine months.

These findings carry a number of implications for the expressive therapist. Given the relatively earlier development of visual (as compared to auditory) skills, it would appear that art therapy, which entails the creation of imagery, may be a more effective means of getting at issues involving earliest object relationships than would the use of an auditory medium. Furthermore, if patients are sensitive to auditory reflections of the therapist's mood, they may be even more attuned to visual clues, e.g. body language.

The capacity of the infant to recognize the face of the mother and distinguish it from other objects appears to emerge at the age of three months. Recognition of the same object in a different shape is the first step in the development of object constancy, which consists also in the capacity to attach meaning to an object over and above its direct sensory image. Presumably, then, objects that are introjected prior to the age of three months must be those that are not characterized by the latter definition of object constancy. A question then arises regarding the nature of these first-quarter introjects and their impact upon the infant's subsequent development. It is assumed that in the absence of object constancy such internalized objects are characterized by vague boundaries, anxiety, and distortions. It is also hypothesized that in subsequent introjections, the same objects in the presence of object constancy will not only have firmer boundaries, less anxiety, and fewer distortions attendant upon them, but will eventually supersede the original introjects and become the primary objects. Problems emerge when this process is interrupted, as, for example, when the mother is absent for an extended period beginning in the second or third month. In such cases, the infant is not provided with an opportunity to revise the earlier, distorted internalizations, and these may come to constitute the sole introjects on which a lifetime of object relationships will be based.

The expressive therapist should therefore be aware that the structure and nature of objects internalized prior to the age of three months—and thus their artistic representations—are likely to be fantastical and distorted, especially if the patient suffered a separation from the mother around that age. Images created in art therapy may well reflect the nebulous boundaries of early visual impressions, contain percepts of anxiety and loss, and assume forms that are bizarre and misshapen.

Spitz (1965) speaks of the combined oral and visual mode in the early months of life as the "cradle of perception." He draws our attention to the significance of visual imagery and we imagine that the earliest memory traces are laid down in this "oral-visual" kind of imagery. According to Spitz, the nursing baby feels the nipple in his/her mouth while he/she stares intently at the mother's face and in this way visual and oral modes become intricately interrelated. Spitz differentiates contact perception from distance perception and views the nursing as leading to the preference for *distance* perception, which is seen in this way as the earliest beginning of object relations.

> When the infant loses the nipple and recovers it, contact with the need-gratifying percept is lost and recovered again and again. During the interval between loss and recovery of *contact* the other element of the total perceptual unit, *distance perception*,

i.e., visual perception of the face remains unchanged. In the course of these repetitive experiences, visual perception comes to be relied upon, for it is not lost; it proves to be more constant and therefore the more rewarding of the two (Spitz, 1965).

Jacobson (1964) also speaks of the combined oral-visual experience of the breast and its relevance to earliest memory. She states, "The memory traces left by any kind of libidinal stimulation and gratification in the past are apt to cluster around this primitive, first *visual* mother image" (and here she equates mother with the breast or "primal cavity," in Spitz's terms). The visual mode is clearly highly cathected from very early in infancy.

Movement

White, Castle, & Held (1964) have identified a sequence of movement skills that infants acquire during the first months of life. At two months, the child is able to swipe at objects, to raise a hand unilaterally, to raise both hands, and to alternate glances between a hand and an object. At three months, the infant has learned to place both hands at midline and clasp them, to raise one hand and alternate glances between the hand and an object while the other hand clutches the clothing at midline, and to orient the torso towards an object. At four months, the child is capable of Piaget-type reach, of top level reach, and of simultaneously placing both hands at midline, clasping them, and orienting towards an object.

The overall pattern of this sequence suggests the development of a capacity to focus attention on a frontally-located object and to orient the body and hands toward that object. The stages comprising the evolution of goal-directed movement, especially in relation to the development of visual skills, form a process that can provide a focus for the work of movement therapists.

The skills acquired during the first four months, especially eye-hand, hand-mouth, and finger-to-finger coordination, are crucial to the development of a sense of self and differentiation of self from other (Mittleman, 1954). They also enable the child to gain control over his/her environment, thereby signaling the beginning of separation from the mother. The process is rapidly accelerated with the acquisition in the second year of locomotion skills, which allow the child to move physically away from the mother and contribute substantially to the development of self-esteem and reality-testing (Mittleman, 1954). Thus, major foci of movement therapy might become the dissolution of symbiosis and the establishment of self-concept through movement. For instance, it might be possible to develop a sequence of movement activities associated with the patterns described above in order to identify and deal with issues of individuation and separation, self-esteem, and reality-testing.

Motility plays a significant role in the development of communication as well. Emotions, first manifested as affect-motor responses, acquire, through validation by the environment, a "communication element" (Mittleman, 1954). This notion may be particularly useful to therapists working in the field of psychodrama, or as a means to encourage appropriate facial affect among patients.

Language Acquisition

The development of language is a remarkable and complex process, which raises new issues regarding the structure and nature of the objects and relations among objects seen within the child. While traditional language theorists have emphasized the importance of learning in language acquisition, recent developments in the study of linguistics and in the study of language acquisition raise questions whose impact has yet been untouched in the field of psychotherapy.

Chomsky has questioned the role of learning theory (either operant or classical) in the acquisition of grammar, a key element in the capacity to use a language, in a review of Skinner's book *Verbal Behavior* (1957).[2] The key issue being investigated involves the question of how the structure of language is derived from its elements. Miller, Galanter, and Pribram (1960) have raised a serious question in asserting that it is not possible to learn grammar inferentially from the experience one has with language. Then how is language acquired? Different cultures speak different languages; how does this occur?

The most radical view held by linguists is that which characterizes the structure of language as innate, at least with respect to grammar. Chomsky (1956, 1957, 1963, 1965) has postulated the existence of certain universal properties that all languages share, and of a transformation process by which the underlying universal language is converted to the surface or visible language. Languages differ in the transformational rules by which they become manifest, but all languages are essentially the same at the universal level. Further, Chomsky (1965) postulates the presence of an in-built language acquisition device (LAD), which facilitates the acquisition of the specific language that is to be learned.

While most linguists today consider Chomsky's theories to be a valuable contribution to the field, the full impact of these ideas has not yet been felt. Specifically, the notion that at least the grammatical portion of the linguistic mechanism is somehow built into the organic structure of the brain has raised a number of questions that appear to have direct implications for the process of learning and development, especially with regard

[2]In some sense, it may be that this review signaled the beginning of the end of radical behaviorism in the United States. While the effects of this review have been felt most strikingly in the fields of child development and language acquisition (previously termed verbal learning or verbal behavior), more recently the areas of social psychology and clinical psychology have begun to show evidence of similar impact. Witness, for example, the introduction in the former of the study of scripts and stories in personality research, and in the latter, the recent rapprochement with cognitive psychology demonstrated in the works of Lazurus.

to the psychoanalytic point of view. If language in its structural form is largely determined by the neurology of the brain, its acquisition is not dependent on learning, at least in the terms that psychologists typically view that concept. Should this notion be supported by future research, previously accepted explanations regarding the structure and functions of the ego may also be called into question. These, too, may be less susceptible to early learning experiences than we have believed—a likely prospect in view of the fact that the course of development is remarkably similar for the vast majority of persons and seems to be less dependent on learning than on unfolding cognitive capacities. This notion is in direct contradiction to the traditional views of expressive therapy and psychoanalysis, and may wreak havoc with therapists' assessments of their power to effect change.

It may be, however, that if the structure and organization of the ego are biologically determined, the contents of the ego are acquired through learning. In this view, a set of rules similar to Chomsky's transformational rules govern the development (within a preordained structure) of ego functions peculiar to the culture, the family, and/or the individual. While such rules are as yet unknown, they may mirror those that, according to Chomsky, regulate the acquisition of language. This notion is consonant with the views traditionally held by psychoanalysts and other therapists.

Cognitive Development

The development of cognitive abilities has been cogently described by Piaget, although there are other well-established cognitive perspectives in academic psychology. The linguistic views presented by Chomsky presume that the development of language is essentially maturational, that is, that it does not differ substantially from the development of an arm or a leg. Piaget's emphasis on the importance of interaction between the child and the environment in order for development to occur renders his view more consonant with psychoanalytic theory than is that of Chomsky.

Cognitive change occurs by two processes, assimilation and accommodation. Assimilation is the process of taking from the environment information which corresponds to preexisting cognitive structures, which Piaget terms *schemata*. Only that information that "fits" these structures is taken in. Accommodation occurs when information cannot be assimilated. New structures or schemata are then created by the person to handle this new information. Thus, change occurs by the creation of or change in schemata.

Development or change occurs in three stages: the sensorimotor stage extends from birth to roughly two years of age; the concrete operations stage extends from two to eleven years; and the formal operations stage develops after the age of eleven. During the sensorimotor stage, mental organization is dependent only on the inborn reflex responses and the schemata that have evolved from them. Thus, the cognitive capacity is seen to be very limited in the young child. The second stage involves play activity and make believe, but as the label suggests, the child is bound by the concrete aspects of the stimulus situation. Finally, the highest level of cognitive development occurs after the age of eleven when the child is able to develop formal thought processes that are abstract.

As we can see, the cognitive theories of Piaget imply that early development of cognitive structures is dependent on the simpler reflex and sensory activity of the child. Linguistic theories imply a much more active and biologically based process in the child. These views in regard to language acquisition and cognitive development may not seem to be important for the expressive therapist who is concerned with essentially nonverbal or preverbal experiences of the patient. Yet, it is clear that the implications of these views for the structure and understanding of these early experiences are constrained in ways that dramatically shape the young child's ability to understand his or her environment.

The expressive therapist should be particularly concerned about these two processes, for much of the goal of therapy is to help the patient learn to verbalize experiences that previously had seemed to be not understandable. Piaget suggests that the capacity of the child to develop formal understanding of these experiences cannot develop before the age of eleven, and not until the two earlier stages have been effectively mastered. Many of our adult patients are still functioning at one of the two earlier levels of cognitive development.

CONCLUSION

The goal of this chapter is to introduce the creative therapist to themes and issues from the academic child psychologist's point of view. The implications for theory and treatment are substantial for any therapist, but have particular importance for the expressive therapist. Traditional verbal therapies do not provide direct access to the preverbal early life experiences of the patient. While these activities clearly play a role in verbal therapies, i.e., the nonverbal aspects of treatment are often implicitly present, direct access to these phenomena may be easier through the artistic media.

While it was not possible in a short chapter to thoroughly and extensively raise all issues from child psychology, it is hoped that the reader will pursue some of the issues raised in this chapter. The rule that we found to be helpful in our reading was to ask, What implications does this point have for the expressive therapist?

The issues from genetics to cognitive development each suggest that the maturation of the child occurs within rather severe limits for understanding the environment. As therapists, we take our patients back to a time when they were trying to make sense of the world through these sets of constraints. Our understanding of the nature of these boundaries to understanding should make it easier for the therapist to appreciate and comprehend what the patient has reexperienced.

REFERENCES

Arena, J. M. Drug dangers to the fetus from maternal medications. *Clinical Pediatrics,* 1964, *3,* 450, 465, 471

Baker, J. B. E. The effects of drugs on the fetus. *Pharmaceutical Review,* 1960, *12,* 37–90.

Bower, T. G. R. The visual world of infants. *Scientific American,* 1966, 80–92.

Carmichael, L. The onset and early development of behavior. In Mussen, P. H., Ed., *Carmichael's manual of child psychology.* New York: John Wiley & Sons, Inc., 1970

Conel, J. L. Histologic development of the cerebral cortex. In Milbank Memorial Fund, *The biology of mental health and disease,* vol. 60. New York: Hoeber, 1952.

Chomsky, N. Three models for the description of language. In *IRE transactions on information theory.* 1956, IT–2, 113–124.

Chomsky, N. *Syntactic structures.* The Hague: Mouton & Co., 1957.

Chomsky, N. On the notion "rule of grammar." In Jakobson, R., Ed., *Structure of language and its mathematical aspects, proceedings of the 12th Symposium in Applied Mathematics.* Providence, Rhode Island, American Mathematical Society, 1961, pp. 6–24. Reprinted in Katz, J. & Fodor, J., Eds., *Readings in the philosophy of language.* Englewood Cliffs, New Jersey: Prentice-Hall, 1963.

Chomsky, N. *Aspects of the theory of syntax.* Cambridge, Mass.: M.I.T. Press, 1965.

Chomsky, N. Appendix A. The formal nature of language. In Leeneberg, E. H., *Biological foundations of language.* New York: John Wiley & Sons, 1967.

Deese, J. *Psycholinguistics.* Boston: Allyn & Bacon, Inc., 1970.

Gottesman, I. I. & Shields, J. *Schizophrenia and genetics: A twin study vantage point.* New York: Academic Press, 1972.

Jacobson, E. *The self and the object world.* New York: International Universities Press, 1964.

Miller, G. A., Galanter, E., & Pribram, K. H. *Plans and structure of behavior.* New York: Holt, Rinehart and Winston, 1960.

Mittleman, B., Motility in infants, children, and adults, patterning and psychodynamics. *Psychoanalytic study of the child* 1954, *9,* 142–177.

Mussen, P. H., Ed. *Carmichael's manual of child psychology.* New York: John Wiley & Sons, 1970.

Peiper, A. Sinnesempfindungen des Kindes vor seiner Geburt. *Mschr. Kinderheilk.,* 1925, *29,* 236–241.

Simpson, W. J. A preliminary report on cigarette smoking and the incidence of prematurity. *American Journal of Obstetrics & Gynecology.,* 1957, *73,* 808–815.

Skinner, B. F. *Verbal behavior.* New York: Appleton-Century-Crofts, 1957.

Spitz, R. A. *The first year of life: A psychoanalytic study of normal and deviant development of object relations.* New York: International Universities Press, Inc., 1965.

White, B. L., Castle, P., & Held, R. Observations on the development of visually-directed reading, *Child Development,* 1964, *35,* 349–364.

Chapter 8

EXPRESSIVE IMAGERY AS A RESPONSE TO THE INNER WORLD OF DREAMS*

Arthur Robbins, Ed.D.

The dream is a very personal message to the therapist, encompassing energy, imagery, and a variety of psychic levels: it is the patient's unique symbolic creation of his/her past, present, and potential future. It contains power. It can be primitive and raw. It can be a resource by which to discover the true nature of our conflicts. At times, if we are fortunate, we can harness the wisdom of our dreams to reveal the answers to our problems.

Dream life is expressed in the language of our earliest mode of communication, in which time and space are bound by the laws of emotional logic rather than by the laws of the rational world of secondary process thinking. In the dream, as in art, our personal bias, or frame of reference and receptivity, will have an important impact on how we relate to the message. All therapists agree that emotional investment in the dream material is a prime requisite for analysis. Their approach, how-

*Printed in the proceedings of the eighth annual meeting of the American Art Therapy Association.

ever, as well as their understanding of the symbolic language of the dream can vary greatly. Some therapists, for instance, approach the dream as a detective story in which the therapeutic dialogue appears as a search for clues. In this approach, associations are woven together and, finally, a cohesive story may unfold. Other therapists may enter the patient's dream world and embark on an adventure into another realm of reality in which there is little emphasis on associations. The dream in this approach is an uncompleted story whose end must be acted out through fantasy or dramatic play, with the therapist as an ally who encourages the patient to go back into the dream and conclude his journey. Still other therapists see the work of dream analysis as facilitating the integration of polarities, the dream being a reservoir for the hidden aspects of the unconscious, which call out for integration with their conscious counterparts. Yet, others approach dreams from the vantage point of the ego, and emphasize the adaptive or defensive function of the communication. Finally, for some therapists the focus is upon the hidden infantile wishes that lurk within the symbolic language of the dream.

First, we must examine the fact that patients, too, have different styles or approaches as they review dreams. Some merely need to externalize their inner world and make a statement of their problem. In this case, the dream is simply an introduction to a long novel that will take many sessions of intensive study and review. Other patients are ready to associate and follow their dream imagery along with the therapist. But, as is the case with many a journey, on this dream voyage the map can be blurred or confusing, and some intervention may be required. The effects of dreams need harnessing, but the patient's associations may bog down and he/she may find him/herself wordless, that is, his/her ego may temporarily lose its capacity to attend, to conceptualize, and to integrate inner experience, perhaps because he/she is threatened by the breakthrough of a difficult and alien force. As the expressive therapist reviews these divergencies in the approach to dream analysis on the part of both therapists and patients, and as his/her own bias towards creativity emerges, he/she is presented with a challenge: can a framework be conceptualized that will have the flexibility and latitude to embrace all these divergent attitudes within a more unified system? First, the expressive therapist must define the function of nonverbal responses in therapy.

A nonverbal response to a dream, a drawing, or a painting has a unique place in therapy. While often a verbal metaphor is not within the patient's grasp to enable him/her to explain the profound experience of the dream, a dream drawing can sometimes capture its difficult, inexplicable, irrational, or primitive aspects. The nonverbal response represents reflections of our inner life that come very close to being an authentic synthesis of primary and secondary communication.

Like verbal ones, nonverbal responses to a dream are associative material, leading through association to the unfolding of the latent meaning, or aiding in the integration of polar forces within the personality. In the case of the patient threatened by the breakthrough of an alien force, nonverbal material invites a sense of play, where control is temporarily given up. As the nonverbal image takes form, the reality principle fades and the pleasure of exploration and sensation takes over. In this way, the patient has the opportunity to distance him/herself, observe, and synthesize his/her response. Relationships, missing parts, and connections emerge as both participants are able to observe the drawing or painting together. The image becomes a connecting link to the secondary process world, and the patient's ego can once again gain mastery as the tools for integration are supplied.

At this point we must consider the role of the therapist's own imagery and symbolism. The therapist sees him/herself within the patient's dream world, and becomes immersed in the drawings. As in viewing a motion picture, the therapist becomes lost in the action in a very active psychic engagement, giving rise to his/her own symbolism and imagery. His/her symbolism and imagery can then be used as the stimulus for questions and explorations.

Some patients, however, require a more intense involvement from the therapist, whose nonverbal response to dream symbolism or dream associations acts as a perceptual link that broadens the engagement. If it is truly resonant with the patient's dream life, the symbolism of the therapist can reveal the missing integrating forces, the solutions that are too deeply hidden in the latent content of the dream to be accessible to the patient. On being presented with the therapist's symbolism, the patient may observe, engage with, reject, or possibly reintegrate some of his/her own dissociated material. This experience can be very healing, as both parties meet and understand each other on a most intimate and revealing level. Moreover, the therapist has the opportunity to view his/her therapeutic inductions and separate them from the countertransference reactions, and the patient has the chance to view his/her partner in a deeper, more multi-dimensional fashion. In working with a patient on this level, timing and dosage are most critical: the therapist should be wary of intruding or infringing upon the patient's boundaries; the therapist should participate only when invited to do so. And even then, the sharing of imagery should be viewed with caution. The therapist may ask him/herself whether the sharing of imagery facilitates the process and leads to greater autonomy and ego integration, or gives rise to signs of fusion and regression as a consequence of his/her interventions.

Diagnostically speaking, the ego resources of the patient must be held in constant consideration; they should determine the direction of the symbolic communication. With the neurotic patient, dream symbolism and expressive imagery can be used to uncover hidden wishes and polarities to go inward. Conversely, with the psychotic patient, the primitive symbolism of his/her dream should and can be a bridge to an interpersonal world, rather than a spiral downward and inward, regressive and self-alienating. The nonverbal rasponse to a psychotic dream may thus well include the missing sense of reality that, hopefully, will place primitive feeling within a human, interpersonal context.

In order to clarify the use of expressive imagery in response to dreams, a therapeutic session will be presented. No attempt will be made to discuss dreams in depth; instead, the focus will be placed on the nonverbal interchange.

CASE DESCRIPTION

The Patient

Francine is twenty-eight years old, married, and a nurse. A good-looking, blond woman of medium build, she speaks in a somewhat squeaky, tense voice. She is both likeable and disarming. She has been in group and individual treatment on a once-a-week basis for approximately four years. She came to the present therapist after four years of previous treatment, which was described as frightening and demoralizing. She described her past therapist as an authoritarian "take-charge" type who would tell her how to handle relationships and her life. Although she found this advice helpful during the early stages of her treatment, as she grew she felt it difficult to follow his guidance, and when she openly disagreed with him, she experienced him as cold and deprecating. This attitude made her furious, but she was unable to express her anger about it. She found herself in a stalemate with the past therapist, and refused to go back to see him and attempt to work out her problems. She felt a change in therapists might be of help in gaining some perspective as to how much could be attributed to the personal problems of her former therapist.

Francine describes her mother as strong on the surface, as looking and acting like a "Russian Rock of Gibraltar." Yet behind the mother's tough exterior was a childlike person who constantly needed support from her own daughter. Both Francine and her mother perceived her father as passive and incompetent; the mother usually took charge and made family decisions. Francine describes her relationship with her three brothers as sexual, taunting, and teasing.

Ambivalent about starting a family, Francine worries about the strain that children would place on the marriage. Although the relationship with her husband has considerably improved, as both parties now feel more free to share their feelings with each other and are more able to give support as well as freedom within the relationship, her marriage has its ups and downs. Both parties are alternately demanding, withdrawn, and passively hostile with each other.

The Dream

In Francine's first session after a seven-week summer break, she reported that she was both happy and unhappy to come back; the summer had gone too quickly; it felt like it was still July. Everything felt much better. In fact, she wondered why she was here, for she was handling things in a way she never had before. She offered the example of being able to talk to her supervisor who previously had always made her anxious because of his quietness and passivity. She never knew where she stood with him. Regardless, she reported, she stood up to him in a conference and stated very explicitly what she was doing in her work, without any approval or encouragement from him. Everything went fine.

After a pause, she mentioned that she had heard that one of her group members had left and reminded me that she had not been present at the last session, when this had taken place. She was both sorry, sad, and relieved: Lily, the member of the group who had left, was quite formidable. She had a "big mouth" and always related to things in a sexual manner. Francine reported that she always felt inhibited by Lily. The group, said Francine, was such a lonely place. Nobody related to anything. Why did she need it? She then reported a dream:

> I walked into a crowded bar where a murder had been committed. I wasn't supposed to be staying in this bar but needed to go into it; to pass through it on my way to somewhere else. Near the exit I was stopped by a man who committed the murder. He

looked mean and diabolical—tall with narrow eyes. He grabbed
me by the hand and would not let go of me; there were sexual
overtones. I knew that I would have to let him hurt my hand in
order for me to get away from him. A tall, black man who was
supposed to help or protect me stood nearby. Somehow he did
not help; either he didn't understand or couldn't help. I ran out
of the door, allowing the first man to hurt my hand—to cut it
or something. I couldn't allow the man to know how afraid I
was, I had to make myself small and inconspicuous. I ran into
the street but couldn't wait to look for a taxi. I ran into a store
or shop of some kind in order to hide.

As she was talking about this dream she smiled. She felt
that the dream had something to do with her wish to leave
treatment and her fear that I was going to hold on to her. She
complained more about the group. It felt like her family, very
lonely. I asked her more about the man at the exit. Could she
give more details about him? It was all unclear. "How would
you like to draw this man," I said. She said that was fine.

As she looked at the man she drew, I asked her how he
looked. "He looks hollow, like a pumpkin-head." "Well, how
does this compare to the man you were frightened by?" I asked.
She did not know, but he certainly wasn't frightening. "Well,
what about this other man (the black man)—let's draw him."
"You know," she said, "this man looks like my brother, my
middle brother John who was supposed to help me but never
did" (long pause). I then brought her back to the man who was
holding her, who she thought might be me. "That is hard for
me to think of, you as a killer, it makes me very scared." "Well,
how about drawing me?" "I couldn't do that, I just couldn't.
I just couldn't draw you." "Why don't you just draw the feeling?" "Okay." As she looked at her image, her attention went
to the upper part of the drawing. "That jagged top is you,
pointed and sometimes cruel . . . looks kind of sexual. This
scares me and yet intrigues me, but let's not talk about this
anymore. In fact, we are sitting too close to one another. Let's
go back to our usual seats." (We had moved over to the drawing
board, and we now went back to our usual chairs.) Then she

said, "This may seem like I'm changing the topic, but I'm interested in doing some work with Estelle. There are certain kinds of basic procedures that you might know as to how to start and initiate your own corporation." (She then went into detail as to what kind of venture it was that she and Estelle, a group member, had planned to start.) I said "You seemed to be much more comfortable with Estelle now that she is not in the group." "Oh, I think that she is a fine person. I like her very much. But when she was in group, I could hardly talk to her. She also was a sexual threat. I guess I felt that even when I was drawing and speaking of you, I thought of you in sexual terms. I felt it would be nice to have you all to myself, but don't expect me to say that to the group. I feel so lousy there. I feel like a mouse and I am not. I am actually quite vocal, only not in this group."

The patient said that she was starting even to dream that she was analyzing her dream in her dreams. She laughed about that, but she felt much better. She felt like a load was coming off her shoulders, as if she was putting things together.

Discussion

In the dream, both therapist and patient face the chief protagonist, the murderer. There are no associations or memories, and so the therapist and the patient resort to the drawing board, where the patient can play, and have room to move. A vehicle, the metaphor of the drawing, provided to externalize an image. Words then follow: she sees the man as an empty-headed pumpkin, an object scary by night, but by day as inanimate and immobile. This charade that masks her contempt. The man is seen as neither evil nor monstrous; he sits there like a jack-o'-lantern.

The second drawing brings her brother into focus. He seems weak and ineffective, his hands lying limply at his side, his demeanor having an aesthetic, feminine quality. We do not see the prominent teeth featured in the first drawing.

Figure 8.1

Figure 8.2

Figure 8.3

Finally, in the third drawing Francine moves closer to her real protagonist, the therapist. It is hard for her to think of him as a killer. It makes her scared, for she knows she needs him too much as a source of protection and care. But she is also frightened of the therapist, for her dream tells her that he is a murderer. She cannot deal easily with her feelings concerning this relationship and the safety of the drawing board now seems to offer her some relief. She produces an abstract image that pulls together the polarity of her externalized and idealized libidinal self. We see merged into one symbol the hostile and sexual part of herself, an image which is both penetrating and round. On top, it is sharp and pointed, the middle more circular and receptive. Her associations soon bring her sexual feeling into play and we are reminded of the continual teasing quality that characterizes the relationship with all her brothers. They were the source of nurturance, care and also disappointment. She loved her brothers, adored them, found refuge in playing with them, and thus attempted to cover some of her

Figure 8.4

early disappointment with her mother through these relationships.

The third drawing represents a synthesis of Francine's growing sense of identification. It speaks with a sharp cadence: "I am proud; I am grounded and centered. I am sharp and soft and I am neither afraid nor worried that my head or power will penetrate or destroy." Some of this image she still attributes to the therapist, but in reality it is an externalization of some of Francine's past as well as her present and future. If this woman is a mouse, then the mouse indeed will soon roar and cut down to size the fantasized omnipotence of her therapist. These drawings are a record, a visual diary that will weather time and secondary elaboration. They are there for Francine to constantly refer to and review. The drawings capture energy and hold it forth for Francine to inspect and touch.

We see, therefore, that the expressive image, as a response to dream materials is more readily able to tolerate ambiguity, polarizations, and the irrationality of the primary process than the ordinary form of verbal communication. For unless we are poets, our words tend to be logical, linear, and rational, and do not always afford us a creative response to our dream life. Expressive imagery, on the other hand, may well give us the opportunity to roam and to harmonize, if not resonate with the symbols of our primary dialogue. For some patients, expressive techniques offer an excellent vehicle to enter the manifest dream material. In Francine's case, the drawings permitted a flow of associations that facilitated the therapeutic response. Thus, we can creatively engage patients in their dream life through the aid of nonverbal expression. The power of the dream symbol can be experienced, enabling past battles to be fought again and, hopefully, new solutions of all problems to be found.

Chapter 9

ART AND DANCE AS TREATMENT MODALITIES

Julie Joslyn Brown
Arlene Avstreih

Pictures can be read in aftertime. They persist, control time and overcome its passage. In this very fact there is magic.
Ernst Kris (1952)

When the individual reacts to his own body, he is stirred and aroused in a manner that rarely occurs when he reacts to the non-self world.
Fisher and Cleveland (1965)

In beginning our comparative discussion of the use of art and dance in treatment, we would first like to summarize the essential points previously explored in our paper, *Some Aspects of Movement and Art Therapy as Related to the Analytic Situation* (Avstreih and Brown, 1979). We have been particularly interested in incorporating art and movement into a more verbal psychoanalytic approach and have attempted to address the various issues that arise in the synthesis of nonverbal and verbal therapies. We have found that there are a variety of uses of these modalities in analytic therapy: as alternate routes to the unconscious, triggering associations, affects, and memories; for reflective mirroring and other restitutional processes; for cathartic release as well as neutralization of drives; and for the formation of reconstructions in analysis.

The concrete and symbolic nature of the modalities helps

to bring overwhelming and powerful affects into the ego sphere, thus facilitating the "taming," mastery, and integration of these affects. We also suggested that the recapturing of preverbal memories may only be accomplished on a sensory level. The use of movement and art has particular value in that it allows for the reexperiencing of these memories as well as the later interpretation and integration in the verbal sphere, through symbolization. Traditionally, communication in therapy through actions rather than words was considered a defense against remembering. It has been our contention that the "action" that is involved in the use of art and dance in analysis is not "acting out" but is in fact a different kind of remembering; a way of remembering that is perhaps more akin to the original experience. Finally, we considered some of the problems intrinsic to the use of art and dance in therapy. If one initially accepts the position of "teaching" art or movement this inhibits the development and examination of the transference and endangers the therapeutic relationship. One must also be aware of certain defensive patterns that are in danger of being *supported* by the use of the modalities, rather than being interpreted and worked through. Of particular note is the concept of "affectualization" as a defense, as introduced by Valenstein (1962), "There is the possibility that affects in themselves are used as defense." Another important point, although not covered in the aforementioned paper, is the tendency of the therapist, in encouraging art or movement productions, to enact with the patient the masochistic transference. In conclusion, we cautioned that while catharsis and abreaction have their place in treatment they are only one aspect of the working-through process, and as creative therapists we must not be satisfied with expression alone as an end in itself.

In considering the similarities and differences between the use of movement and art in treatment, we are struck by the perhaps most obvious and yet most critical difference intrinsic to the two modalities: that is, that art exists and endures outside of the self while dance is a fleeting, yet intensely vivid experiencing within the body. While one has a timelessness, the other an immediacy. We will attempt here to understand some of the implications of these essential differences in their use in therapy.

Because of the concreteness, observability, and independent, continuing existence of the "product" as it were, the use of art allows the observing ego to operate more readily and to be further developed in treatment. This is of particular importance in working with patients where there is a disturbance in impulse control or a danger of ego disintegration. The durability of the art materials may allow a safe exploration, whereas the fluidity, evanescence, and impermanence of the movement work, along with the extremely intense feeling experience, would possibly create too much anxiety around these issues. We must remember that in its origins, dance therapy was used primarily as a group or adjunctive therapy. In a group movement session the circle formation and the use of rhythm provides a structure within which strong aggressive components and fears of engulfment can be diluted. As the dance therapist begins to move into the role of primary therapist, one needs to be increasingly aware of these issues. The first job of the therapist is to help the patient stay in treatment long enough to form a therapeutic alliance. When using movement there is a danger of prematurely tapping unneutralized aggression and fear of engulfment.

Whereas the art product, regardless of how "unstructured" it might be, is observable and separate, the movement work is inextricably bound to the self. According to Fisher and Cleveland (1965):

> First, the body as a perceptual object is unique in that it is simultaneously that which is perceived and also part of the perceiver . . . No other perceptual object ever occupies such a dual position or participates so intimately in the perceptual process. Second, an unusually intense level of ego involvement is evoked by one's body as an object of perception.

Or, as Yeats wrote so beautifully, "How can we know the dancer from the dance?" It is this unique property of dance that is at times our greatest ally in treatment and yet in other instances our greatest foe. Two interesting examples occur to us.

Donna, a twenty-year-old gymnast, was seen in analytic therapy for one-and-a-half years, three times weekly. She came into psychoanalytic treatment after a year which could be characterized by a progressive decompensation in ego functioning, with a good deal of psychotic and suicidal symptoms. She had never been hospitalized, nor did she ever truly cease functioning in her day-to-day existence. She had since childhood expressed herself through her body. Physical activity, athletics, as well as dance gave her as a child a sense of self and vitality. So, too, was there a history of a wide range of somatic symptoms. For Donna gymnastics and dancing were truly a "compensatory structure" as Kohut (1977) describes it. In the course of treatment this patient's mother emerged as a rather disturbed woman who was overwhelmed by her large family. She, too, expressed herself predominantly with somatic symptoms: she had "fits," headaches, "fell ill," and developed a "neurological disease," which was never substantiated medically. Imagery pertaining to both parents as "cripples" came up repeatedly in dreams and associations.

What is unusual and surprising about this case is this patient's use of art. After the first week of therapy this patient began to experience a severe breakdown of ego function with the return of many of the previous psychoticlike symptoms. At this time, she did a series of drawings at home of a dream she had of a running antelope. She had hoped at some time to choreograph this elusive, impressionistic dream into a dance. At this time, however, she drew a series of drawings in black charcoal of a figure whirling as in a dance. The drawings became more disorganized, until the total structure became fragmented, dramatically illustrating the parallel dissolution of body boundaries and ego disintegration she was experiencing. These drawings, shared with the therapist one year later, seemed to have played a pivotal role in helping her survive this crisis, which came so early in treatment, thus allowing her to continue through some very deep and important analytic work. We have many such cases, but what is particularly interesting in view of this present discussion is that here we have a patient who uses her body expressively, who continued in treatment to use a predominance of movement or "kinetic" imagery both in her dreams and in therapy sessions, but did not work on a body level in this period of crisis. The symbolic and concrete nature of art allowed her to explore, yet, at the same time, to encapsulate her frightening inner experience. To experience this fragmentation in her body would have been far too threatening to her already fragile ego. Incidentally, this patient has gone on to more creative use of dance and is now after some time able to use movement work to deal with emotional issues as well.

The next example is of a patient whose case was supervised.* Ralph is an artist in his early twenties who was in treatment with an art therapist. He began with vague, generalized complaints, focusing on difficulties with his parents and girlfriend. Issues revolved largely around autonomy and dependence. Underlying, one sensed a deeper difficulty with depression and fears of merging. In the sessions there was an overabundance of verbal material and the therapist continually experienced Ralph as whirling and spinning around and around. Upon exploring this, we began to suspect that perhaps this verbal whirling was a resistance to a sense of stillness that was frightening for this patient. The therapist began to work in movement with Ralph, allowing him to actually whirl in the sessions. When the whirling stopped, Ralph was able to contact the feelings he had been struggling to defend against: a deep sense of depression as well as a fear of merger. Out of this, the working alliance was solidified as well. In this case, with a patient who is far more intact and whose defensive structure functions far more adequately, the direct experiencing of the

*Our many thanks to Kathy Hynes for the use of this case material.

resistance in his body resulted in a greater degree of insight and eventual change. What, of course, is interesting in this case is that using art, even though it was the more familiar and seemingly appropriate modality, would not really have helped this patient to deal with his resistance. It needed to be experienced in the most direct, least symbolic form. He needed to feel it in his body.

It is this direct, visceral, experiential aspect of movement that provides a chance to reexperience a kind of nonverbal empathic environment. It is this aspect of dance therapy that embodies its greatest potential for healing. It also accounts for its particular effectiveness in working with the autistic child, the psychotic child or adult, and the client who suffers from emptiness and severe depletion of inner objects and images. Following are excerpts from a case to illustrate this point.

Michael, a young man in his early twenties, had been in the theater for a short period, but at the time he entered treatment he was working as a waiter. He sought therapy because of panic states and "feelings of unreality." Michael had a history of losses. The eldest of two boys, his brother was born when Michael was 13 months old. His parents were divorced when Michael was four, at which time he moved with his mother, brother, and maternal grandmother far from his original home, rarely seeing his father. He and his brother shared his mother's bedroom until her remarriage eight years later, when Michael was twelve years old.

The therapist was immediately impressed by the discrepancy between Michael's presentation of himself as a "happy-go-lucky fellow" and his description of his inner distress. These feelings were apparently so split-off that it was difficult to get a real sense of what he was experiencing. He didn't know what to do the first session and thought the therapist should perhaps teach him "some dance routines" to enable him to "move more gracefully and to feel less like a robot." He walked around the studio wondering if and how the therapist was going to decorate it, experiencing her as preoccupied with these thoughts during the session. As he walked, he talked a great deal to fill the space. When he moved at all, he danced a silly, mocking ballet. The dance was light, filled with turns, but had no fluidity or completeness.

One day, he walked into the session and began talking about his friends and he related with surprise that one close friend had commented that "he didn't really know" Michael. This shocked Michael since he felt he was "very open" and then asked, "What does being open mean?" The therapist asked him whether he was able to show his feelings to his friends. He thought about this and reflected that he probably could not. In connection with this, he suddenly remembered that when he used to tell his mother how he felt, she often responded, "You can't feel that way. I don't know anyone who feels like that." Of course, Michael learned quickly that feelings were not to be communicated, if felt at all. He often wondered in treatment whether the therapist could really understand him either, and would often blame himself for not being clear.

In movement, he and the therapist could meet this nonempathic introject and replace it with one that could tolerate and validate a wide range of emotions. They worked for months, moving together, almost as mother and child, reflecting and mirroring both in movement and in words. As Winnicott (1971) so aptly describes, the child seeing himself reflected in the mother's face develops the origins of a reliable sense of self.

One session in particular stands out. That day Michael walked differently, more slowly, his chest slightly concave and his shoulders slumped, and he said, "I think I'm depressed; I think I've been depressed a lot in my life." The therapist validated his feelings and asked him to describe them further. He was able to relate in detail what his body felt like, connecting this with his inner affective state. At this time, too, the panicky and unreal feelings began to subside. This shared movement experience provided a context in which he could begin to fight the amorphousness of alienation: a place to regain his body and his self in the reflective containment of the therapist.

In discussing the restitutional function of dance we cannot neglect the role of play. The quality of impermanence in dance and movement is very closely related to the earliest forms of play, where the important thing for the child is to *do*, not to *produce*. The child plays in order to recreate and to gain control by mastery and understanding. Certainly, the ability to play is essential for the success of any form of therapy (Winnicott, 1971), however, the work of dance therapy is very close to the original experience where the child grows and gains control of his reality by physical manipulation and mastery.

Another essential difference between the use of art and dance in treatment lies in the projective-introjective nature of the art process. Ehrenzweig (1967) describes this process in detail as he conceives of three distinct phases of the "creative ego rhythm". First there is a projection of split-off parts of the self out into the art work. Next comes a period of what he conceives of as "unconscious scanning" and integration, where the artwork acts as a "receiving womb," containing and integrating fragments into a whole. The final phase is one of reintegration of the work into the artist's ego. Through this process it is possible in treatment to reintegrate and synthesize the projected image in a more neutralized and detoxified form. This is particularly important in gaining distance from exceedingly bizarre, alien, or malevolent introjects, while maintaining the therapist as a good object.

Using movement, on the other hand, would perhaps have a more limited usage here. As the self is first a body self, "becoming" the alien and frightening introject with one's body could tend to foster an integration into the self of these destructive introjects. This would, of course, be detrimental to the patient as, in our view, the goal of treatment is essentially to rid one's self of these introjects in order to replace them with more sustaining and nurturing ones.

We would like to conclude that we are not posing the two modalities in opposition to each other or to the more traditional modalities of verbal interactions and dream interpretation; but rather we feel that a thorough knowledge of and comfort with the use of art and movement in treatment adds an important dimension to the therapist's repertoire.

REFERENCES

Avstreih, A. & Brown, J. J. Some aspects of movement and art therapy as related to the analytic situation. *The Psychoanalytic Review.* 1979, *66,* 49–68.

Ehrenzweig, A. *The hidden order of art.* California: University of California Press, 1967.

Fisher, S. & Cleveland, S. Personality, body perception and body image boundary. In *The body percept,* Wapner, S. & Werner, H., Eds. New York: Random House, 1965.

Kohut, H. *The restoration of the self.* New York: International Universities Press, 1977.

Kris, E. *Psychoanalytic explorations in art.* New York: International Universities Press, 1952.

Valenstein, A. The psychoanalytic situation. *International Journal of Psycho-Analysis.* 1962, *63,* 315–324.

Winnicott, D. W. *Playing and reality.* New York: Basic Books, 1971.

Yeats, W. B. Among school children. In *Collected poems of W. B. Yeats.* New York: Macmillian, 1958.

Chapter 10

POETIC, SPONTANEOUS, AND CREATIVE INGREDIENTS IN THE THERAPIST

Emanuel F. Hammer, Ph.D.

In Freud's Vienna, it was Hysteria. In the modern world it's Alienation, which is *the* psychiatric condition of man. Isolates adopt "roles" that do not truly represent them, accepting others in *their* "roles" as masks to be nodded to, escaping deeper contact. Lionel Trilling, in his sensitive essay on Jane Austen's *Emma,* wrote: "There is no reality about which the modern person is more uncertain and more anxious than the reality of himself. For each of us, as for Emma, it is a sad, characteristic hope to become better acquainted with oneself."

Responding to this state of man, Jean-Jacques Rousseau, when perhaps more than a little mad and suffering from old age, consoled himself with a daydream of a world like our own, except that in it connections and impressions are more vital. The people of this world experience a greater closeness to each other, and as an expression of this their words embrace the truth of each other more. Language speaks with full emotional texture, so that feeling and knowing become one. Could we but speak in such a manner, Rousseau sighs, it would put us more closely in touch with ourselves and with one another. In a parallel statement, John Updike (1977) asks for "something live that surfaces out of language." We analysts—those of us who dream—might also fantasize just such a language.

Among us, it is our poets who most closely approximate Rousseau's hopes, poets who shape speech in a manner enabling us to understand more deeply and feel more richly.

At the interface between novelist-playwright-poet and clinician is to be found common ground. Like T. S. Eliot, we know that "each venture is a new beginning, a raid on the inarticulate." Isaac Beshevis Singer (1978), the recent Nobel laureate, elaborates further when he speaks of the task of the artist as holding up the truth "then twisted about to show a new and unexpected view." Is this not, at the same time, exactly what the psychotherapist strives for with his patient? James Baldwin asserts Singer's view all the more boldly: "If you're an artist . . . you see things others don't admit are there." If you're an analyst, you should too.

In his essay, *What is Art?*, Leo Tolstoy wrote, "It is on this capacity of man to receive another man's expression of feeling and experience those feelings himself, that the activity of art is based." The same statement could as validly be finished with the word therapy substituted for art.

Herbert Marcuse in *One-Dimensional Man* writes, "Art gives us a vivid, concrete experience of our condition." So does properly conducted therapy. W. H. Auden (1977) has said of poetry that, "We hope that someone reading it will say, 'Of course, I knew that all the time but never realized it before'." Isn't this just what the *ah ha* moment in therapy is? We merely need poets, and other strangers (hopefully therapists among them) to point out such truths to us.

The poet, wrote Sir Philip Sidney over 300 years ago, "yieldeth to the powers of the minde and image of that whereof the Philosopher bestoweth but a wordish description." Similarly, interpretation in the clinical setting falters when the therapist becomes wordish. Intellect, as Saul Bellow reminds us, "is an excellent thing in fiction, but, like grease in a pan, it tends to congeal when the heat is turned off beneath it" (Prescott, 1970). And in therapy also, we look for that intervention that connects not only with the patient's intelligence but also his feelings and, at times, his imagination.

What might we borrow, then, from the poet to approach Rousseau's dream? Intrigued with this possibility over the years, I will draw upon what I have previously begun (Hammer, 1958, 1968, 1978), and here extend it further.

LOOSENING UP ONE'S GRIP OF RATIONALITY

From what particular vantage point might the therapist function with relative creativity? Henry James' prerequisite for a good writer might be considered for a creativity-enabling stance for the analyst as well: James propounded that the novelist needs to be half in life and half out of it; sufficiently involved in life to know what it is about, but enough outside of it to be able to see what is going on within. The reader will see in this the parallel to Sullivan's advocated role of "participant-observer."

The analyst's experience of a flash of insight is much like that of any creative moment—it is felt as a passive opening of oneself to receive that which comes (Hammer, 1964). As one listens to the patient's material with a "hovering attention," not only does one feel a conscious urge to reach out for its meaning and emotional subtleties, but, when one's sensibilities are tuning in, one experiences it as something in the material reaching out to touch one.

Capitalizing on this truth in his possession, the analyst will find that he functions more creatively, with honed intuition more available, not when he focuses his concentration, but rather when he relaxes it—actually *unfocuses concentration.*

SOME NOTES REGARDING MY OWN EFFORTS AT CREATIVITY IN SESSIONS

I might here share with the reader the evolvement of *one* style of functioning: when responses seem to emerge from relatively deeper within me. If I speak from the personal perhaps it may be more helpful. As I have instructed my patients on the couch to allow their thoughts to follow their own lead, to go —when there is a tug in such directions—off in tangents, to pay attention to marginal ideas, peripheral feelings, and also bodily sensations, I then do likewise. I tune in on the patient and, as I do, pay attention also to my own darting ideas, feelings or sensations as they reverberate to the ongoing process in the patient. I have a reclining chair in which I lean back to listen, not so much trying to be alert but rather absorbed. My mental posture, like my physical posture, is not one of leaning forward to catch 'clues', but one of leaning back to let the mood, the atmosphere, come to me—to hear the meaning between the lines. As one gives oneself up to be carried along by the affective cadence of the patient's session, one may sense texture and subtleties.

There is an interesting report of the creative process in painting that appears strikingly parallel to both the patient's free association and this approximation to a similar process on the part of the analyst. After an initial phase, "I look at flies, at flowers, at leaves, and trees around me," Picasso (1971) then works as follows: *"I let my mind drift at ease, just like a boat in the current.* Sooner or later, it is caught by something. It gets precise. It takes shape" (italics added).

When more open, in this manner, to resonating to the patient from the processes within me, what I find is that pictures form in my creative zones, an image crystallizes, reflecting what the patient is experiencing.

To illustrate: To a masochist I once observed, "How nice to get a wound you can lick." "Wham! That connected," he said. I was struck with the degree to which this communication reached the patient as other conventional interpretive explanations had not. What fleshed out the understanding for the patient was the imagery.

To backtrack, the first thing that had struck me about this patient was his tendency to enjoy ill luck as some people enjoy ill health. He liked, also, to dramatize to himself the inevitability of his latest and of his next defeats. Though well established financially, he would "talk poor" as if to ward off the Furies who might come and take away what he owned. His insistence on his misery was, in part, an extracting of an identity from it. Once when I walked him to the door after a session, and by way of parting commented, "Enjoy this lovely spring day," he quickly countered with, "What, and step in all the dog shit on the New York streets?"

All in all, this was a man who gave to troubles the assurance that they had fallen into the right hands, as when a rough stone comes to an experienced stonecutter. "You know, Bob," I had expressed to him, "you take some small failure you've had and tar-and-feather yourself with it." Then he *felt* what he had, from our previous discussions, only understood.

All the more helpful than the therapist's images, are the uses of the patient's own metaphors. Bob had had a dream of picking up large and heavy stones and putting them in a bag to carry around over his shoulder. His associations to this included a memory of having, five years ago, suffered a broken car headlight when a metal bolt lying on the road had been jumped up by traffic into his light. When he brought his car to a garage and the cause of the difficulty was established, he had asked the garage mechanic to put the greasy bolt in a bag, which he has ever since carried in the trunk of his car. It was as if it were to show Fate or God that he had already paid his dues, already had his troubles, and should thus be exempted from subsequent ones. Reference now, whenever the occasion arose, to his carrying his "greasy bolt" or to his self-imposed burden of "stones" or to his world of "dog shit on the streets" became a meaningful shorthand to illuminate his masochistic strategy whenever he unknowingly engaged in it. After a while he moved on to where he would himself, with a smile of recognition, come to identify a maneuver he caught himself in as, with the lightness of mood he was beginning to attain, his "dog shit shtick."

When, some years later, his analytic trea nent was being completed, he had loosened up, had liberated his imaginative and creative zones enough to produce the following rich imagery in a dream he may have been extending to me as a parting gift.

> "A slide in a projector throws out its picture, large and lavish in color. The slide picture than turns to a movie . . . and then that gives way, as in one of Chaucer's tales a painting comes alive, to the picture coming to life." His associations were to the use of imagery in his treatment now ending, and also to "that which was obscure within me having been made visible, and having come alive for me"—an elaboration of the metaphor in the dream of his attained *affectively*-relevant insight and, now, fullness of experiencing.

To a young psychiatrist in analysis who was "interpreting" to his wife almost everything she did at home, I found the most effective thing I ever communicated to him about it to be: "It's important not to get so used to tearing away people's masks that you no longer hear the rip." Here, auditory *and* visual imagery were jointly employed to put the patient in touch with the raw affect of hurting others, the emotion beneath his defensive intellectualizations.

Communication through the senses is via a more basic, elemental route than is communication through mere thought. The tactile may be called upon to join the visual or the auditory as the sense addressed.

For example: A woman, 28 years of age, was describing a situation I received and understood as a wallowing in gloom. She had told herself her boyfriend had forgotten her birthday, and she settled down for an evening of despair. Suddenly the doorbell rang and there was her boyfriend with flowers and a present under his arm. Instead of a sense of fulfillment, she experienced, "strangely," she said, "a feeling of deprivation."

"Why?" she turned to me, feeling at a loss. There seemed two directions in which to explore: one, the losing of her feeling of current *justification* for anger, and, two, the disruption of her self-consoling self-indulgence.

The second seemed closer to awareness, and I chose to address that aspect. But how could I most usably express my understanding of her reaction? Listening, I had felt an empathic linkage, which formed an image at the back of my mind, and I shared it. "Could it be," I inquired, "that you had prepared *a warm bath of unhappiness to soak in* for the evening, and Bill interrupted before you could really settle into the tub?" That worked. It served to draw out, and connect her with the subjective undercurrent of her experience. Then she knew, and felt, its emotional texture.

At the same time it served another goal. Patients early in the treatment enterprise need a response from the therapist to their unvoiced question: "Do you really know how I feel?" A patient worries himself with doubts over whether he will ever be able to take the therapist figuratively by the hand and say, "Here is where I stood," "This is how I felt," "Do you hear my heartbeat, or silent laughter; can you sense my fear, or the tears behind my eyes?" An empathic image, formed within the therapist and shared with the patient, serves as one form of demonstration in response to the patient's needs in this direction. It facilitates the therapy moving toward that empathically necessary uniqueness each treatment encounter must attain—if it is to be anything at all.

An affectively-textured, discrete image of the patient's inner reality initiates a two-way movement. It helps the patient connect with the therapist as he extends a vivid communication; and it helps the patient deepen down into his own feelings. The effect is to enable him to emerge from constriction—to stretch himself, to experience himself simultaneously more outwardly, and more inwardly; in essence, to *expand.*

DISCUSSION

Conventionally expressed interpretations, even when true, are often not nearly enough. When the patient's response is flat, there may be many reasons but one wonders if what might help, at times, is the muscle and surprise of language. The use of imagery, by virtue of its concentrated expression, its enlivening quality, its tone of playfulness, and most importantly its emotionally-richer texture and capacity thereby to connect with a patient beneath his intellectual layer, is particularly helpful at the following times, or with the following patients.

1. *In the long middle phase of treatment* the work often tends to go repetitious with a patient, it is all familiar ground. Involvement hollows and loses its zing. The work tires, interest flags. The therapist speaks in the by now too-familiar tongue, reflecting, commenting, describing, interpreting. The attitude of the patient half dismissing it all—something more general than just *resistance*—can be felt by the therapist. The shift to a richer interpretive style at this point can freshen the process.

2. *Obsessive-compulsives* try to shut out the pulsating currents of their lives. The therapist feels as if these patients' processes run sluggishly, as if the sap of affect has run thin. Communication from the therapist should, hence, all the more be warm, alive, concrete, and if possible to deal in images that may prove evocative. The obsessional patient may then become less someone in therapy as a tourist, and more deeply a participant.

3. *Depressives,* like obsessionals, require a sprightly style on the analyst's part to supply a vitalizing ingredient. Lightness of approach is thus balanced with seriousness of intent. The richness of emotional tone the patient experiences in his therapist, when the latter employs imagery, may offer an example for the patient

that work and play can harmoniously coexist. At the same time, a metaphor is an intuition, a flash of empathy. Receiving it, the patient feels genuinely understood.

4. *The creative individual,* seemingly paradoxically, since we have just recommended imagery for the obsessional, is also someone for whom this style is singularly desirable. The creative patients feel the therapist, when using images, speaks their language. The creative are particularly responsive to the terse and the visual. Imagery, like wit, expresses a meaning that is accomplished in intense compression.

Thus, we have, if we borrow from the poets, a method whose special efficacy lies not in any greater profundity, but in its ability to create dramatic images. The interpretation is thereby made not only to the patient's mind but also to his emotions.

When the therapist, tuning in to the patient, feels an unmistakable tug on the fabric of his creative zones, he may reach down into his reverberations, experience there the imagery reflecting the patient's state, and share this with the patient. Applying one's imagination to the images suggested by a metaphor enables one to see as someone else has seen. Analyst and patient, when sending and receiving on this more subtle wireless, are then not so much *having* a session, as *composing* it.

REFERENCES

Auden, W. H. *The Paris Review interviews (4th series).* In *Writers at work,* Plimpton, G., Ed. New York: Viking, 1977.

Hammer, E. *The clinical application of projective drawings.* Springfield, Illinois: Charles Thomas, Publishers, 1958.

Hammer, E. Creativity and feminine ingredients in young male artists. In *Perceptual and motor skills,* 1964, *19,* 414.

Hammer, E. *The use of interpretation in treatment.* New York: Grune & Stratton, 1968.

Hammer, E. Interpretations couched in the poetic style. *International Journal of Psychoanalytic Psychotherapy,* Vol. 7, New York: Jason Aronson, 1978.

Picasso, P. In Gaunthier, S., Picasso. *Look Magazine,* Feb. 10, 1971.

Prescott, P. Looking at books. *Look Magazine,* Feb. 10, 1970.

Singer, I. B. Interview, *New York Times Book Review,* July 28, 1978, 1–24.

Updike, J. On poetry. *New York Times Book Review,* April 10, 1977, 3.

A JOURNEY OF EXPRESSIVE THERAPY DISCOVERY WITH THE HELP AND TEACHING OF DON JUAN (CASTANEDA'S)*

Anna Falco, M.A., M.S.W.
Arthur Robbins, Ed.D., A.T.R.**

The field of expressive therapy constantly draws from the theoretical tenets and constructs of psychoanalysis and psychotherapy. All too often, these notions do not capture the uniqueness of the expressive therapy experience (typical transference, character structure, past and present reality, with an overall orientation toward relatedness and self-direction). An expressive therapy relationship can attend to these issues, but can also open up for the patient levels of consciousness that are either overlooked or simply neglected in the usual therapeutic experience.

When one approaches the notion of levels of consciousness, complex sensations, multiple imagery, and altered ego states become important avenues of communication that de-

---

*Printed in the proceedings of the seventh annual meeting of the American Art Therapy Association.

**This is a coauthored paper. The authors are listed in alphabetical order.

mand a broadened theoretical framework complimenting the standard therapeutic approaches. Out of the works of the anthropologist Castaneda and his ten-year relationship with Don Juan, the sorcerer, we discover certain concepts that clarify these dynamics.

Essentially, Don Juan views life as a flow of perceptions and imagery, and he introduces Castaneda into this world through a number of techniques and experiences that facilitate a relatedness to cosmic forces. Don Juan helps us to understand our relationship to a broader vision of existence that goes beyond object relations theory, ego psychology, or intrapsychic conflicts.

When one refers to this sphere of the cosmos, reference is made to a broad reservoir of energy that ebbs and flows and becomes interchangeable into both the organic as well as the inorganic states. This energy is at times confined by time and space, but also breaks these boundaries and flows into new dimensions of existence. The physicist would find these notions compatible to Einstein's theory of relativity; the psychologist can understand these concepts in terms of ESP experiments; the Jungian analyst would talk of temporal contiguity. Perhaps the psychologist may also talk in terms of right hemisphere mental operations; by this, he refers to a holistic, intuitive, gestalt approach to existence. None of these concepts however, really gives a full dimension of the cosmic experience. Thus we turn to Don Juan and his teachings and see how some of the experiences of the mystic can be translated into a theoretical perspective.

Don Juan introduces us to the *nagual,* the indefinable part of ourselves that existed before conception and continues to exist after death. It is the unknown, the heart of creativity, and it cannot be described through words. It is a power that can help or hinder us. Don Juan also introduces the reader to the *tonal,* the part of us that is our earthly self, the self of being, seeing, feeling, knowing, and apprehending; the rational self that gives some notion of who and what we are. Perhaps an analyst or therapist might broadly term this part of ourselves the ego.

According to Don Juan, for man to experience the totality of himself or to be self-actualized, he must intergrate his tonal with the nagual. It is our belief that the expressive therapy process can facilitate a balance by attempting to bring a patient into some degree of harmony where by a flow of outer cosmic consciousness and relatedness to oneself and others are all interconnected. To accomplish this task, the actual expressive therapy task will be described in another section of this chapter.

Don Juan sees life as a process of unfolding perceptions and energies that can unleash sensations and that contain within them the power of creative existence. Contained within this flow are the potentials and the actualities, the wishes and the solutions. This process is neither a problem-orientated nor symptomatic-orientated approach to life. The individual discovers his need and his own solutions through the process. Life is not broken down into compartments, goals, or judgments. All of this can be viewed in the context of what Don Juan calls *the process of seeing.* Connections are made spontaneously, if at all, rather than through interpretations by the therapist or the teacher. In other words, understanding comes through perceptions. These perceptions form their own matrix that may or may not be elaborated by words. The importance however of this notion is that "insight" comes from perception as the basic foundation for cognition. There is no vacillation in decision making. Choice is a mind-body action that does not entail a thought out plan of action. It is a doing that is not even questioned by the very quintessence of synchronization of mind, body, and perception in one harmonious unit. One sees, one experiences, and one acts as a complete being.

Expressive therapy is a process, a working out, a balance between the tonal and the nagual. To achieve this, an expressive therapist does not give interpretations of symbols nor make connections, but does provide an atmosphere that is conducive to allowing a natural flow of images and perceptions. Expressive therapy is nonjudgmental, nonanalytical, and nonrational. What the expressive therapist effects, as in most meditative methods of focusing, is a way to stop the "internal dialogue."

When Don Juan refers to stopping the internal dialogue, he addresses himself to a crucial therapeutic tenet; if one does not talk to oneself, a flow of nothingness can accrue, which sets the state for the production of images and symbols that arise not only from our unconscious but from this broader level of existence that we call the nagual.

The expressive therapist provides at times the appropriate sensory experiences to aid the process of image making. As a result, the therapist must be extremely aware of the particular temperamental problems and issues that each patient poses so that he may use the appropriate material to stimulate the perceptual functions. For instance, the therapist may offer materials as a polar contrast to a patient's particular affect state, i.e., warm rich colors to a cold tight patient, materials serving to exaggerate a certain temperamental issue. Materials, therefore can stimulate and move energy so that a dynamic flow of perceptions occurs. Without this movement, the entire process of perceptual exploration can be bogged down.

A basic assumption in the Castaneda text postulates that humans discover what they need once the flow of perceptions takes place. Out of this process, images bring the person further along a journey of self-growth and discovery. Central to the concept of expressive therapy is the perception and apprehension of an image. The artistic experience encompasses a multitude of levels where words offer but a rough approximation. Thus, to the extent that the expressive therapy experience stimulates imagery, an experience is offered to the patient that can go far beyond the typical therapeutic communication.

Central to our notion of psychotherapy is our concept of imagery. An image captures the perception and holds it for the patient so that his vision can be apprehended. At the same time, the image does not interfere with the perception of other images but indeed acts as a stimulus to generate other internal representations. These images are often loaded with affects and have their own problem-solving qualities. Often in an expressive therapy relationship the patient may well start with a very innocuous image. However, as often the case, perceptions and sensations are often generated that find their way to central life issues.

According to Don Juan, there is nothing to know. Basically we are what we see. Once we see, we are totally responsible for what happens to us. At this point of seeing we are not bombarded with our usual "internal dialogue" or talking to ourselves. The internal dialogue stops us from giving ourselves what we need for it is predicated on preconceived notions, beliefs, and traditions. By stopping the internal dialogue, we automatically discover our needs and become more related to the stark totality of existence.

A central theme implicit in mediating or balancing of the tonal and nagual is Don Juan's notion of the *double*. The double is that part that goes crazy and the part that comes back to our earthly selves. Don Juan offers a means of apprehending the double by slowly developing techniques of entering into one's own dreamlife and actively taking over the direction of dreaming. This is also comparable to the creative art experience where the artist or patient may well be able to transcend his or her earthborn self and enter a larger level of existence: the world of the cosmos. Thus, if we are able to help our patients transpose energy from one world to another through images, experiencing the unfathomable on the one hand, while seeing, hearing, and being on the other, we approach what Maslow would call the peak experience. Others might call this the creative experience, or self- actualization. Thus, in the creative act, one often has the experience of being completely lost and exposed and at the same time he or she is there guiding and directing the entire experience.

The expressive therapist provides an imagery experience with the patient in order to discover a creative means to fill a need. The function of the artwork is one of harnessing on a multilevel plane of existence, feelings, affects, and sensations that crystalize a particular aspect of a life cycle. The expressive therapist helps the patient to be with the image, experience the image, be part of the image, and to grow with the image; and as this imagery changes within the expressive therapy relationship, a transformation of energy takes place as affects, experiences, and sensations build to other levels of self-actualization and self-affirmation.

A patient might well say, "Well, I'm feeling nothing. My mind is flooded with words and thoughts . . . or images. What do I do?" Don Juan's answer might be, You simply stop what you've been doing. The expressive therapist proceeds to avoid any further explanations or elaborations, he literally cuts through the intellectual defenses of the patient and provides a structure where there must be a response, even if that response is confusion and perplexity. Thus the patient is forced not to take distance from himself but to enter into whatever experience can arise. The expressive therapist attempts to break in to all routinized acts and customary habits that interfere with the breakthrough of new and surprising material. Thus the patient who is constantly complaining is requested to stop the complaining and learn that those complaints have been the means of avoidance of new material and experiences in life. But no explanations are ever needed. Once you stop doing something, a new something happens. In other words, one stops doing what he or she has been doing to make room to start doing something else.

The various techniques that Don Juan teaches Castaneda are geared to produce "seeing." They are running while looking straight ahead or focusing on an object. Shocking, surprising, keeping in mind a state of live drama from one session to the next. Those techniques enable the giving up of the internal dialogue so that one can see.

Expressive therapists can transpose some of these techniques and utilize them within the therapeutic relationship. For instance, it is possible, and often necessary, to use the element of surprise with patients who tend to function on the dull repetitive level of pictorial production. At times the therapist may introduce materials that overwhelm or shock the patient. The tight, constricted individual might be exposed to sensations and feelings while blindfolded so that the element of surprise completely takes over. Other patients may well need a combination of motion and movement combined with color and form. Music and rhythm, on the other hand, may allow the person to move with kinesthetic sensations along with color and motion. Thus, functions of perception, motility, and cognition become integrated in a total imagery experience.

Patients may also need to experience being part of the material they are working with so that boundaries are temporarily lost between the central perception and the outside object. This kind of continuity and connection exists between materials and the eyes of the beholder. As a result, energy starts flowing from a unified world where there is an integrated experience of sensations, perceptivity, feelings, and apprehensions. Patients can be helped to lose some of their controls and take a chance by erasing the boundary between themselves and the material. The atmosphere that facilitates this is one where there is a good deal of trust and an emphatic sense of understanding by the therapist as to the patient's need for distance, stimulation, and relatedness.

Implicit in the above is a belief that you do not have to stop and say what you are or what you learned, for the transformation is made by being part of the total therapeutic experience. The process of stopping the internal dialogue is in actuality a process of separation. We give up the traditional knowns and encounter archetypal experiences that connect to our past, present, and future. We also separate from the known world of temporal space and action. But of equal importance, we give ourselves the opportunity to create new roles and means of communication that are not part of our immediate past.

Separation leads to a sense of responsibility and direction for one's destiny. With our patients, we may inquire, "Is that what you want. Don't judge it. Don't analyze it. If you want it, it's okay." Thus it puts total responsibility on the patient. Don Juan is in tune with Castaneda and offers a very supportive relationship to accomplish this. The therapist must also learn to stop his/her internal dialogue in order to join the patient. At the same time the therapist has his/her own experiences and yet has the capacity to be completely with his patients.

The therapist finds ways of introducing to the patient methods and means of keeping the flow of imagery going. This is a cornerstone of an expressive therapy relationship. At times the expressive therapist is an opponent or adversary. He thus offers a means of combat and by doing so externalizes an internal demon. Don Juan believes that all of us need an opponent to bring out what is best in us. We need, in fact, both an ally who helps and supports us as well as an opponent who challenges, stimulates, and confronts. In some respects, psychoanalysts may reduce this notion to one of combatting introjects. Or a Jungian might call this an archetypal kind of experience. But perhaps we are dealing with much more. These images are the connecting experience not only with our past and present but also with the indefinable, prehuman phenomenon that at best belongs to a universal world of cosmic existence. The expressive therapist may find ways of producing this experience through materials, such as making masks, puppet play, or role playing. In these instances, both parties, patient and therapist, become lost and reborn in a very primitive and primary dialogue.

Expressive therapy is a here and now experience. We create an environment where the nagual can be free to flow and the tonal is synthesized. By so doing patients develop a capacity to both lose themselves in the art experience and become more connected to the self that needs mastery over its world. The patient is then able to have his feet planted in the tonal while venturing in the cosmos. In essence, we are developing a double or a creative self that mediates between these two worlds. Therapists might call this process the development of an observing ego. This reduces a complex concept to a very simplistic level.

More accurately, we believe another state of existence becomes apparent: the blending of the world of the tonal with the world of the nagual. Object relations therapists speak of that indefinable, indescribable schizoid or alienated part that exists in all of us. Perhaps they are addressing themselves to our nagual, the part that can never be related to on a verbal therapy level. It is that part of us that is alone; alone with ourselves, with or without another person.

Castaneda describes the important character traits that are necessary to prepare oneself to make a journey into the unknown. He refers to the "impeccable warrior," a person who has a sense of values to live by, who does not compromise but is able to stand alone and deal with all the paradoxical polarities that surround him. He is also able to take risks and be responsible for his choices. He is fully responsible for everything that happens to him. He can see, as he has learned to stop his internal dialogue. An impeccable warrior, therefore, has a profound sense of autonomy to prepare him/herself for a dangerous and exciting journey into the unknown self. In the words of Don Juan, one needs to "have death on one's shoulder." To understand the importance of the present, the importance of being able to live fully now, to recognize that one's life is finite, to not be overly involved in indulgences, or compromised by rewards, to see: these traits are the strength of any therapist who dares to risk the unknown and invite his patients on a joint journey to discover the unfathomable.

As part of being an impeccable warrior, the expressive therapist develops a very clear sense of who and what he is; he/she makes few compromises and is able to hold his or her ground. This entails the development of the will; an internal sense of discipline and control. This will has power and force, and can be developed by concentrating on focusing and remaining for long periods of time within the same image. The will is enlarged by expanding the state of being in one's double. The will of the therapist helps him/her to go from the nagual to the tonal and keeps a delicate balance between the two.

The great majority of expressive therapy experiences is often preoccupied with bringing about a great balance between the tonal and the nagual. Many patients, in fact, need their earthbound self or ego (the ability to see, hear, and apprehend) strengthened, and reinforced. All too often they are inundated by cosmic, archaic forces that reduce and enshroud the tonal and, so, narrow their lives to a fragmented and compartmentalized level. Other patients, however, need experiences that bring about a greater harmony with their nagual. Still others use their expressive therapy experiences towards facilitating a self-actualizing self where the very essence of creativity and growth is afforded. In these instances, the patient has both the will and capacity to feel and experience the world of the unknown, the world of the cosmos to be able to have his feet anchored here in this world of reality, to see, hear, and explore both worlds, to have the feeling of energy and enlightenment as he travels within both spheres. Only then can he/she experience creativity in the fullest sense of the word. His/her art, life, knowledge is one of process, is one of seeing, is one of discovering. It is this dynamism that makes expressive therapy a mystical, religious, alive experience. In this sense, we believe there is a meeting ground between the psychotherapist, the mystic, and the artist.

Part II

EVALUATIONS

Chapter 12

THE INITIAL INTERVIEW
Diagnostic Considerations for the Expressive Therapist*

Arthur Robbins, Ed.D, A.T.R.
Amelia Strauss

This chapter will attempt to clarify some of the diagnostic problems of the initial interview in expressive analysis, since often the treatment diagnosis, goals, and techniques in expressive analysis differ from those of conventional psychotherapy. An expressive analyst is concerned with the development of a patient's creative life potential. Consequently, a theory of creativity development is woven into a therapeutic framework that includes the capacity to shift into various ego states and to synthesize unconscious symbolism into an organizing force. No attempt will be made to summarize the principles of good interviewing, as these are readily available in the psychotherapeutic literature. (MacKinnon & Michels, 1971)

GENERAL DIAGNOSTIC CONSIDERATIONS

In the initial interview, the expressive therapist not only assesses the patient's cognitive functioning as seen in the opera-

*Editorial assistant, Heather Wilson.

tions typical of the holistic (right) and analytic (left) hemispheres of the brain, but also studies the psychodynamic structural organization, which facilitates a flow from one ego state to another. S/he evaluates the patient's capacity to be direct, linear, and verbal (left hemisphere operations) and the ability to be global, spatial, and perceptual (right hemisphere operations). Right hemisphere functions are seen in the predisposition to the use of metaphor and in nonverbal modes of communication. The relative strength and reliance upon each hemispheric mode and the problems inherent in facilitating an integration of each style are the areas of study and the ultimate treatment for the expressive therapist.

SPECIFIC DIAGNOSTIC CONSIDERATIONS

Involved in the evaluation will be a review of the patient's self and object representations, capacity to lose control, ability to tolerate complex stimuli, and his or her receptiveness to preconscious imagery, as well as the ability to harness strong libidinal drives.

In the initial interview, the strength of early internalization of the self-representation and the degree of clarity in the delineation of self and object will be of major concern. For example, those patients in whom self and object representations tend to be fused will more often than not utilize global or holistic styles of communication in order to avoid reality contact and communication with the outside world. Such patients, in whom right hemisphere functions prevail, will often be excessively vulnerable to strong affects, have limited capacity to absorb shock, and possess limited capability within the self to integrate their strong affects.

Patients' communications are studied for the presence of strong libidinal drive and the ability to harness this energy: Are there channels for sublimation or does the patient rely upon restrictive defenses that cut off his or her creative energies? The therapist will, therefore, note whether the patient is inundated with primitive material that interferes with a capacity for mastery and integration and restricts his or her ability to use secondary process levels of communication.

There may be anxiety associated with the loss of control that interferes with the patient's ability to use the spatial, intuitive, or holistic modes in his/her approach to life. Patients of this order often have difficulty organizing a continual feedback system between sensations, perception, and cognition. They force their fantasies and symbols to be reality-related, to have meaning within some kind of social context. Such patients, indeed, block off from consciousness a wide range of bodily sensations and nonverbal communication; they are direct and verbal, or mathematical in their approach to life. The fear of a loss of self in a state of out-of-consciousness or cosmic being is too esoteric, too foreign for these patients who are more comfortable going from one outer problem to another as a way of handling frustration and emptiness. Symbolization and fantasies, however, may be used by other patients as a means of avoiding realities that interfere with a real integration of the self.

Some patients are able to use creative artistic work as a safe means of losing control. Although these patients feel overwhelmed by primitive drive material, they are able to achieve some form of integration. Other patients, however, are basically intuitive or nonverbal in their approach to problems, yet distrust this mode of relating, relying excessively on direct, verbal forms of communication. By denying intuitive functions for the sake of more socially acceptable forms of thinking, they produce anxiety within themselves. Thus, any breakthrough of the imaginative material causes threat and damage.

The capacity to be related to metaphorical or global cognitive functioning can, of course, be fused to either a productively nonconforming or a negatively nonconforming approach to life. The patient who is able to be both paradoxical and metaphorical within a social framework has the capacity to rise above sterile, rigid, empty forms of problem solving. By the same token, s/he may easily shift to being more global and holistic as a means of being negative or rebellious. If this is the case, indulging in the loss of ego control acts as a way of living out primitive fears connected with early experiences around closeness and intimacy.

In most instances, patients tend to be stronger in one cognitive mode. Ideally, one should be able to combine both hemispheric functions so that one can lose control: be nonverbal and symbolic, and yet have the ego mastery resources to conceptualize and rationally assimilate one's impressions. Involved in the integration of both areas are manifold complexities.

SUMMARY

The expressive analyst studies the interconnection between the patient's verbal and nonverbal methods of communication, how this interconnection relates to the patient's sense of self and how it integrates the self with outer reality. As s/he studies this balance of forces, the therapist makes some judgment as to the depth of life experience to which the patient is able to be receptive. The expressive analyst's value system regarding mental health is inherent in his/her approach, as are his/her convictions about self-realization. At the root of the expressive analyst's convictions lies his/her belief that the creative use of one's self is a crucial contributor to an inner sense of vitality and well-being. S/he is, therefore, less concerned with symptoms and behavioral adjustment than with the richness and complexity of functioning.

Through treatment, then, the expressive analyst hopes that the patient will be able to develop breadth and receptivity to his/her inner life as well as to develop ego controls. Only then can there be a great facilitation of energy stemming from deep relatedness to inner and outer stimuli concomitant with ego integration. The patient's very sense of self may thereby be intensified and affirmed. The expressive therapist thus assesses the holistic and analytic cognitive modes of functioning and develops a treatment plan to deal with the various issues that presently interfere with the integration of the two hemispheres.

The case that follows illustrates typical diagnostic problems presented in the initial interview in expressive therapy. The initial interview explores the strengths and weaknesses of the patient's ego functioning and the treatment plans of expressive therapy.

INITIAL INTERVIEW: CAROL

Referral and First Interview

Carol was referred to the Center for Expressive Analysis by a friend of hers who is an art therapist. Later, she told me she had applied to only one center because she wasn't interested in shopping around. At the center she was seen by an intake therapist who referred her to me. When we spoke on the phone to arrange a time and place for our first interview, Carol sounded pleasant and businesslike.

Carol arrived precisely on time. She seemed full of vitality, gave me a bright smile, and introduced herself. (I was very aware of being quickly scrutinized, and also had the impression that Carol sometimes spoke in a lower register.) Carol's gaze darted about the reception area. Her body seemed to be in constant motion, particularly her head and hands. She chatted cheerfully as we walked from the reception area into the office and swung her mass of blond curls (as if to be sure I would notice). Still talking about what an interesting place this studio/office was, Carol perched on one of the stools. Her tall, slim body became concave; she crossed her legs. Carol was dressed casually in jeans and a knit top and wore some jewelry, which enhanced her appearance.

It was hard to judge her age. She could have been any-where from twenty-one on. (Her large, deep-set eyes stared, which didn't quite fit with her bubbly, almost offhand attitude.) During our discussion, Carol made only fleeting eye-contact with me.[1] At times, she turned her head and body away from me. Her speech was very rapid; at times I needed to ask her to repeat herself. While Carol's body remained quite still, her hands darted about as if to punctuate her rapid speech. (I was most affected by the lightness, almost gaity, with which she answered my questions. Her apparent attitude—that this whole thing was just another lark—seemed incompatible with the content of the material she presented.)

History

Carol is a single, twenty-nine-year-old, white female. She describes herself as a nonpracticing artist. She expects to begin graduate courses in the fall. Currently, Carol works as a secre-tary for a research foundation. This is the fourth job she's had in the eight years since she graduated from college with a B.A. in fine arts. Carol describes herself as an active person who enjoys life. She frequently goes to the theater, museums and so on, and says she has many friends.[2]

Carol is the youngest of three children: she has a brother who is ten years her senior and a sister who is five years older then she. Until she was fourteen her family lived in upper Manhattan where, as Carol describes it, she had a normal child-hood. She did well in school and enjoyed a wide range of friends. When she was fourteen the family moved to Long

[1]Anxiety seemed very close to the surface.

[2]Carol appears to be self-sufficient and declares she has no problems. She says she wants to make changes, yet expresses satisfaction with her present life and is unable to elaborate about what it is that she would like to be different.

Island and there Carol had difficulties. She felt out of place among her new classmates and had difficulty making friends.[3] Nevertheless, she completed high school and went on to college.[4] In her senior year she became engaged, but broke the engagement shortly before the wedding, feeling she was not ready to marry.

Family Relationships

Carol offers little information about her family life. She describes her relationships as "never close," but does not elaborate. Currently, no two members of the family live in the same state. When Carol was twenty her mother was stricken with cancer. She died one-and-a-half years ago after a nine-year illness. Carol feels there is nothing further to to be said about either her mother or her mother's death.[5] She did note that since her mother's death she has become closer to her sister. They now have frequent phone contact. Carol informed me that unless she initiated the discussion, she did not want to talk about her family.

Other Relationships

Carol describes herself with friends as sometimes being stubborn and sometimes giving to an extreme. To paraphrase her, "I'm a very giving person, usually willing to concede in an argument unless I definitely feel I'm right, and then I'll fight to the finish. I'll give a lot, but if I feel I'm being taken advantage of, I'll withdraw." Carol was unable to clarify these rather

[3]The loss of peer support during adolescence is often critical in precipitating illness: the identification process loses momentum when there is a loss of support from familiar structures.

[4]The presence of ego strength is indicated by the fact that in spite of stress, Carol completed both high school and college.

[5]A good deal of denial and dissociation seems to be in evidence here.

confusing generalizations.[6] She said her friends object to her decision to enter treatment and complain she has "changed." Carol believes her friends are uncomfortable with her plans to return to school.[7]

Patient's Reasons for Entering Therapy

Carol feels she has given to others and now would like to give to herself.[8] Additionally, she expresses dissatisfaction with her present work and social life; she is looking for "greater personal fulfillment."[9] She is not unhappy, yet something is missing from her life; she wants to "find herself."[10] Carol has observed some changes in herself that concern her. Three years ago, after breaking up with a boyfriend of several years, she stopped painting.[11] While she has seen another man since then, she feels they are not compatible and has refused to live with him. Carol is also concerned about the fact that six months ago, at the time she began applying to graduate schools, she stopped dreaming.[12] Her dreams had been pleasant and generally re-

[6]The patient's defensive system may well be a primitive one, as large areas of her life seem disconnected. The affects of anger, depression, and pain are encapsulated within a wall of narcissism, which is supported by Carol's tendency to withdraw and exert omnipotent control over her very strong need for support and contact.

[7]This is one of several contradictions in the patient's interview. At one point Carol spoke of herself as a loner without friends. Here, they are against her return to school and her entry into treatment. However, this may indicate the patient's own ambivalence.

[8]Giving to others is a way of giving to herself.

[9]Vagueness of expression, "greater personal fulfillment," goes along with the mechanisms of denial and dissociation.

[10]Perhaps this emptiness has its origins in an unresolved symbiosis.

[11]It is likely that this boyfriend was an extremely important anchor for this patient. Loosing him may well have intensified her defenses and blocked access to her unconscious and creativity.

[12]This is further evidence of a general shut-down in possible networks of self-affirmation.

lated to something in her daily life. Usually she would return to a dream after having awakened in the middle of it.

Therapist's Reaction to the First Interview

Carol left me feeling rather confused. (She talks about difficult times as if discussing the purchase of a pair of window shades.) Indeed, as much as she talked, she showed little affective change and did not communicate much of a sense of either Carol the artist or Carol the person. (My internal reactions were curiosity, boredom, and withdrawal, and increasing irritation. I kept wondering why this chatty young woman, who reiterated her contentment with her current life, would want to embark on a course of introspection where feelings and changing internal states are the primary order of business. I was impressed both by the contradictions and the gaps in the information she gave.) Carol conveyed a general sense that something was missing from her life that she'd like to find. Although I asked her to elaborate on this several times during the interview, she was unable to do so. She spoke of her family's lack of closeness and her mother's recent death in a manner that indicated an absence of any personal discomfort. This puzzled and concerned me. (She seemed to be saying, "I want help, but I won't help you to help me; you do it, but don't tell me about it.") Carol left the interview in the same cheerful and chatty manner that she had come in. I felt exhausted and had no clear idea about what she really wanted out of treatment. I realized I would have to find another way of discovering what Carol was all about, and decided to suggest we do some drawing exercises at our next meeting.

Second Session: Drawing

Carol agreed to try drawing although she expressed some reluctance saying she preferred acrylics and was not used to pencil or cray-pas. She added that she was uncomfortable with unplanned art production. First, I asked her to draw herself or a free-form representation of herself without looking at the paper. Carols' drawing was a skull-shaped top on a long, squiggly bottom, encased by a circular line. Carol described the top—the head area—as a lima bean and thought it needed additional work.[13] She felt the encircled body was well-shaped. Then I asked her to draw me while looking at me. (I was interested in her perceptions of me because she had expressed a great deal of curiosity about why I had been selected to work with her and what my credentials were.) Although Carol knew this drawing was supposed to be of me, she said it was also another portrait of herself. She said little else about this drawing other than noting it was shaped like a bowling pin and encased in a rounded-cornered square.[14] My support of her analysis seemed to please her, but she continued to press me for my "expert opinion." Carol seemed to have genuinely enjoyed making connections between herself and her drawings.

Diagnostic and Therapeutic Considerations

The death of her mother and subsequent blocking of Carol's energies produced a breach in her character armor. Until recently, the armor had protected her against intolerable feelings. She denies there are any internal experiences with which she can't cope. In fact, her feelings of anger, hate, confusion, and genuine affection must be defended against to protect both herself and others. Carol is genuinely convinced she is a happy, well-adjusted person who is giving almost to a fault. Particularly in the early phase of treatment any probing of these ego syntonic defenses will be experienced as narcissistic injury.

[13]The patient moves in a vague, undifferentiated world and is unable to put together her feelings and knowledge about her past and present. She cannot describe to the therapist what has happened to her. Secondary thought processes are poorly developed.

[14]The patient describes herself as being encased in a rounded-cornered square.

When threatened, Carol uses projective devices. She wondered why I, an older woman, had been selected to see her and wondered what my qualifications were. When I reminded her of her option to "shop" for someone else, she backed off and denied any wish to investigate other therapists. Carol had perceived my reminder as rejection. She described her feeling during this interchange as mild annoyance of no consequence. Her inability to acknowledge feelings of closeness and anger is depressive in nature. This is demonstrated by the lack of affect with which she described her family's lack of closeness and the death of her mother. Carol's joviality and good-natured optimism have a hollow ring.

Her drawings probably provide the clearest indication of the schizoid Carol has constructed around what is essentially a depressive core. Neither drawing has definition of distal parts nor suggests intention or direction. Both drawings are encased. While there is some detail in the torso of her self-protrait, it is nonspecific in meaning and form. Difficulties around fusion and separation are expressed by Carol's association that her drawing of me is actually another portrait of herself. A juxtaposition of the drawing of me (as representative of the mother figure) onto her self-portrait reveals frenetic activity layered over an empty, amorphous blob. In both pictures, the encircling lines serve to contain themselves and the other.

From this it could be theorized that Carol experienced deprivation of a mothering figure very early in life. Possibly this was due to her mother's inability to tolerate the developing infant's oral sadistic expression. These feelings remained unresolved and safely encapsulated in Carol's schizoid armoring until her mother's death. Then feelings of loss and rage emerged once again. Because of her need to remain fused with the Good Mother, these feelings were intolerable and Carol cut off once more. To avoid resolving her feelings toward her mother, Carol has sacrificed the libidinal drive of her creative energies.

Carol's amorphous reasons for entering treatment are somewhat clarified within this context. Until now her art had served to fulfill unresolved needs through sublimation (she prefers to keep her works). Now her art is unavailable to her. Carol's vague sense of incompleteness is rooted very early in life. Her motivation for treatment can be seen as a need to reclaim something she's lost. However, in doing so, Carol will run the risk of facing her feelings about her mother, which are now manifested by denial and projection.

In both interviews Carol's message is "don't push me." A sense of her fragility comes both from her words and her slim, light body, which seems unable to tolerate any pressure. Presently her ego is too fragile to integrate transference interpretations and they would be experienced as an assualt. Using expressive, nonverbal techniques the therapist will serve as a container for Carol's feelings. Within this framework Carol can begin to experience a sense of trust in herself and in the therapist.

It will take a good deal of time for Carol to begin to lower her defensive armor. Artwork will serve as a metaphor for communication until she feels sufficiently organized to relate directly in the context of a strong therapeutic alliance. Only then will it be possible to begin the process of working toward freeing the depressive core that has remained out of conscious awareness for much of Carol's life.

REFERENCE

Makinon, R. A. & Michels, R. *The psychiatric interview in clinical practice.* Philadelphia: W. B. Saunders Company, 1971.

Chapter 13

DIAGNOSTIC CONSIDERATIONS FOR THE EXPRESSIVE THERAPIST

Arthur Robbins, Ed.D.*
Anne Sternbach, M.P.S.

IINTRODUCTION

Diagnosis and treatment are inextricably related processes. The former defines and structures the latter while, conversely, changes in treatment modify diagnosis. By implication, diagnosis makes a statement regarding a particular set of treatment interventions. A subcorollary of this can be drawn in the following terms: diagnosis constantly changes as the patient moves from one treatment level to another. Diagnostically, the expressive analyst identifies and relates to the particular ego states and defenses that interfere with creative and therapeutic development. The purpose of this chapter is to demonstrate this process in motion. The authors will utilize diagnostic testing material as well as clinical data to clarify this process. Finally, therapeutic interventions will be culled from this material in order to

*Both authors share equal responsibility for this chapter and are listed in alphabetical order.

demonstrate the interaction between diagnostic and treatment considerations.

PRESENTING THE PROBLEM

The patient complains of an overwhelming sense of powerlessness and immobility. Working as a secretary, Barbara sees herself at the age of forty as wasting her potential. She has been unable to develop creative work outlets or satisfying love relationships. Social contacts are now mainly with women. Previous treatment of sixteen years' duration led to little change. Barbara sees her current treatment as her last chance, though she is not particularly optimistic as to what can be done for her.

THUMBNAIL SKETCH OF FAMILY HISTORY

The patient comes from a lower-class home, both parents working in a laundry and struggling to eke out a living. She pictures her mother as a martyred, pained woman, constantly pulling support and succor from her daughter. During Barbara's early years, she loved and idealized her father. However, as her need to be freed of the mother-daughter relationship became intensified, her disillusionment with a very passive father grew. During her preadolescence, Barbara was a good girl who waited in pain for her day to come, hoping someday to be heard and attended to. In the meantime, the family's hopes and dreams were placed on the eldest daughter, who was encouraged and supported through law school. The latter became a tyrant who demanded obedience and silence from all around her as she nobly sacrificed her life to carrying out the family myth of success and achievement. What she experienced was a family anointment of adhesive glue that allowed her little room to find her own autonomy. Her younger brother was a positive force for Barbara. She seemed to have a genuine affection for him and a feeling of mutual support.

TREATMENT CONSIDERATIONS

During Barbara's two years of treatment, the direction has been a movement from distrust to grudging acceptance of the therapist; from control and constriction to fear of loss of control and sporadic eruptions of rage; and from fear of sexuality to a wish for recognition as a female. Transferences range from the unrelated, unresponsive parent, to the powerless and ineffectual father, and, finally, to the brutal sadist who would withhold and demand a humiliating surrender. Each transference confrontation appears to strengthen Barbara, yet she seems to feel a sense of staleness and stagnation in her life outside the treatment situation.

Throughout the course of her treatment, Barbara has insisted upon being clearly and acutely perceived by her therapist. She has met platitudinous or stereotypical formulations with a tight-lipped negativism or outward hostility. At the same time, she resents her therapist having any knowledge of her, and only with reluctance has she been able to allow him into her life. Constantly demanding strength and substance from her therapist, Barbara has meanwhile often doubted his capacity to produce and come through for her. Detecting any degree of ineffectuality, she feels rage, which soon evolves into a fear of loss of control or balance.

During an early period in treatment, Barbara spent many months unemployed and was content to sink into a state of passive immobility. Occasionally she would face herself and recognize the devastating waste of her life. With each period of increasing intimacy, the depressive immobility seemed to diminish as the world seemed less threatening and overwhelming.

Barbara has spent many sessions speaking about her sense of womanhood. She has feared the aggressive part of herself and has viewed it as somewhat unfeminine. While she likes to putter around with hammer and screwdriver, she also has had some access to a soft, receptive aspect of herself. However, the emergence of this component is accompanied by fears of surrender, humiliation, and sadistic penetration. Meanwhile Barbara acknowledges her positive feelings for men and desire for their companionship.

Defensively, her obsessiveness would often tie strong, libidinous impulses in knots, though this too has subsided as she has become more incisive and comfortable with her aggressive thoughts.

TEST OBSERVATIONS: THEMATIC APPERCEPTION TEST, FIGURE DRAWINGS, EMBEDDED FIGURE TEST, BARRON-WELCH ART SCALE

Barbara seemed to view the testing situation, in part, as an opportunity to try to confront some of the difficulties highlighted by the test. In this attitude, we see some of the patient's strengths. While there were many aspects of the testing that aroused Barbara's anxiety, defenses, and wish to withdraw, she showed a good deal of determination. With time, Barbara seemed progressively able to discuss her feelings and to permit into her consciousness more threatening material. She was able to playfully express, rather than deny or obsess about, some hostility toward the examiner as well as to relate with a degree of intimacy. Transference-like elements seemed present in some wish to identify with the examiner, and in some attendant competitiveness and need to establish a separate identity in the situation. At the same time, the patient seemed able to view the examiner realistically and maintain interpersonal contact over a rather long testing period.

With every test, a variety of associations were aroused. Barbara seemed to share them with the examiner partly to make herself known to another, and partly to clarify for herself the significance of her thoughts and feelings. Each test thus seemed to become part of a process of increasing self-awareness and definition. In stating her preferences (marking "like" or "dislike") on the Barron-Welsh art scale, Barbara often equivocated and sometimes obsessed before making a choice. She explained that her taste seemed to be changing, and she was pleased that she was becoming less rigid than in her college years, when she feels that her controlled, intellectual design work was often "noncreative" and a "cop-out." She found herself in the testing situation struggling to allow herself new reactions rather than being bound by the tight strictures about mathematics, a subject that she has tended to reject although she has talent in it. She feels she has also made some progress in accepting this aspect of herself. Barbara's relatively high score on the Barron-Welsh scale indicates that she may have made some progress in terms of breaking through her self-imposed constriction.

The embedded figures test seemed to present a challenge for Barbara to prove that there was an area in which she was very competent. She seemed to struggle with disappointment in herself for a lack of perfection in completing this task. As she was able to complete some of the unfinished figures after the official testing time, we see some indication that this woman's ability to perform certain tasks can be limited by her anxiety and her need to use such tasks to demonstrate her worth. In this light, it is noteworthy that she assumed it was better to complete all figures. The manner in which she struggled with some of the disembedding tasks would seem to indicate a similar struggle for the establishment and maintenance of her identity, and some fear of entrapment.

We have seen in Barbara's Thematic Apperception Test (TAT) stories some development within a limited context of her ability to allow sexual and aggressive material to consciousness and to be honest about some of her problems. Along with this seems a genuine desire and capacity to confront some of these issues, even if this occasions anxiety.

Barbara came to the task of drawing after having completed the other tests. At this point she seemed to feel relatively comfortable with and supported by the examiner. She expressed that she had anticipated such a task with a mixture of dread and hope, and described her inability to draw within her regular treatment situation. She seemed to regard this test above the rest as an opportunity to try to confront her fears. The drawing experience became for the patient an experience of the creative process. In a series of drawings, she struggled, sometimes painfully, to make a statement on paper, and to clarify some issues about definition of womanhood and manhood. During this process, Barbara showed frequent displeasure and some anxiety about what she had done, and yet she was able to enjoy herself. She kept working to make changes until she achieved some degree of satisfaction on individual drawings and on a progression through a series. She became very involved with her drawing of the examiner, in a way that seemed quite loving and seemed to bespeak a desire to really perceive the other and to make contact. It was important for her to state that "What I was thinking of was that I was willing to look at you—you can't take that for granted." Her other comments showed an appreciation for the examiner's personal style and expression of femininity. In a full figure drawing, which used three pieces of paper, Barbara drew an image of her nephew's wife. As she spoke of this young woman, of whom she is very fond, her own voice and manner became softer and more feminine. She seemed to use both these drawings as a source of identification with women who were more comfortable than she with their own sexuality. Barbara was quite pleased with herself that she was willing to acknowledge such feelings verbally and on paper.

Troubled at not having a model for a male, Barbara struggled to draw a man. She saw in his face her father (whom she had intended) and her analyst. She was surprised to find that the drawing looked like an old woman reminiscent of one of the TAT pictures.

Barbara had a great deal of difficulty in drawing the full figure of a male. As she made her first attempt, a surprised smile spread on her face. "Oh, Christ, you're not going to believe this!" she exclaimed as she showed me that she had unwittingly drawn a bull. She had originally meant to draw David, a man she had been involved with, in his soccer uniform, and was surprised to see his hands turn into hoofs.

Barbara seemed quite delighted with this development, which seemed to help her push to continue. In the series of drawings that followed she confronted issues of merging and differentiating images of her therapist, her brother, David, and a generalized representation of the male. During this process she struggled with back-front reversals, with difficulty in portraying a sense of power and gentleness, and with reluctance to giving a clear identity to a figure. It seemed at first that she literally could not draw a frontal view of a full male figure, but would not allow herself to stop until she had completed the task.

Barbara was quite tired, though pleased with herself when she had completed the pencil drawings and discussion. She initially balked when asked to do crayon drawings, but, again, wanted to face the task. She was asked to draw a full figure as quickly as possible without thinking about it. Holding a green and yellow crayon, she drew quickly and with loose, open movements. Barbara commented that she rebels against anything that makes her feel like a child, and that she needed to plunge into the task in order to do it at all. "It's a woman, by the way, a flowing one, very weird." Barbara was then surprised by an association to her menstrual cycle and some conflict about it. In spite of the problems, she said she liked this evidence of womanhood. There was some discussion of a greater feeling of ease and fluidity at this point in the process.

The prospect of drawing a man in crayon was more threatening. It was suggested to Barbara that she just "think man" and draw quickly. With the same crayons, she bore down heavily on the paper to write "man" and then took another paper and quickly drew. Again, she was pleased and surprised with the results and said that the suggestion stopped her from obsessing about details. She said she felt she couldn't portray the sense of male strength that she wished to, so she tried to do so by pressing very hard and starting with the shoulders. She felt this method did produce a powerful image. Then, holding the two drawings up together, she said with a tone of pleased discovery, "I think this one makes this one look more like a woman and this makes this one look more like a man."

Barbara expressed that being able to draw in this manner was a new and valuable experience for her. It seems that in this instance, the testing was allowed to become part of a creative therapeutic experience with implications for future possibilities.

TEST EVALUATION

Barbara links her inability to play and be spontaneous with her difficulties in working creatively. Reporting that she never completes any project she begins, she says that even her home of many years looks as if she has just moved in. We have noted throughout the testing situation the patient's inability to make decisive choices. It appears that she fears attack and annihilation if she takes a definite stand, as if she would find herself standing naked in heavy traffic. Barbara seems to be saying that she feels anything she creates will be destroyed, and, by implication, she with it. Her unfinished projects seem to reflect her sense of incompleteness; her creations cannot exist because she lacks a sense of her own existence.

One of the assumptions of the expressive therapist is that the capacities to play and to create are interrelated, and that both require an ability to stand alone. With Winnicott, we feel that aloneness may take different forms, but that a "sophisticated aloneness," established during the Oedipal phase and later deeply rooted in very early experience, which "is that of being alone, as an infant and small child, in the presence of mother. Thus the capacity to be alone is a paradox; it is the experience of being alone while someone else is present" (Winnicott, 1965).

From the patient's presentation of herself, and from her

history, it would seem that she was short-changed of this experience. Rather than being present in this special way for her child, the mother appears to have expected the patient to serve that function for her. Later, it seems, Barbara created in fantasy a father to serve this function for her, but was finally disillusioned to find him ineffectual and to experience him as not present. For Winnicott, "Cultural experience begins with creative living first manifested in play," and, "The place where cultural experience is first located is in the *potential space* between the individual and the environment (originally the object)" (Winnicott, 1971). For Barbara, there was no such space; there was no room for her.

Barbara now seems to be searching for a place in which she can play, and hungrily craving a playmate, but her experience is such that she cannot believe such a person can exist. The tremendous deficits in her self coincide with her lack of ability to experience the other. Barbara is not capable of truly being with another or of being alone; she cannot exist in a relationship nor can she exist separately. If there is no Barbara, in her experience there is also no one else.

Terrified of seeing nothing if she looks at herself, and of feeling nothing if she tries to touch another, the patient tries to reach out in spite of her fear. What does she risk if she acts on her own desire for contact? She feels she may destroy or be destroyed by her hunger and rage, and her sexuality arouses her fears of annihilation. She does not feel a sense of self strong enough to contain powerful emotions, nor does she trust that another would or could do so for her. Intermixed with Barbara's self-protectiveness, we see also spite, which seems directed in a variety of generalized transferences at the human and inanimate object world. It is as if she says "no one was there to play with me. Now just see if you'll get me to play with you, goddammit!"

Meanwhile, Barbara is painfully aware of the self-deprivation resulting from taking this position. Another voice from within alternately pleads and demands that someone find a way, if only through trickery, to engage her. We have seen that she can be willing to respond. Barbara seems to need at times an interaction with someone who can be both soft and strong, supportive in a way that does not detract from Barbara. This individual needs to be able to withstand Barbara's attack, and be able to respond in kind without retaliating or coming on too strong. This would seem a rather difficult balance to achieve and maintain, particularly because Barbara has a difficult time in sustaining her end of the volley of playful hostility.

While at times Barbara is all too aware of her wishes, she tends to discount, discredit, and deny them. Why play if there is no wish to mastery? What use play, if one has no wishes to fulfill? Play does not, at an early age seem to have served these functions of mastery and wish-fulfillment for Barbara. It is as if she denies having powerful experiences, or brackets them out. However, when she can allow herself some playfulness, she is capable of being surprised and delighted to discover expressions of powerful experiences emerging from her, as when she produced the bull. This experience, in turn, seems to have sparked more desire to assimilate and harness, rather than deny this brute force. Thus we see that drawing can be an avenue of play experience for Barbara, and an experience through which she can possibly meet some of the developmental needs served by play.

Barbara's tremendous difficulty in making an unambivalent statement in word or image is connected with her ambivalence surrounding her passive wishes and need for mastery. Again, her inability to play is an issue: She has not learned to use play to effect transformation, from passivity to activity. Barbara has difficulty producing a story with aggressive or even assertive content or meaning: such stories often deteriorate into defensive obsessing. The character who is aggressive or assertive is punished, or the move toward self-assertion and autonomy is met with lack of interest on the part of others and feelings of isolation. However, we see in Barbara's growing playfulness and acceptance of her own hostility during the testing situation an active desire to be more assertive.

While Barbara is obviously quite imaginative, her ability to use her imagination in a gratifying manner is limited. We see obsessional defenses come to the rescue when the patient feels threatened by incipient awareness of the pain she will experience if she truly confronts the discrepancies between her fertile fantasies and her basically sterile reality. She is thus limited to her ability to fantasize freely about real objects as well as to create objects of fantasy. This is linked with her deficit in establishing both self and object representations. Barbara needs to be helped to allow life to the frequently aborted creations of her imagination in a transitional space from which reality and imagination may begin to have a cohesive meaning.

Related to all of the issues discussed above is Barbara's lack of development in the area of sexual identity. Her inability to indulge in oral and anal play had not established a good basis on which to achieve genitality. Many of her fears and fantasies concerning sexuality have a pregenital ring. Along with this we see Barbara's struggle to establish clear male and female representations. Not only are the feminine and phallic principles within Barbara not on good terms with one another, but each has been stunted in its own growth. The creative interplay between these aspects of herself, which can bring better definition to each, is missing, as is the interaction with men, which could bring greater definition to Barbara as a woman. Again, we have seen in Barbara's TAT stories, and particularly in her response to her drawing experience, a conscious attempt to confront this problem. Barbara's history indicates that while she waited for someone to listen to her, her ability to conceive of the space in which to play dwindled. It seems as if she was looking into a room that she could not enter for so long, it ceased to exist. It is as if the place where this space should be is a vacuum in her experienced reality, or a place that she regards as dark and dangerous, populated, if at all, with untrustworthy beings. The implication for treatment is that Barbara needs to be helped to find the way into a space she has dreamed of but never been to. Once there, she needs the guidance of someone who can sensitively modulate the level of intimacy and help Barbara learn to play together and alone.

TREATMENT CONSIDERATIONS

From a treatment point of view, the therapist is faced with a choice regarding the essential core problem. If he sees Barbara's diagnostic issues as belonging in the realm of conflict theory, he will attempt to analyze the neurotic defenses, lessen the superego forces, and free the impulse life. Though these issues are important, treatment with this focus could be futile and disastrous.

We believe that Barbara's problems are rooted in a severe disturbance of the self. Deeper than the rage and attendant guilt is the emptiness and despair of the lost self who was not perceived or related to on the most basic of levels. The therapist's creativity will be called upon to hear through the static of her verbalizations, touch her with metaphor, and mirror what he perceives of her. The patient will need to hear, see, and visualize the scope and depth of the painful dilemma of her existence. In this treatment, the use of the patient's and therapist's imagination and preconscious imagery will be crucial in the opening of a space in which this patient can find her identity. In order to help Barbara emerge with a sense of self that has true integrity, the focus in treatment must be on the integration of polarities, and only secondarily on the resolution of conflict. The split between good and bad, light and dark, pure and evil, must be healed. The patient must also assimilate the powerful masculine urges and rescue the female from her helpless victim image. With a new internal relationship between the feminine and phallic principles, we would hope Barbara would be able to take further risks with men.

The importance of the therapist's presence cannot be understated. The patient needs a real person with whom she can engage in dialogue, so she may begin to test out her vague self and object representations and more clearly differentiate herself. If the lost girl within her needs recognition, so does the male intruder, who can be ambitious, powerful, and brutally incisive. The good little girl who is so masochistic needs a proper introduction to all these opposing forces.

This woman has a cognitive sweep that constantly stops in the middle. Needing a refuge from her strong urges, she must be challenged when she withdraws. However, this can only be accomplished in the context of understanding and sensitivity.

Barbara aspires to be more in touch with her essence; to be primitive, earthy, and sensual, if not erotic, and eventually she must emerge from the bathroom and not feel so private about her inner hungers. She will need from her therapist a very active confrontation so that the irascible bull will not be experienced as ugly or castrating.

SUMMARY

The authors have attempted to demonstrate the complex interconnection between creative and therapeutic growth as well as to show how diagnostic considerations affect a therapeutic stance. We have shown the pervasive damage in Barbara's self-development and the various secondary forces that accrue. She is threatened and terrorized by powerful hostile and erotic impulses that are rooted in the very early pregenital past. Not having a strong enough sense of self in which these feelings can be contained, Barbara takes refuge in her cognitive processes, as a means of avoiding confrontation by the powerful archaic images that make her feel crazy and out of control. Her need for clarity and specificity are her strengths, but they really do not help ground her in a more organic sense of herself as a person. Her verbalizations can become elaborative in a nonproductive way when she feels only a tenuous connection to a larger libidinal force within. While Barbara wishes to have some impact on the world, she feels powerless, and her deep narcissistic injuries make it difficult for her to seek recognition through her work. Ironically it is precisely this step she cannot take that could probably start her on a healing journey. She has the potential to use creative work as a transitional space in which she can feel protected from her debilitating hurt and rage, and also reach out for self-affirming contact with another. She needs to create a child, if only in her work, for in her injury and deprivation there is an opportunity to find restitution in a creative and therapeutic dialogue that begins with a therapist but must ultimately be directed at the world.

REFERENCES

Winnicott, D. W. The capacity to be alone. In *The maturational processes and the facilitating environment*. London: Hogarth Press and The Institute of Psychoanalysis, 1965.

Winnicott, D. W. *Playing and reality*. New York: Basic Books, 1971.

Part III

CLINICAL MATERIALS

Chapter 14

CREATIVE INTERVENTIONS IN PSYCHOANALYTIC PSYCHOTHERAPY*

Jane Mattes, M.S.W.
Arthur Robbins, Ed. D., A.T.R.

In this paper we will describe the use of creative techniques, particularly verbal and visual metaphors, as means of strengthening the ego, lessening the superego and overcoming resistances. Essentially, we will describe a very intricate therapeutic relationship in which the deepest part of the patient's sense of self is tapped and touched. As we see it, the field of the therapist-patient communication is overdetermined, replete with inductions and counterinductions, and overlaid with highly-charged transference and countertransference reactions. In many respects the therapeutic session can be compared to a work of art. There is a multiplicity of levels. The feelings and communications cannot be readily reduced to words, and there is a sense of excitement when both patient and therapist have experienced an encounter that is healing and growth-produc-

*In press, from the *Psychoanalytic Review* through the courtesy of the editors of the National Psychological Association for Psychoanalysis, New York, N. Y.

ing. The past, present, and future become concentrated in a very delicate balance, and at the close there is a sense of completion and integration.

Each session poses a creative challenge to both therapist and patient. In any one encounter, many parts of a patient's psychic structure need attending. The metaphor, be it verbal or visual, often serves this purpose. At any one time, one word or image can touch a variety of psychic structures and, at the same time, can cope with resistances, recognize reality, and respect the patient's need for safety, distance, and contact. It also serves as a frame for our images and play. With the verbal or visual metaphor, complex affects fall into a structure that has a beginning and an ending but is still timeless. For in the act of creative communication, energy becomes bound but not static.

The metaphor can serve as a bridge for raw, primitive communications, which are not easily translatable into secondary process communications. This is particularly true for complex introjected phenomena, which reflect presences that can be captured better by images than by words. What we are therefore proposing is a framework that allows both therapist and patient the freedom to play. But, as in any good artist's work, play and discipline, freedom and structure, all become necessary parts of a very interdependent process. For the therapist to play with his imagination and creativity as a response to the patient's communication, the structure of the analytic relationship must be constantly upheld. (All too often, in the attempt to facilitate symbolic communication, there is subtle acting out of fusion fantasies and wishes on the part of the therapist. While imagination is object related and serves as a bridge to object constancy, fantasy, by contrast, is a retreat and a withdrawal from the outer world, and is neither creative nor adaptive [Rosen, 1960].) Thus, like an artist, the therapist is able to enter an ego state that permits him to roam in any direction. At the same time, his observing ego is constantly noting and recording both his own process and the mutual one between himself and the patient. To put it succinctly, he plays with a degree of objectivity. Also like an artist, his interventions are not show-stoppers, but act as catalysts to enlarge the perceptual field and to maintain a flow of ever deepening communications. Creative communication implies touching the very essence of the therapist's and patient's selves. Words are no longer flat or hollow, but offer an indiscernible feeling of self-recognition. These concepts will be illustrated with examples from the treatment of a thirty-year-old woman patient.

The history of this patient is notable mainly in the number of losses she suffered during the first years of life. From a middle-class, Catholic family, she was the first child born after her mother had several miscarriages, and in the year following her birth her mother became pregnant again and gave birth to her first brother. There were severe illnesses of both maternal and paternal grandparents, and one grandparent died. The mother became pregnant again in the patient's second year. We can speculate that the patient's mother was depressed and narcissisticly involved with her pregnancies and the invalided grandparents, and was thus unable to provide a satisfying symbiotic phase for the patient at the developmentally appropriate time. Given the lack of "good enough mothering," the patient could not firmly establish a good internal object (Winnicott, 1969). Consequently, separation-individuation was not completed and she was unable to sufficiently neutralize drive energy needed by the ego for adaptive functioning. Her fantasy life became the main source of her libidinal investment.

Quite masochistic, she experienced everyone as powerful while she was powerless. Strongly invested in suffering, she tried to turn the therapy into punishment, suffering in her sessions. Right from the beginning, the therapist's imagery was stimulated by her. Nursery rhymes, song lyrics, and creative responses came to the therapist with startling frequency. For example, after having worked on the patient's need to suffer for some time, the therapist suggested that the patient might organize a group called V.O.W. (Victims of the World), and further suggested that since she had perfected the art of suffering so

well, she should be its president. In this "suggestion" the therapist was doing several things at once; saying that she understood both the patient's need to suffer and that she got
something out of suffering, recognizing her need for grandiosity
and omnipotence in the masochism, and pointing out a basic
paradox in her need for both those positions (Nydes, 1963). The
therapist was also teasing her, and in her use of tamed aggression was both recreating the patient's bad mother while being
a new mother who saw the world differently. From a countertransference point of view, the patient's masochistic orientation
most likely freed the therapist's playfulness while, at the same
time, it unlocked some sadism. The sadism and playfulness then
became converted into creative communication. The question
remains, Why did the therapist's interventions come out playful? One might hypothesize that the therapist's masochistic
aspect became infused with energy from the transference-countertransference communication, and, through the use of the
therapist's observing ego, the energy could be contained and
translated into a creative act, rather than an acting out. The
principle of polarization is also called into play. In order to
really make contact with this patient, the opposite polarity of
fun, playfulness, and freedom had to be mobilized.

Another example involves the therapist's response in the
form of nursery rhymes. Different ones were used:

Mary, Mary, quite contrary. . . .

There was a little girl, who had a little curl,
Right in the middle of her forehead.
When she was good she was very, very good,
And when she was bad she was horrid.

Baa, baa black sheep, have you any wool?
No, sir, *no,* sir. . . .

The patient could hear what the therapist was saying about her
negativism, but didn't feel criticized. In fact, she felt understood
and given to. The creative communication then becomes a gift.

She is not reprimanded for her resistances, but is appreciated. Resistance is no longer something to be made ego-alien in the therapeutic process, but is seen as a way of contacting the world as an outgrowth of identification. Mary, Mary, quite contrary is a girl all of us have known and been at one time of our lives. She is no longer separated from an essential part of our experience in life while being analyzed as a resistance. It is of note that the therapist learned several years after this phase of treatment that the patient's grandmother, who was the closest person to her until she died when the patient was nine, had put her to sleep each night by reading or reciting nursery rhymes to her. Of further note is that this was also an important form of communication between the therapist and her own mother.

Another example of the therapist and patient communicating in an unconscious way came at another phase of treatment when the patient expressed a desire to *play* and the therapist thought she heard the patient ask for *clay*. Giving the patient some clay led to the creation of many imaginative objects in the sessions for a period of several months. Some of them are discussed here.

The first object the patient made was a bird on a branch (not shown). Looking at it, the patient was reminded of a vulture and began associating to it, recalling early feelings of her mother being more attuned to death than to life. The vulture was a primitive representation in which there were powerful affects, and through their externalization the patient could get in touch with them. Another object was a cute Easter bunny (Figure 14.1) with a basket of eggs in many colors; the eggs, however, were poison eggs. We can see here how this patient hid the angry parts of herself beneath a sweet exterior.

It is clear that the clay had meaning to her on many levels. It was a gift from the therapist, and in that was an implicit recognition of her existence. It also had symbolic meaning as feces, a part of her that she regarded as dirty, and from which she could now create something that was recognized, valued, and kept by the therapist. With it she could put form to what

Figure 14.1

had been formless before, convert global affects into secondary process, and then communicate them to the therapist and get feedback from her. A dream that the patient had during this phase a few months further on, shows progress in the working through of some of these issues.

> I was in a coffee shop. I ordered a corn muffin and then I ordered a cake. There were cakes all over the place. The woman left the counter to go back to the kitchen to have a special cake made for me. I also ordered something with egg, like an egg sandwich. While they were away I added something yellow to the egg, but realized that they would find out, so I stopped. She brought my cake out. It was different from the white and blue one I'd been looking at. I started eating the corn muffin and the thing with the egg, and a couple of pieces of cake, but I realized I had to go to a meeting. But I wanted to finish the cake. I wondered how I was going to bring the rest of the cake, then I put it in my purse.

Her associations were that the dream (like the bunny) had a sneaky quality, that she felt guilty because she was getting too much from her sessions, and that it was stimulating her wishes to be the therapist's only patient. While there is continued guilt over oral greed in the dream, we can see that the eggs, which were poison earlier in the Easter bunny figure, were now sources of nourishment and were able to be taken in. We can speculate that the cake was the clay, a "special" material that was different from the kind of feeding she had gotten from the therapist in the past.

Many of her clay figures were two-sided, usually representing a primary process and secondary process level, as in the prehistoric monster and angry award (Figures 14.2 and 14.3). Here, once more, we see the formless, global, monster-like feelings being transformed into communicative, imaginative, secondary process symbolization.

Figure 14.2

Figure 14.3

The therapist's cat appears in many of the figures and has been an important part of the therapy, both as a representative of the therapist and as a projective representation of the patient. In a figure not shown, there is a cat along with other creatures, identified as members of the patient's therapy group. They are all on a life raft. This figure was created in a session prior to the patient taking a vacation, while she was dealing with her fears about the consequences of her separation from the therapist and the group. The cat symbolizes the therapist and the life raft is symbolic of the patient having begun to achieve object constancy in the human environment.

The monster family (Figure 14.4) is, of course, her family. The patient is moving more and more into the human environment and these figures are the most like humans thus far. She depicts herself here as the embryo on the shoulder of the large maternal figure. Her coming into the world is definite, although in the beginning stages. A dream illustrates this phase.

> I was pregnant; I was ambivalent about giving birth, happy and scared. Then I was a baby, a newborn, with an awful case of diarrhea. The adults around were upset and concerned.

Among other things that came out in associations to this dream was the fact that she had smeared feces after the birth of her first brother, and that her mother had "never seen such a mess." She imagined that she must have been angry as a baby and caused everyone a lot of trouble. Here we have some indication of why the gift of clay may have had such strong symbolic meaning for this patient; the smearing of feces in infancy was undoubtedly one of the few experiences of herself that had been available to her at the time.

Figure 14.4

The above illustrations demonstrate how diffuse and chaotic energy, which is manifested in primitive symbolism, becomes transformed into more manageable and object-related communications. Poison eggs, which are thinly disguised behind her bunny cuteness, now become the wellsprings for food and nourishment that truly give impetus to the beginnings of a creative and autonomous personality. We see how imagery gives a thread of continuity to the treatment, how it becomes, in fact, a visual, biographical account of the self struggling to emerge. We can see the ebb and flow of her monsters struggling for human contact and sunlight as they become de-invested of their scary qualities through creative play. Vague, frightening feelings now have space to find more specific differentiation. Symbolic communication becomes a way of discovering love, for the creative act converts the patient's unwanted products into something worthwhile and valuable. The self becomes repaired as creativity becomes an avenue for taking the therapist in. Indeed, creation and love meet and produce change, while the patient reconstructs her unwanted mess, and gives order and organization to a new feeling of mastery. Her products are now an extension of a positive sense of self, and they, in their organization, have become reintrojected as a more stabilizing and synthesizing source of nourishment. With each externalization of symbolic material, the self becomes more differentiated, representative and, consequently, more autonomous. Fantasy is no longer a retreat but is a means to rediscovering productive imagination that leads to a firmer grasp of reality.

And, in her life, the patient masters graduate school and goes on to becoming a productive professional; gets married and risks changing her scary monsters for real object relatedness.

In conclusion, we have shown how the use of expressive and creative techniques can enable a patient and therapist to recreate a primary relationship in which there is an opportunity for neutralization of drive energy and reparation of the self, while working through resistance to change.

REFERENCES

Nydes, J. The paranoid-masochistic character. *Psychoanalytic Review,* 1963, *50,* 215–251.

Rosen, V. Some aspects of the role of imagination in the analytic process. *Journal of the American Psychoanalytic Association,* 1960, *8,* 229–251.

Winnicott, D. W. Transitional objects and transitional phenomena. *Through Paediatrics to Psycho-Analysis.* London: Hogarth Press, 1969.

Chapter 15

MUSIC IN EXPRESSIVE THERAPY

Alice Shields, D.M.A.
Arthur Robbins, Ed.D., A.T.R.

A Psychodynamic Theory of Music

Psychodynamic music therapy can assist verbal psychotherapy in facilitating the release of repressed affects and memories through ego mastery. This takes place through the psychodynamic structure of music itself. Within music occur archetypal conflictual situations where very intense personal experiences find a structure and format for expression (Friedman, 1960). These conflictual situations are expressed most predominantly through melody, which represents in our view a structure onto which the listener projects an inter- or intrapersonal conflict. Melodies, or pitch sets, may be, then, the carriers of object relation information, which run horizontally in time. By horizontally we mean going forward in time, i.e. melodic, whereas vertically in time means simultaneously in time, i.e. harmonic, several events happening at the same time, as in Jung's synchronicity.

Contrary to Friedman, we believe that the melodic line

does not represent affect itself, but is a symbol, a container for a conflictual relationship projected upon it by the hearer, almost as a mathematical formula is a shape into which content is projected. Mathematical formulae and melodic lines, then, have meaning only in terms of relationship, not in substance or content (Langer, 1942). If the conflictual situation is represented by the melodic line, then the basic affect of that conflict is represented by the timbre or color of that melodic line.

For example, a flute playing a certain melody would produce a significantly different affect than a full brass section, the one producing a lonely, fragile affect, and the other a powerful, dominating one. The *degree* of the affect implied by timbre will be represented by the dynamic or loudness of the melodic line: in the flute example above, a very soft dynamic might create a *very* lonely, fragile affect, whereas a mezzo-forte or medium dynamic in the brass might create a *somewhat* powerful, dominating affect.

Rhythm represents the libidinal content of music; *density*, the number of simultaneous conflictual situations, as in counterpoint, where several simultaneously sounding melodies establish different "personalities" of their own. By the same analogy, the experience of the mother's rhythm by the child (and vice versa) binds and structures free-flowing energy into meaning and harmony with the world. The very foundations of rhythm seem to enhance, embellish, and reinforce the underpinnings of a symbiosis. Counterpoint moves into the area of differentiation and may well also act as a structure to demarcate problems in introject formation.

Finally, *harmony*, or simultaneity in music, represents the vertical object relationships, the general social environment in which the melodic conflict finds itself. The harmony or simultaneous sounds of the music of any culture tend to represent the composer's psychological response to what he perceives as the social structure and typical object relationships of his time.

For instance, tonal harmony seems to present hierarchical characteristics of the social and familial structures of western Europe in the period of the seventeenth through the nineteenth centuries. Further, in the serious music of the twentieth century, one finds a predominance of simultaneous dissonance, perhaps representing the composer's response to the distress of a chaotic society, and the present conflicts within the nuclear family. Paradoxically, one can also hear in the mathematical formulae, with which some serious music is written, fears of the automatism of society, while in the random simultaneities of other contemporary music, the dissolution of clear social roles.

The mechanism that connects all these seemingly abstract musical symbols with the psychological conflictual situation is probably association, according to Noy:

> "If music resembles in its form the structure of unconscious experiences and conflicts, it should activate the latter according to the rules of association" (1967, Vol. 4).

EGO MASTERY AND PLAY IN MUSIC THERAPY

Assuming familiarity with the style of the music played (which implies learned response to the particular way in which the conflictual situation is expressed in the melodic line), and assuming that the music is "good," that is, that it is competently composed, and that it effectively sets up and resolves the conflictual situation, then the listener's ego will experience mastery over the conflicts that are aroused in him by the music. By the same token, the patient's *inability* to synchronize his inner affect and symbolic states with that of the composer provides a vehicle for exploration, clarification, and trial adoption. If there is an experience of ego mastery then there is an integration of the affect of aesthetic pleasure in which the particular dyad of the patient meets and harmonizes with that of the composer. Ego mastery through music then becomes a way of discovering an early part of oneself through the externalization and joining of the composer's and performer's creations and recreations. Thus in musical activity, as in play, the ego reenacts painful past experiences, but this time with the secure feeling that it will succeed in overcoming its difficulties.

To simply experience music as a listener is therefore an active experience in ego mastery. To experience music as a performer, however, increases the intensity of ego mastery by directly involving the body image and kinesthetic, spatial metaphor, thereby increasing right hemisphere involvement in an activity that is refined by the secondary process. Finally, to experience music as creator and performer at the same time, as in the improvisatory play of music therapy, is to combine the intense experience of ego mastery of the performer with the original and most intense projection of one's own conflicts into one's own aural symbols: one creates a transitional object and performs it as a transitional phenomenon.

SINGING: A TRANSITIONAL PHENOMENON

The process of playing an intrument external to the body, then, displaces onto a safe, transitional phenomenon the projection of conflicts that in singing—where one's body is one's own instrument—are expressed in a more potentially threatening but instinctually more intense form. Singing is potentially more threatening than playing an instrument, because

> "Inner psychic reality has a kind of location in the mind or in the belly or in the head . . ." (Winnicott, 1971)

and it is precisely from these areas that singing seems, to the singer, to emanate from. Thus the connection between one's feelings and one's voice can seem dangerously direct. Singing, then, becomes a transitional phenomenon as it was in the infant's early babbling and the older child's singing of his repertory of songs while preparing for sleep. This singing activity is

> "vitally important to the infant for use at the time of going to sleep, and is a defense against anxiety, especially anxiety of depressive type" (Winnicott, 1971).

One can conclude from clinical experience that the music lover has conflicts around mother-child symbiotic formation. Music is for this person a kind of defense, where the person feeds on, experiences, and reenacts the feeding tone-quality of his early maternal relationship. Thus the singer or musician may supply for himself the modality of affective interchange that was lacking in his infancy. On the other hand he may be unable to sing or play because of the very nature of this early feeding and, consequently, we discover a painful repetition of the past in his voice or instrumental sound; that is, the voice or sound may be starved, weak, tumultuous, etc. Thus the "feeding" can be reparative or repetitious. The singer, then, is feeding himself by creating his mother's voice answering his own in need. Especially interesting in this line of thought are the studies of musicians' personalities, which have shown a general profile of dependency conflicts and depression, indicating early disappointment with the mothering one.

In the expressive therapy session, which focuses on music and aural metaphor, visual, spatial, and verbal metaphors are also used. The experience of singing, involving as it does the use of verbal and visualized metaphor in the text, and body ego through coordinated, goal-directed movement, combines the three senses of vision, movement, and hearing in a synaesthetic whole, thereby unifying percepts that in infancy, the original period of seeking resonance, were quite disparate, not yet assimilated into a whole object (Spitz, 1972). Thus, even though all musical skills strengthen the body ego by stressing muscular coordination and goal-directed actions, and even though in our belief playing any instrument extends the body ego to the acoustical parameters, the synthetic functioning of the ego is most aurally enhanced by the act of singing. Indeed, singing is the prototype for all music, for any instrument's musical tone may be considered a transformed scream (Racker, 1951), just as singing itself may be considered the very early outreaching of the infant's cry.

All music

"presents to the ear an array of auditory patterns which at a purely formal level are very similar to, if not identical with, the bodily patterns which are the basis of real emotion" (Pratt, 1952).

Musical rhythm is similar to the heartbeat in its regular pulse and its accelerations and ritards; pitch resembles the rising and falling of the voice in relation to the degree of emotion felt. It is obvious that singing, being produced in the body, is closest to the bodily patterns, "which are the basis of real emotion." Further, singing, being very close to shouting or screaming, can be a way of playing with the loss of control.

THE PSYCHODYNAMICS OF THE VOICE AND MUSIC THERAPY

It is generally accepted among professional singers that there are at least two basic registers in the voice. These are "head register" or "head voice" and "chest register" or "chest voice." It is our view, based on clinical experience, that head register, which is experienced as resonating above the mouth in the cavities of the head, psychodynamically represents vulnerability, or the ability to be receptive, self-object dominated; and that chest register, which is experienced as resonating in the chest and throat, psychodynamically represents the ability to be agressive, the ability to act, to be reality or ego-dominated. Further, the head register generally represents the female imago, and the chest register the male imago. A patient whose speaking or singing voice is harsh, chest-register-dominated would need to work on opening up the head register, whereas one whose voice is delicate, head-register-dominated would need to work on developing the chest. In the descriptions of the two vocal music therapy sessions that follow, a case of both types is presented. It will be seen that the ability to play with metaphor and imagination plays an important part in the improvisatory sections of each session.

In singing, the tone is produced by subtle muscular tension, tension that may be considered to reflect the pressure of the drives on the inhibitions. A high pitch or key, then, requires a greater amount of instinctual energy than a low one. It will be seen that this principle is used when choosing the key of a song or improvisation in the music therapy session: when a more exhilarating affect is desired, the music is sung in a higher key.

CASE ILLUSTRATIONS IN VOCAL MUSIC THERAPY

The above concepts will be illustrated with examples from the music therapy sessions of two female patients. One case will be examined in some detail, the other will be summarized.

The first patient, a forty-year-old social worker, came to music therapy as an auxiliary to her verbal psychoanalysis. She wanted to sing in the music therapy sessions, and was already quite accomplished in singing folksongs while accompanying herself on the guitar. At the beginning of music therapy she sang in the sweet, head-register-dominated voice of a latency-aged child, and each song, regardless of the differing affects of the texts, had a hollow sadness in it because of a lack of high frequencies in her voice, and a feeling of fragility because of the relatively low overall volume. At the same time her voice lacked precision and structure, as the soft head register seemed to flow towards an early affect state that had the quality of being fused and symbiotic. Her early family constellation consisted of a mother who was pushy and controlling and attempted to define her feelings and needs for her, and a father who did not relate to her or anyone else in the family, hardly ever spoke, and never knew what was going on. Her mother wrote books, and her father was a minister. The patient was the first child, and had four younger brothers. The patient needed, as she said, to be more in touch with "anger, nastiness, and sexiness." Her basic psychological responses are of the nondominant hemisphere: she is intuitive and global in her imagery. Her head-register-dominated voice indicates a certain lack of discipline, and she needs secondary process abilities to help her focus her singing with a mixture of chest register. Her voice problems vividly symbolize both the regressive wishes and frustrations of her early family relationships. Her voice, on the one hand, yearned for some type of mothering softness, while on the other ruled out feelings of domination, aggression, or control. In a real sense the voice represented an imbalance of mother, father, and child.

The twelfth session began with a brief discussion of what had just happened in the patient's group therapy meeting the previous hour, and how she was feeling now. Patient: "I feel tired, and as little like singing as I've ever felt during the past ten years." She was asked what register she would sing in if she could. "Low." And what kind of sound would she make? Patient:

This improvised fragment sooned changed to:

It was sung in head register. She was asked to add chest, and the fragment was vocalized upwards until a very high chest register was reached, which naturally brought about an intensification in the energy level resulting in a dramatic sound with high frequencies, quite different from the diffuse, gentle sound with which she began the improvisation. The therapist commented on a particular hooded, heavy-lidded look that had suddenly come into her eyes during the warmup improvisation. Therapist: "Can you watch your eyes in the mirror while you sing?" The patient sings while looking in the mirror. She laughs: "That's a terrible look! I wonder if I was looking like that all evening."

Therapist: "What are you thinking or feeling when you look like that?"

Patient: "Nothing! I'm not thinking of anything! That reminds me of a patient of mine who says, 'Oh, Mary, I'm not mad at you, please don't make me mad at you!' "

Therapist: "Could you be mad at me now?"

Patient: "No."

Therapist: "Well, to me you look angry when you look like that."

Here, the therapist leaves the verbal level with this interpretation and returns to the non-verbal sphere.

Therapist: "That look keeps the tone from being more brilliant. Try focusing your eyes very carefully on one eye in the mirror."

The patient sings. The sound becomes angrier, more brilliant with high frequencies.

Therapist: "Can you put the sound farther forward by your front teeth? Try biting on the bottom note."

The patient sings.

The sound becomes still angrier. As the vocalize ascends, the patient has to experience going in and out of the angry-feeling lower register.

Patient: "I sound like a tenor! That sounds just like a man to me!"

Therapist: "It's a very gutsy sound. That's what it feels like when a woman belts; it feels very strong."[1]

The therapist suggests a vocalize on the vowel "ee" to emphasize the feeling of the biting front teeth. The patient sings up through high "C" with a mixture of head and chest. The tone is relaxed and yet rich-sounding.[2]

The patient chooses to sing a folksong, "The Lily of the West," and sings it in a tentative, head-dominated sound.

Therapist: "Try to make the tenor sound in this song. How do you feel about the words?"

Patient: "Bragging. Look at this verse. It could be his comeuppance." The patient sings while standing with legs wide apart, arms akimbo. She belts it out on a low key, but on certain words the sound weakens noticeably.

Therapist: "You seemed insolent most of the time, but on the word 'jealousy' the sound suddenly became delicate. If you think that word in an obnoxious way it will come out strong, even though you're going across the transit from chest to head."

Patient: "I have no compassion for this man at all."

Therapist: "Then have him have no compassion." The patient sings the song again, with a barroom coarseness very different from her usual refined manner.

Patient: "He's really a nasty man and is blaming Flora for everything."[3]

[1]The patient slowly meets the male imago in her, while allowing herself to discover the chest register. Associated with this stance are a whole series of affects that threaten the patient. We see also her resistance in admitting the male into her private space. As a result, both patient and therapist decide to go along with the resistance and move towards more familiar territory. Hopefully they will have an opportunity to blend both affect states when there is not such a sharp discrepancy.

[2]Thus the patient makes a successful attempt towards blending, and moves towards a sphere of male-female wholeness in her voice. The patient then retreats from this threatening integration and takes refuge in a more familiar ego state.

[3]Thus the patient, instead of denying and dissociating herself from a threatening male introject, re-experiences it and acts it out, and by so doing gains some mastery over the figure.

Therapist: "What image comes to mind of someone who's insolent in a graceful way."[4]

Patient: "I was thinking of an eighteenth-century gentleman with a high hat. He'd kill you with a smile. But I don't know how to do it."

Therapist: "How would he stand?" The patient stands on one leg, gracefully turning the other out in front of her. From the pelvic emphasis of the previous "bragging" posture, the emphasis is now on the gracefully suspended carriage of the torso and the high-stretched neck.

Therapist: "How would this eighteenth-century gentleman talk?"

Patient: (enunciating very clearly) "*I d*on't *k*now."

Therapist: "When you said that, it was very much in your teeth. You can be very smoothly obnoxious with this character: he can enunciate very clearly." The patient sings. On the higher notes she has difficulty maintaining the tone, especially on the words "ruby lips." She is asked to sing the phrase on "ah" without words.[5] Then the patient is asked to sing with the words, doing a minimum of closing the mouth for diction. She sneers while singing.[6]

Therapist: "It worked well that time. I think this is because you thought the feelings—of relaxed sneering—first, and your mouth automatically took the right shapes for the tone. That sneer also brings your attention to the teeth in the front of your mouth."

[4]The therapist is asking for an aggressive body image without the excessive muscular tension found in "belting."

[5]As the patient moves into the world of metaphor and primary process the patient holds onto words because of the anxiety associated with sensual expression. In short, she finds it very difficult to simply let herself go with the affect.

[6]Here we see a beginning amalgamation of various affect states that are associated with different parent-child dyads. She moves from the mother-father-child relationship in the first part of the session towards the hate-spite-love relationship of mother and child in the second part of the session. Pregenital hate starts coming closer to oedipal hurt and disappointment. Hate and love as a consequence start to move towards a better balance.

The patient purses her lips in front of her mouth, making a humorous face. The therapist does the same.

Therapist: "It's a fun feeling. There aren't too many times in life you get to make faces like that." (Both laugh.)[7] "OK. Now let's try your eighteenth-century gentleman down lower."[8]

The patient sings in a smooth head and chest mixture, but with few of the expressive components functioning. Yet she was visibly sneering.

Therapist: "Your face looked very involved, but I didn't her the sneering in the sound."

Patient: "I didn't either."

Therapist: "Could you make more of the insolence go into the sound? Could you, say, slide insolently from note to note?"

The patient sings, sliding from note to note, with examples by the therapist.

Therapist: "That's good. The previous time the insolence was going into your face but not into the sound. So there was a split between your voice and your face: if I looked at your face it was well acted, but I didn't hear it in the sound."

Patient: "That's something I do all the time. My analyst tells me how expressive my face is, but I'm not aware of what it's expressing."[9]

The patient sings. The tone includes a little more chest. The expressive components of subtle loudness changes, special attacks, and sliding are present.

Therapist: "Did it feel different?"

Patient: "That time I could feel my voice and face were

[7]Here we see the importance of mirroring as part of the reparative process.

[8]The intent is to diminish the extent of energy required to simply sound the pitches, so that more of the expressive components of music (subtle changes in loudness, short glissandi or expressive sliding, sudden attacks, etc.) can be easily used.

[9]The therapist is aiming at synthesizing the body responses to internal imagery, so that the senses are not split off from one another in an infantile, dissociated manner.

together now and then." The patient starts to sing again, and then stops.

Patient: "You know, I can't remember all those things at once."

Therapist: "Basically, there is only one thing to remember, and that is, what are you expressing. It's easy to forget that amidst technical details of head, chest, mouth, diction, breath, and so on, but nothing really works without a clear feeling. Without it singing becomes inexpressive, a mere technical feat. Do you feel like singing something else?"

Patient: "Yes."[10]

Therapist: "How about a very gentle song? A very great contrast to what we've been doing."

Patient: "I want to sing a lullaby."

She chooses "Hush Little Baby," and sings in a childlike voice dominated by head-tone. The therapist suggests singing it on "ah." The patient sings with a gentle chest mixture, a warm, mature, womanly sound, but slightly too full for the soothing quality of a lullaby.[11]

Patient: "My two-year-old daughter wouldn't let me sing it that way a few months ago, but she's used to that sound now." (Laughter.)

Therapist: "I wonder if you can do it even softer with the words, but keeping the open feeling of 'ah' behind everything?"[12]

The patient sings, with a warm but very soft, womanly sound, a very gentle mixture of chest.

Patient: (Nearly whispering, keeping the mood of the song.) "I've sometimes sung like that before, but I lose it."

Therapist: "You can sometimes remind yourself of the

[10]The therapist realizes that there is resistance to going further at this time, since the patient stopped singing, so she decides to offer a more familiar experience.

[11]The challenge here is to feel soft and sexual as a woman instead of soft and vulnerable as a child.

[12]The therapist is trying to maintain the open position of the oral cavity, quite like, for a woman, relaxing the muscles around the vagina.

way the tone feels by singing it first without the words on 'ah.'[13] Then sing the words as an afterthought. The way you sometimes sing, the words come before the tone, so that the tone suffers."[14]

Therapist: "What else could we do with this song?"

Patient: "I could sing it humorously to my daughter." The patient sings in a lilting manner with expressive components, but the resonance is only part head and throat, with no chest, the words predominating over the tone quality.

Therapist: "That seems very easy for you."

Patient: "Relating to a baby is not my problem."

Therapist: "What would happen if you were to sing this to your husband?"

Patient: "I'd get embarrassed."

Therapist: "Do you want to try it?" The patient sings, with basically the same timbre as she sang to her daughter, but with blockings on certain words and inserted laughter, ending with uproarious laughter.

Patient: "Jack and I sometimes joke about my being his mama, which he hates!"

Therapist: "It sounded much the same as you sang it to your two-year-old, except the pauses on 'diamond' and 'looking-glass.'[15] Could you sing this to some other adult?"

The patient sings gently in a very light chest, very slowly with expressive components and a very hushed feeling, very smooth and soft with a rich but not womanly sound, more like an adolescent's voice. She created a very hushed and gentle mood, which neither she nor the therapist broke.

---

[13]That is, by focusing on the melody, which divorced from the words carries much of the affective burden of the song when expressed through the vocal timbre.

[14]In other words, the patient generally emphasizes secondary process—word—elements in her communications at the expense of powerful affects.

[15]The therapist realizes the patient resists going further into sexual material at this time.

Therapist: (In a hushed tone.) "It sounded very soft and soothing."

The patient explained that she was singing it to a close female friend who was very upset.

Patient: "I can sing to a friend, I guess. But anger, nastiness, beltingness, sexiness, those are the things I've been working on a lot in analysis."

In this session we see the patient moving both towards and away from a more complete genital integration of her conflicting identifications. As the patient goes through many trial adaptations, the therapist harmonizes and resonates with her. Thus we see a reexperiencing of some of the symbiotic relatedness through the vehicle of trial adaptations. At the same time, along with the resonance, we see also some counterpoint in their relationship. The therapist is often induced into the role of being more dominant and aggressive, and gives the patient ample opportunity to dialogue and interreact as well as reintroject the feared male imago.

The second patient is a forty-five-year-old German-born businesswoman with two grown children. She came to vocal music therapy when she terminated her analysis, because she had always wanted to study voice. She had acted a good deal in high school and had wanted to be an actress, thinking that she had an expressive speaking voice. She had never sung or played an instrument, but her father had had a beautiful voice, and she had loved to hear him sing. At the beginning of music therapy she sang in a constricted, chest-dominated voice, which was overly focused with too many high frequencies and not enough head-tone. Regardless of the text, she sang with a harsh, forced quality, which, although piercing, gave an impression of instability, due to the breath being overly supported by extreme muscular tension. The third child among four sisters and brothers, her family had fled the Nazi influence in Germany. This patient needed to be more in touch with the gentle, vulnerable parts of herself. Her basic psychological responses are of the ego-oriented sphere, which cruelly represses warm affects. She needs to let primary process melodic lines flow without undue tension in the throat and head. She needs to become more diffuse, more head-tone oriented, less chest-tone oriented, less over-focused in her voice.

In the third session, after discussion of how she was feeling that day, and after initial warmup exercises in head register, emphasizing a relaxed throat and jaw, the patient was asked how it made her feel to use her head register. She responded with the image of the Little Match Girl. When asked how the Little Match Girl stood, she adopted a posture with arms and hands held out, pleading piteously. The patient was asked how this character would walk. She moved around the room in a halting manner, while the therapist imitated her. The patient was then asked if she could make a sound that would express what the Little Match Girl was feeling. She sang, in an insecure and throaty voice full of chest register:

The therapist asked her to relax the back of the tongue, to let the throat stay open. The patient sang again, this time with a head-dominated sound. She was asked what words the Little Match Girl would sing to these sounds. She sang:

"please, please" in German. The patient seemed surprised at this pathetic image emerging from her, who was so cynical and bitter and hard-edged. The therapist then asked her to vocalize "bitte, bitte" upwards in increments of a minor second until

was reached, at which point the patient exclaimed on how powerful the sound had become, that the Little Match Girl was no longer beseeching and pathetic, but was powerful, demanding, and assertive. After further vocalizing on this improvisation, the patient had a sudden association to the melody: "It's like the ko-ha-ne-cha, 'your priests will wear the mantle of righteousness' from the Saturday morning temple service." The patient was struck by this association, and exclaimed on its importance, because she was deeply religious.

In contrast to the first case illustration, the patient struggles to integrate the more diffuse, receptive parts of her personality. The dependent, lost little girl that is associated with loss of control, humiliation, and pathos, is re-met via the vehicle of the Little Match Girl. As she becomes less threatened by this imago and its concomitant affects, a move towards real control and power is initiated. Softness is not equated with powerlessness. The vulnerability of being a lost, frightened child in the Nazi police state is reexperienced.

The Use of Music to Overcome Resistance in Therapy

Friedman says of music:

"The fact that the entire presentation is non-verbal and seemingly remote from psychological problems may enhance the listener's willingness . . ." (1960).

Because of this nonverbal nature and seeming remoteness from psychological problems, singing becomes an act of displacement from talking: one can sing about things one cannot talk about (Racker, 1951). Music in general can thus bypass a good deal of resistance, conceivably more than art or dance at times, because of its seemingly abstract, formulaic nature, and the difficulties involved in verbalizing or making rational statements about its meaning. It seems possible that hearing is the sense that belongs more than any other to the affective sphere (Knapp, 1953) and is therefore capable of appealing directly to the emotions. Further, the aesthetic distance created by the details of musical form and presentation removes the conflict from the realm of the self and projects it onto a safe third party: music, the not-me, the transitional phenomenon, is given the conflicts of the self.

Thus we see painful affect states that are accompanied by self and object representations, being sharply brought into focus through the vehicles of musical and vocal expression. The expressive therapist thus has at his disposal a very powerful tool. The affect states can be tapped in very short order. In instances where this would prove overwhelming, a much more controlled modality may be in order. In summary, musical expression touches upon some of the most basic forces of human experience. Within a psychoanalytic framework, it offers a structure to demonstrate the use of energy with its harmony and disharmony as well as counterpoint, to describe the temporal nature of our most primitive experience.

REFERENCES

Cambor, G. C., Lisowitz, G. M., & Miller, M. D. Creative jazz musicians: A clinical study. *Psychiatry,* 1962, *25,* 1–15.

Friedman, S. M. One aspect of the structure of music. *Journal of the American Psychoanalytic Association,* 1960 *8,* 427–449.

Kohut, H., & Levarie, S. On the enjoyment of listening to music. *Psychoanalytic Quarterly,* 1950, *19,* 64–87.

Knapp, P. H. The ear: Listening and hearing. *Journal of the American Psychoanalytic Association,* 1953, *1,* 672–689.

Langer, S. *Philosophy in a new key.* Cambridge, Mass.: Harvard University Press, 1942.

Noy, P. The psychodynamic meaning of music. *Journal of Music Therapy,* 1966–1967, Vols. 3 and 4.

Pratt, C. C. *Music and the language of emotion.* Washington, D.C.: Library of Congress, 1952.

Racker, H. Contributions to the psychoanalysis of music. *American Imago,* 1951, *8;* 129–163.

Spitz, R. A. *The first year of life.* New York: International Universities Press, Inc., 1965.

Spitz, R. A. Fundamental education. In *Play and development,* New York: W. W. Norton & Co., 1972.

Tyson, F. Music therapy in the community: Three case histories. *The Psychiatric Quarterly,* Part I, 1966.

Winnicott, D. W. *Playing and reality.* Harmondsworth, Middlesex, England: Penguin Books, Ltd., 1971.

Chapter 16

INTEGRATING MOVEMENT AND PSYCHOANALYTIC TECHNIQUE

Elaine V. Siegel, D.T.R.

TRADITIONAL DANCE THERAPY

Dance-movement therapy has been defined as a form of psychotherapy in which the therapist utilizes movement interaction as the primary means for establishing therapeutic goals (Schmais, 1974). It is further postulated that movement per se reflects personality, that the interpersonal relationship established through movement with the client supports and produces changes in functioning, and that significant changes occur on the movement level that may affect the total personality. *Psyche* and *soma* are seen as continuously interactive. Thus, Trudie Schoop, a pioneer dance therapist, wrote in 1971: "Where a psychoanalysis brings change in the mental attitude, there should be a corresponding change in physical behavior. When a dance therapist brings about a change in body behavior, there should be a corresponding change in the mind. Both methods want to change the total being, body, and mind." This holistic approach to the entire human being is a major concern in all dance-movement therapy. After all, we live in, with and through our bodies and contact all of life's tasks through bodily means.

If task completion is inhibited by real or fantasized obstacles the resultant frustration causes restrictions of creative endeavors, with distorted adaptations as result. A split between felt experiences and thought processes occurs that establishes repression and feeds intra- and intersystemic conflict. Dance-movement therapy is concerned with closing this ubiquitous split between the body and the mind, in whichever form this split might manifest itself in the various nosologic categories (Siegel, 1973 a,b,c, 1974, 1977, 1979). In the narcissistic disorders this might be primarily an inability to connect overwhelming tension states to appropriate, rather than global, discharge. But a person who has fallen ill with a compulsion neurosis may literally freeze his entire body into a permanently rigid unit that operates like a fortress under siege while mental content and fantasy lie unexpressed in the lower dungeons of the mind. To help bridge this gap, dance-movement therapists are always on the look-out for an avenue through which the hidden contents can penetrate and be expressed without overwhelming the client with renewed tensions and anxieties caused by the strength of the very forces he or she has so valiantly hidden from view. In other words, the adaptational purposes of repression are not overlooked in the pursuit of creative expression. It becomes necessary to provide a structure in which the client can once more venture forth safely to rebuild what originally went astray. Dance-movement therapy in its expressive aspects allows for such a structure, in that the therapist enlists the cognitive functions of the ego by inviting the client to observe and feel himself in movement. That is, it is the self-observation possible during the externalization of bound feelings that is a first step in bringing about change. In this, dance-movement therapy is not different from any other expressive arts therapy: As the client sees and feels himself reflected in his production, he may make another choice than the one expressed in his creation, or stick with it, whichever suits his own psychic time-table best.

In its broader applications, dance-movement therapy has been utilized in a wide variety of settings as an adjunct therapy, which helps to draw off bottled-up and overwhelming affect, builds motor skills, and facilitates body-image building (Schilder, 1950). In the case discussed later, however, it was employed as primary intervention.

DANCE-MOVEMENT THERAPY AS PRIMARY INTERVENTION

In this form of dance-movement therapy, the writer sees motility as an indicator of developmental levels, as an expressor of internal conflict and as a receptor that is imprinted with the reactions to all past and present experiences. Given all these properties along with the fact that it can be influenced, motility is viewed as another tool for therapeutic intervention, i.e., it is seen as another primary ego apparatus that has access to unconscious processes as well as to the ego (Hartmann, 1970). Mittelman (1957) postulated the presence of a motor urge in the same sense as the oral, excretory, and genital urges. By this he meant that there are identifiable body organs that carry out and/or are the sources of the activity that has the quality of urgency. Following this urgency leads to pleasure and satisfaction (Freud, 1905b).

The development of motility is connected with the physical maturation of the individual, of course, but it does carry identifiable, phase-specific patterns. For instance, obsession-compulsion, which is said to have its origin in the anal phase, carries with it general body tensions, particularly around the sphincter and buttocks, as well as rigid spines and often the body-posture of a toddler (Siegel, 1974). Since all this can be present in an otherwise fully matured individual, it does not seem farfetched to hypothesize the presence of a somatic crystallization of the fixation point, or, as Laban phrased it, "We show a frozen effort shape to the world" (1950). If one adds to this the "tendency to persistence in psychologic function and development" (Sandler & Joffee, 1967), it becomes clear that the way a person moves also reveals the time in his life his major conflicts were formed. Sandler and Joffe suggest that primitive modes of functioning do not disappear but stay active in the present under the cover of more complex adaptive behavior. This, as well as Schilder's (1950) hypothesis that every sensation has its motility, gives credence to the widely held but as yet only empirically substantiated view of primary dance-movement therapy that there is a body-memory, i.e., that all experiences are stored in the body and specifically in the muscle systems and are recoverable under appropriate circumstances. An example of this "persistence theory" would be as follows: When watching a dance performance or athletes at games, there is often an inclination to move slightly and rhythmically in time with the performers. A form of very early confusion with self and other is expressed motorically in a minute fashion. The tension produced temporarily by this fleeting regression to an earlier form of being is thus discharged quietly and without anxiety. In a similar fashion, a synchronistic "dance" often occurs between partners in a conversation. As one leans forward, to make a point, the other "closes up" by crossing legs or arms, or becomes receptive by shaping his body in a complimentary fashion. People who do not respond on this level are often considered with less than affection by their peers. They are considered "haughty" or "distant" because they do not bend their spines with the shifting winds of conversation. Yet it would be erroneous to speak of conflict here, certainly not of an inner one, on such scant evidence. These individuals may indeed express a need to be distant but their upright posture could also reflect training and thus may merely reproduce the ideals of their environment as well as their own.

All of these are considerations the primary movement therapist must be acutely aware of and work into the sessions. If, on investigation, an individual is unable to relax upright posture, there might indeed be something amiss. But there is no one-to-one correlation between expressive behavior and pathology or normalcy except in its developmental aspects. Specific pinpointing depends on examination of personal life histories and adaptations. It may be safely stated, however, that constriction of movement, i.e., the inability to learn or to adapt new movement patterns and sequences, indicates the presence of conflict, provided there are no organic causes.

Once developmental levels and areas of conflict in the motor area have been ascertained, it becomes important to deal with the affects shown. Do they match the developmental phase imprinted upon the individual's movement? Are they separated from content of verbal productions; are they forced to make a circuitous appearance in blushing, sweating, trembling or in one or the other body phobias, such as an inability to meet another's gaze or to look at something or someone?

The affective state of the client is the guide toward the hour. Freud (1915) saw affects as manifesting themselves "essentially in motor, secretory, circulatory changes in the subject's own body without reference to the outside world, motility in action designed to effect changes in the world." He distinguished between affect and feelings, Jacobson (1953) points out. The word "affect" seems to designate all psychophysiologic discharge phenomena. The physiologic components express themselves in body changes that are under the control of the vegetative nervous system. The voluntary skeletal-muscular system may be activated as well. Posture, facial expression and tone of voice would be mediated by the peripheral nerves. The psychological components are experienced as "feelings." Rappaport (1950) sees affects in their psychosomatic completeness and maintains that "if there is no direct and momentary expression on either the physiologic or psychologic level, a chronic alteration of the physiologic process as seen in psychosomatic disorders or of the psychologic process as seen in neuroses, psychosis and character disorders may occur." However, immediate or complete discharge of a given stimulus will not necessarily prevent the untoward events proposed by Rappaport. Rather, one must postulate that when a person is forced by external or internal events to adapt to life in a manner that is constricted for him, there might be something in these events that does not allow him to integrate or "digest" affect sufficiently. Most often it is found that the person in question lacks "frustration tolerance." Freud (1915, 1905d) said that in order for adequate reality testing to take place, immediate drive gratification must be relinquished so that, by postponing it, more adequate and complete gratification can be achieved later (Kris, 1951). Spitz (1965) enlarges on this when he says that: "The capacity to suspend drive gratification, to tolerate a delay in the discharge of tension, to give up immediate and perhaps uncertain pleasure, in order to gain this certainty of later pleasure, is an important step in the humanization of man. It made possible the progress from internal reception to external perception, from passive perception to motor discharge in the form of action, eventuating in active appropriate alteration of reality. . . ."

This has important implications for therapeutic intervention because it becomes apparent that simple release of tension or abreaction may complete what the original stimulus, expressed in affect, had intended but that the completion of it might stir up conflict because the completion might be unmodulated and, thus, too overwhelming. The affect must be released and completed in such a manner that the person feeling it can link it cognitively with mental representation and life experience so that closure and integration can take place. In the more fragmented personalities, or significantly unevolved individuals, this calls for particularly structured activity on the part of the therapist.

It has been noted by Gestalt psychologists, in particular Zeigarnick (1927), that unfinished tasks are remembered while finished ones are forgotten. Therefore, when a child is told "no" he will recollect this fact easily because he could not carry out his intent. He has been frustrated. But if this affect, frustration, is brought about within a trustful relationship with a prohibitor, the mother, he will identify with her and begin saying "no" himself (A. Freud, 1936). This simple identification with an "old" aggressor (an aggressor from the past) is often a component in affective states and must be taken into account because of this linkage. If only the release of affect is accomplished, the components that caused it may still be hidden and even receive exaggerated importance through their artificial isolation from the emotive part. Release in and of itself does *not* mean completion. If the person in question was not able to establish "frustration tolerance" as discussed above, a release of affect may bring about loss of boundaries. So, before going into the release and relaxation techniques known to any reasonably well trained dance therapist, it is essential to ask: What is the expected result if this affect is indeed completed in its entirety? What kind of new affect will appear in its place and what developmental level will the client come in touch with?

The answer *must* be that the muscular release has to be connected with the original thought and events-representation by careful linking of past and present verbally *and* nonverbally though interpretation and/or mirroring. It is only when the past is mastered that we are free to be in the present. Overwhelming or inappropriate affect destroys the present.

When the client is asked to reconstruct the past, or is propelled by his inner need to do so, he must be provided with a structure according to his developmental level that allows for a shift of feeling within the session and facilitates a new outcome of an old problem so that it can be "closed" and lose its hold on the present. For example, in psychoanalytic dance therapy, a client may habitually carry her shoulders bent forward, in an "old lady's" stance, and correctly identify this as "carrying the weight of the world on her shoulders." Exercises may keep her spine supple, her shoulders open, as long as she is occupied with these exercises and therefore not under the command of the affect from the past momentarily. As soon as she is not vigilant, the depressive posture recurs and does not leave permanently until the original event and all its antennae and inroads into the present have been explored.

These explorations include corrective exercises and relaxation techniques, but only as a starting point for improvisations, coupled with verbal productions.

When the client is in danger of being overwhelmed, or carried away, by the gratification inherent in such a situation or by the force of inner needs, the therapist must intervene by providing an exit through verbal and nonverbal interpretation. The client with the bent shoulders will straighten up without thinking about it when the original affect is brought together with its original contents and the events that caused it. It is the affect's incompleteness that froze it as a weight upon the shoulders. Once fixed permanently, it could then lurk behind the tensed muscles and influence the present. It can be seen that affect can bridge not only "inner and outer" but "past and present."

Further, it must be clearly stated that there is another significant difference between psychoanalysts and dance therapists who practice within a psychoanalytic framework. In the former, speech is the most important communicator and "acting" is to be shunned because it is said to remove inter- and intrasystemic conflict from thought processes. In the latter, motoric expression, in all of its manifestations including states of stillness, takes on equal importance. As in speech as communication, the transference to the therapist is seen as the essential channel through which destructive actions outside of the treatment hour are, hopefully, confined to action *in* the hour.

As mentioned before, because affects straddle the physiologic and the psychologic they fit into the emerging framework for psychoanalytic dance therapy as outwardly visible indicators of feeling states and possible representatives of past events.

In current psychoanalytic thinking, many, sometimes contradictory, efforts have been made at classification of affects either according to presumed underlying instinctual drives or to align them with the ego. Early on, Fenichel (1941) spoke of affects as "archaic discharge syndromes" and of "affect spells." This is echoed by Krystal (1978) in his description of "affect-storms." The implication is that affects ought to be tolerated by the mature adult as signals only and should not be connected with their conscious motor expression, i.e., desomatization of the phenomenon in its manifold forms is sought. This would obviously be anathema for all types of dance-movement therapy not only psychoanalytically-oriented dance therapy.

Jacobson (1953) presents yet another try to classify affects into simple and compound ones, which arise out of intra- and intersystemic tensions, in their various combinations. Overlooked in all these metapsychological constructs is the fact that in bridging the inner and outer worlds of an individual, in linking psyche and soma so completely, affects are concrete, visible, felt, lived, and transmitted expressive agents of the mind-body unity. Depending on their strength and the clarity of their intent and direction, they will fasten on the motor apparatus to find discharge as outlined above. At the risk of belaboring a point, it must be stated again that in psychoanalytic dance therapy the assumption is that an affect ought to be brought into its most evolved form in order to become both a vehicle for discharge and for self-observation.

To have sweaty palms, for instance, may be merely embarrassing, but to raise these same palms in supplication or to hide behind them, i.e., to exploit the motor answer of the affect (Schilder, 1950) will immediately allow the improvising client to see and experience what might be unrealistic or unnecessary or unresolved in the "sweat of his hands."

In the example just cited, the affect in itself was condensed, allowing only part expression of a possible conflict. Affects are not necessarily indicators of conflict, although in their expressive aspects they most certainly are signals that an attempt is being made by the organism to discharge something or to produce homeostasis (Hartmann, Kris, & Loewenstein, 1959). Affects, then, along with somatization may help to discharge tension and become stronger in direct proportion to the amount of drive behind them. Space does not permit the discussion of the existence and dynamic of drive. Suffice it to say that affects in and of themselves have qualitative differences. These differences in intensity may reflect the urgency of the propelling drive but also that repression has been at work and has denied direct motor expression. Before questioning the effect of repression upon affect, it might be fruitful to look at Freud's (1916) description. He maintains that an affect includes motor stillness or discharge and certain sensations. These are of two kinds: The consciously experienced motor action and the specific pleasure and unpleasure sensations that give the affect its basic tone. Nevertheless, Freud thought there was more than this in the essence of affect. He hypothesized that all affects carry a nucleus of traumatic disturbances in the psychoeconomic equilibrium of the species in the distant past. Given the similarity of affective states in most people, this is not an outrageous statement, although at first glance it seems to deny the recoverable specificity of content mentioned before. Another explanation might be the limitations of the somatic equipment. It becomes apparent that one and the same motor response and act may have many meanings within differing contexts.

The important conclusion to be drawn from this sameness of available motor responses is that one needs to talk as well as act in order to be fully understood.

A case history, in which mood and affect swings were particularly marked, will better illustrate some of the theoretical assumptions presented here. It will be illustrated that the completion of this client's many affective and transferential experiences brought about a beneficial change. Interventions were always developmentally geared and were kept to their barest minimum in order to allow for the unfolding of specific life history.

Case History

A nineteen-year-old woman, Alicia, was referred for dance-movement therapy, after two years of combined drug therapy and verbal psychotherapy had kept her from acting-out but had not been able to induce her to return to school or to do anything but "mope around, and hang out." Initially, psychiatric treatment had been ordered for her by a court order after an arrest for soliciting and prostitution. Her upper-middle-class parents were profoundly disturbed by their daughter's history, and tried repeatedly to shake her out of her torpor after the arrest by offers of jobs, schooling, travel. When the father was first confronted by his daughter's antisocial actions, he flew into an uncontrollable rage and hit her repeatedly. This fact was now used by the daughter as a rationale to refuse all offered aid by her family. However, she voiced no resistance to the suggestion by her psychiatrist to come for dance-movement therapy. Her mother brought her for the first few sessions, and anyone unfamiliar with the background would have thought the mother, rather than the daughter, was the patient. While mother wrung her hands, wept, and asked where she might have gone wrong, the daughter comforted her, hugged her, and told her not to worry, she was a fine mother, etc. There was a practiced and somewhat histrionic air about this whole scene, which took place almost immediately upon arrival, as though to impress the therapist with the closeness of the mother-daughter bond. Questioning revealed that the mother was in therapy, also, and that Alicia's "troubles" had begun immediately after a younger, brain-damaged brother had been placed in an institution during Alicia's absence at summer camp, and without her knowledge. The mother claimed "not to have had a minute's trouble" with her daughter before. She described her as moody; charming when it suited her purpose; as an erratic student who exasperated her teachers by just working enough to get by, despite good potential; as a rather lonely person who would have "crushes" on either a boy or a girl for a short time and then drop the new friend suddenly. Although all questions were directed to Alicia, she answered none of them, with her mother eagerly pouring forth great amounts of information. Significant in the family's, and Alicia's, history was the determination with which the younger child's severe disability had been treated. The child was patterned a la Delacato (1962), with little success. He had also been taken to other specialists all over the United States and abroad, so that all family life was centered almost exclusively around him, until it became apparent that existence outside of a hospital setting would be impossible for him. As the older sister, Alicia had been expected to share the responsibility for "the baby" despite the fact that only four years separated them. The final decision to place the brother, however, was made suddenly and without consulting her, as stated above.

Alicia's only comment during the first session was that she liked taking care of people and had thought of becoming a special education teacher. Under torrents of tears, mother confided that this was "just talk," since Alicia refused to finish her high school requirements.

Alicia herself was an extremely attractive girl with huge eyes, dressed in easygoing, but expensive "hippy" style. She moved slowly, with a floating, ungrounded quality and had a curious way of stiffening into immobility when looked at. We agreed on two sessions per week to which her mother would drive her until the time when Alicia "would get it together enough" to take her driver's test. Apparently, this had become an issue within the family. Both parents had agreed to buy Alicia a car if she would get her license and return to school. Alicia, however, had decided that driving a car would add to the pollution of the environment, and made it clear that she expected to be transported. The manipulation and inconsistency of these statements were understood by the parents, as was the offer of a car as a bribe to Alicia.

The borderline aspects of Alicia's character organization were already visible in the mother's sketch of her daughter's behavior, as well as in the refusal to pollute the environment by driving a car, but allowing the same pollution if someone else drove it. The floating, ungrounded way of gliding rather than walking, very harmonious, slow, sweeping movements were certainly Alicia's own motoric adaptation. But the sudden rigidity when she felt looked at also pointed in the direction of a diagnosis of borderline personality organization. The psychiatrist had variously called her a "preschizophrenic character" and an "as-if personality." An unrealness emanated from Alicia, and produced a vague countertransferential unease in the therapist (Siegel, 1979). Watching the skill with which she reinforced her mother's guilt by supposedly comforting her and at the same time conveying to the therapist nonverbally that she was not needed due to the intensity of the mother-daughter relationship, had induced precisely the emotion people like Alicia know how to manipulate so well: unease. As long as the Alicias of the world feel in control, they are able to function well and to figure out, with amazing accuracy, what is expected of them (Deutsch, 1942). This gives their actions the "as if" quality which belies the concrete *accuracy* of much of their behavior when they are not in the impulse-ridden phase. This unease was further reinforced when Alicia reported the psychiatrist whom she had seen for two years as a "fink" who "doped her up" so that she didn't know what she was doing (Siegel, 1974, 1977, 1979). No attachment to the physician who had treated her for two years was visible on the surface. We agreed that she would stop taking her medication, after this had been cleared both with the psychiatrist and the parents. It is my conviction, based on fifteen years' experience, that people who are heavily medicated benefit only peripherally, if at all, from dance-movement therapy. Amount of dosage and type of drug are important also, of course, and vary considerably in each case. Some drugs, such as Haldol, may cause dyskenisia so that the very agency one addresses onself to, the body self of the patient, is not available except in diminished form. It is like doing verbal therapy with a deaf client (Cain & Cain, 1975; Hall, 1978).

Alicia seemed very pleased by the many telephone conferences that were necessary to free her from her prescriptions. As a reward to the therapist, she agreed to participate in movement. An interpretation that perhaps she was treating the therapist as she would like to be treated herself was met with a sneer in her angelic face. Rather, the telephone calls were seen by her as a sign that she had controlled the therapist psychically into sharing her supposed wish for freedom from medication. She began to revile both her former psychiatrist and her parents as old-fashioned and rigid, and requested three sessions per week instead of the agreed upon two. This request was refused as part of the needed educative measures, because the wish to ally herself with the therapist against the important people in her life was viewed as yet another manipulation that could not possibly produce growth.

The unease within the therapist increased because this event occurred very early in the treatment and was a result of the request for cessation of medication, which had fed into Alicia's pathologic control fantasies without being shoved up a transference situation.

After all the verbalizations, arrangements, and setting of boundaries (an indispensable phase, if the course of intervention was to succeed), therapy proper now began.

True to her promise, Alicia "danced." Attired in embroidered Indian gowns, a flower in her long curly hair, she would glide into the room and trace its circumference with slow measured steps. Sometimes she would strike a pose, arms stretched to both sides, head thrown back and then resume her pacing. On occasion, she would hum tuneless songs that accelerated into loud, deep calls without words. When she became aware of the therapist watching her, she would stand still, smile, and indicate with harmonious gesturing that the therapist was invited to join. Refusal or acceptance of the invitation was met with equanimity, but attempts to investigate the meaning of her rite or to change it were simply ignored.

The unease within the therapist now began to give way to pictures of Alicia as a reincarnation of Isadora Duncan. Painstaking self-analysis revealed them as a reflection of Alicia's omnipotence and prepared the therapist somewhat for the next event. Some three months after the biweekly ritual dances, Alicia appeared in jeans with big leather boots, high on marijuana, waving her new driver's license about. She had brought a new raggae record with her and began a triumphal dance expressing ecstasy, sexual arousal, and the unmistakable wish to impress the therapist. Strutting and cavorting, she cynically asked if she would be discharged now since she had "got it together," and received her driver's license and was prepared to return to school to fulfill the few missing requirements for her diploma. Recognizing the shift in her behavior, but also aware that this was the other face of the same control issue we had skirted before, the therapist asked how the effect of the marijuana high differed from that of the drug she had to take previously. "It's the same, you old cow," the ex-Isadora exclaimed. "Bet you haven't screwed a man in ten years!" Here, finally, was an allusion to the behavior that had brought her into conflict with the law. The effect of the marijuana seemed a symbolic bridge to the "fink of a psychiatrist" who had kept her under control. The more neutral stance of the present therapist, and the often-voiced assumption that Alicia could "get it together" if she wanted to, were partially responsible for the swing. More importantly, Alicia accusingly screamed that she was tired of all that slow dance stuff, especially when the therapist was so stupid as to fail to recognize a medieval chanting and court ritual when she saw it. Acknowledging her disappointment, she was told that the therapist had no magic, but needed words as well as movement for communication. It was also strongly suggested that she abstain from smoking before and during her sessions. "You don't give a shit about me, do you?" she yelled and wanted to leave. The information that she was expected to finish her hour had a strongly quieting effect. Grumbling, she removed her boots and began to prod the therapist gently with her feet, obviously an invitation to join the dance.

Alicia's manifold symbolic actions in this hour made the therapist aware that much of the conflict had been brought to the surface. But how to interpret, understand, integrate so much material to a person whose foremost aim is to stay "boss" at all cost!

Alicia had begun to understand that it would be hard to manipulate the therapist, and much was known about her despite her denials. Perhaps the outburst had adaptational purposes. Also, she had at least peripherally mentioned sexual matters, though projected onto the therapist. Questioning the therapist's feelings for her and testing empathic qualities also seemed a step toward recognizing the existence of another human being (Friedman, 1969).

This new, raucous Alicia proved herself a fine dancer who could easily follow any and all instructions, and was so enthused about dancing and moving in general, that she wrote to various dance departments for admission. The parents were pleased, high school was "a cinch," and only the therapist was back with her previous unease.

All of Alicia's movements seemed to begin and end in the same place. They stayed concrete and were said not to evoke anything beside the immediate muscle sensation of "doing." There was no joy in the movement itself, no exploration of new planes or space without prodding, just a dogged pursuit of more and more difficult exercises, structured dances and combinations. Conspicuous, also, was an inability to combine breathing patterns appropriately with the executed rhythms. Most sessions ended with a wild spurt of energetic spinning or jumping of great speed.

Alicia began to read dance publications, became an expert in anatomy, and began to fantasize about becoming a dance therapist herself.

Investigation of the initial outburst that ushered in this phase was angrily warded off, as were attempts to deal with the overt negative transference. Previous experience alerted the therapist to the probability that the present positive manifestations were more likely a cover for rage and disappointment. Joylessness, cynicism, and mechanical aping of the therapist were very much in evidence.

Speculations about Alicia's past had to remain just that because she warded off all questioning and denied and suppressed feelings aroused by sessions. Nonetheless, it can be postulated that the depressions, guilt, and frantic activity with which Alicia's mother surrounded her son prevented her from helping the little girl to integrate opposing feeling states. The brief moments in which the parents' full attention shone onto Alicia's life, alternating with their total unavailability when immersed in helping their son, more likely than not reinforced the child Alicia's perception of the world as cut into two unconnected halves: One filled with loving parents; the other with emotionally unavailable giants who moved other people's limbs about as in the brother's patterning. The father's propensity toward uncontrolled rage was probably also a factor in reinforcing the small Alicia's perceptions of one person being really two strangers. All these theoretical considerations, as well as the countertransferential unease, helped the therapist to bind the temptation to jump on the bandwagon, and to claim a miraculous "cure" due to the healing powers of movement.

During the last half of her senior year in high school, Alicia became a model citizen, indeed. She volunteered some time at a school for special children, took dancing lessons, and appeared punctually for her sessions. However, there was no talk of adding a third one now. The hours were filled with attempts to stretch further, contract more correctly, turn out more widely, and to use dance therapy jargon picked up during workshops with other dance therapists. Alicia was accepted at a prestigious college where the openness of the structure would allow her to continue efforts toward becoming a dance therapist.

Warnings by the therapist that Alicia was not yet ready to leave her present, protected and structured life went unheeded by her parents and herself. Off she went in a cloud of triumphant control.

Just before the Christmas holiday break she was back, wide-eyed, depressed, and with a new set of symptoms. During choir practice, off campus in a church while singing a hymn, she had suddenly felt transparent. She claimed she could see her own veins and heart with the blood coursing through them. Her flesh had become waxen, flexible, and "illuminated.' At the same time, she had seen a vision of the Virgin Mary. Peace flooded her and she determined to convert to the Catholic faith. Apprised of this, the parents brought her home. Because of their own ethnic, but not religious, identification with Judaism, the threatened conversion appeared almost as bad to them as the arrest four years ago.

The therapist was to see Alicia daily and "get her back in shape" for the start of the next semester. Though declining to accept this deadline, crisis intervention nevertheless seemed appropriate in view of Alicia's delusions.

The Isadora Duncan-like performances began again, this time with sound effects. Alicia had unearthed a record of sitar music to which she now danced. The sounds swept her into a hypnotic twilight state during which she lost her fear of being looked at, which she had never verbalized, but always acted upon. Autoerotic activity in the form of wetting her underpants slightly, giggling, stopping the flow of urine just in time, and then running to the toilet also was engaged in during the session.

The therapist responded to this need for both toilet training and approval by her mother with direct gratification by saying: "I am glad you can wait to reach the toilet."

After these episodes, Alicia's general behavior became more primitive during the sessions. She had a need to skip to polka music, sway to waltzes, play hopscotch, or to simply run around in a circle. Every once in a while she would stop smilingly to be admired by the therapist. Finally, a true regression to the fixation point had been achieved. Alicia began to act like a mischievous toddler testing her mother's tolerance. This "toddler-phase" is a regularly occurring event in the successful treatment of Borderline Personality Organization (Siegel, 1979). Hide-and-seek became a favorite game. Her daily arrival was marked by joyous excitement, while the therapist felt in the presence of a warm, emerging human being. Body contact, however, was shunned because Alicia was convinced that her skin would retain indentations from a hug, and become "illuminated" again. She began to read the *Confessions of St. Augustine,* and to compare herself with this saint and his life. Reassurances that past mistakes did not need to be undone by a saintly life went unheeded.

Now, Alicia began to compose poetry and to write it down in beautiful, rounded calligraphy with a special pen producing a medieval effect. The first letter on each page was illuminated as in ancient manuscripts.

An interpretation that possibly Alicia was illuminating letters instead of her skin was accepted.

Just before the beginning of the semester, Alicia announced that she would not return to school. Crushed and angry, the parents withdrew Alicia from treatment. Not yet strong enough to insist on continuance herself, Alicia began to send her lovely poems to the therapist by mail. Approximately a year later, she telephoned to say that she was joining a commune in which healing by laying on of hands and by herbs was practiced. Another year passed before she appeared again for sessions, brought by her mother. In the commune, a young man had a revelation of himself as the second coming of Christ, and sought twelve female apostles to follow him. Alicia was to be number three, with initiation consiting of intercourse with the young man in the presence of the other apostles-to-be. Immediately after this "initiation," Alicia had a recurrence of all her symptomology; including the vision of the Virgin Mary and her own physical transparency. However, she had enough strength to call her parents who immediately flew to the distant state, where all this was taking place, and brought her home.

In treatment for the third time with the therapist, Alicia settled down to an in-depth intervention. She jokingly began to call the therapist "Mrs. Rock," because "she never fell apart." Intervention in the form of effort-shape-based exploration became possible as a true theraputic alliance had finally been formed (Friedman, 1969). Alicia's ego could now tolerate, and even welcome as valuable, work on body fundamentals and conscious examination of her flow qualities. Eventually, she entered a school for Hebrew teachers and there immersed herself in a course of studies of her own heritage. Though many of the mystic qualities of her psyche were reinforced by prayer and ritual there, her parents were able to accept her other-worldliness in this frame of reference.

The latest crisis came at the eve of her wedding to a young member of her religious community. The fear of receiving permanent indentations in her skin was revived, as was the wish to become a saint who is removed from the "blemish" of physical life. The fears subsided on accepting the realities of normal life through interpretation.

At present, Alicia is a young wife earnestly striving to reconcile what she has learned about herself in therapy with the demands of her life. Still fragile, her ability to sublimate is increasing. Her strong need for physical tension release has been translated into leading an Israeli folk-dancing group, and some of her poems have been published. The need for communal sharing and the family life she never had is being met by her devotion to her temple. Most importantly, she has learned to read her own body signals accurately and can thus forestall regression and pathologic splitting.

In summary, it can be stated that Alicia's ability for reality testing remained unimpaired through her main crisis, though her ability to *experience* reality was often severely distorted by the oscillations of contradictory feelings about the self. The capacity to establish true object relationships was severely impaired due to the mechanism of splitting until a combination of educational and therapeutic measures helped to establish a transferential relationship, which could grow organically without manipulative control by the client. Dance-movement therapy was seen as the intervention of choice because it offers tension discharge, body image building, strengthening of body boundaries, and the possibility of integrating diffuse and diverse instinctual manifestations nonverbally, despite the presence of splitting and denial of affect.

References

Cain, R. M., and Cain, N. M. A compendium of psychiatric drugs. *Drug Therapy,* Jan. 1975.

Delacato, C. H., and Dolman, E. *The Dolman-Delacato Developmental Profile.* Philadelphia: The Rehabilitation Center, 1962.

Deutsch, H. Some forms of emotional disturbance and their relationship to schizophrenia. *Psychoanalytic Quarterly,* 1942, *11.*

Fenichel, O. *The psychoanalytic theory of neurosis.* New York: International Universities Press, 1941.

Freud, A. *The ego and the mechanisms of defense.* New York: International Universities Press, 1936.

Freud, S. *Three essays on the theory of sexuality.* Standard Edition, No. 7, 1905d.

Freud, S. *The unconscious.* Standard Edition, No. 14, 1915.

Freud, S. *Introductory lectures on psychoanalysis.* Standard Edition, No. 15, 1916.

Freud, S. *The ego and the id.* Standard Edition, No. 19, 1923b.

Friedman, L. The therapeutic alliance. *International Journal of Psychoanalysis,* No. 50, 1969.

Hall, R. C. W. The Benzodiazepenes. *American Federation of Physicians, University of Texas Medical School,* 1978, *17,* No. 5.

Hartmann, H. *Ego psychology and the problem of adaptations.* New York: International Universities Press, 1970.

Jacobson, E. *Affects and psychic discharge processes in: Affect, drive, behavior.* Ed. by Loewenstein, R. M. New York: International Universities Press, 1953.

Kernberg, O. *Object relations theory and clinical psychoanalysis.* New York: Jason Aronson, 1976.

Kris, R. Some comments on early autoerotic activity. *Psychoanalytic Study of the Child,* No. 6, 1951.

Krystal, H. Trauma and affects. *Psychoanalytic Study of the Child,* No. 33, 1978.

Loewenstein, R., Hartmann, H., & Kris, R. Notes on the theory of aggression. *Psychoanalytic Study of the Child,* Nos. 3 & 4, 1949.

Laban, R. *The mastery of movement.* London: McDonald Evans, 1950.

Mittelman, B. Motility in the therapy of children and adults. *Psychoanalytic Study of the Child,* No. 12, 1957.

Rappaport, D. *Emotions and memory.* New York: International Universities Press, 1955.

Sandler & Joffe. The tendency to persistence in psychologic function and development. *Bulletin of the Menninger Clinic,* 1967, *31,* No. 5.

Schilder, P. *The image and appearance of the human body.* New York: International Universities Press, 1950.

Schmais, C. Dance therapy in perspective. Focus on Dance VII. *American Alliance for Health, Physical Education and Recreation,* Washington, D.C., 1974.

Schoop, T. Philosophy and practice. *American Dance Therapy Association Newsletter,* No. 5, 1971.

Siegel, E. The resolution of breast fixations in three schizophrenic teenagers. Proceedings of Fifth American Dance Therapy Association Convention, New York, 1972.

Siegel, E. Movement therapy with autistic children. *The Psychoanalytic Review,* 1973a, *60,* No. 1.

Siegel, E. Movement therapy as a psychotherapeutic tool. *Journal of American Psychoanalytic Association,* 1973b, *21,* No. 2.

Siegel, E. Motility and developmental levels. Eighth Annual Proceedings of American Dance Therapy Association Convention, Kansas City, 1973c.

Siegel, E. Psychoanalytic thought and methodology in dance therapy. Focus on Dance VII. *American Alliance for Health, Physical Education and Recreation,* Washington, D.C., 1974.

Siegel, E. Transference and countertransference in dance therapy. Abstracted in *Journal of American Dance Therapy Association,* No. 1, 1977.

Siegel, E. Psychoanalytic dance therapy. In *Eight approaches to dance therapy,* Bernstein, P., Ed. Kendall/Hunt, Dubuque, Iowa, 1979.

Spitz, R. *The first year of life.* New York: International Universities Press, 1965.

Zeigarnick, P. Über das Behalten von erledigten und unerledigten Handlungen. *Psychologische Forschungen,* No. 9, Berlin, 1927.

Chapter 17

FROM THE NOTEBOOKS OF MILTON M.*
Art Therapy with the Homebound Adult

Ruth Obernbreit, M.P.S., A.T.R.
Arthur Robbins, Ed. D.

Art therapy with a homebound person presents a particular challenge to client and therapist. The homebound are a population whose losses are far more profound than mere physical disabilities. Confined to the same rooms day after day, the homebound experience a form of sensory deprivation. They do not go outside for brisk walks, feeling fresh air on their faces. They do not feel the snow under their feet. Everything becomes the same. They experience painful ruptures in self-esteem, often more obvious than malfunctioning limbs. The introduction of a nonverbal modality—art—into the lives of those who are physically disabled and homebound achieves important therapeutic ramifications, which perhaps could not be attained through conventional verbal therapy alone.

As a result of the crippling effects of multiple sclerosis, Milton, a man in his late fifties, has been homebound for nine

*Segments of this chapter have been printed in the Proceedings from American Art Therapy Association's Ninth Annual Conference.

years. This illness has left him paralyzed from the neck down, but he has mobility in two fingers on one hand. An outside attendant comes in to bathe him. At times when he has little muscular strength he must have somebody feed him as well. He lives with his wife, daughter, and granddaughter, but relies a good deal on the television for companionship.

It was not without a sense of anxiety that I first met Milton. The introduction of art into the life of an individual with such severe liabilities presented a true challenge. Initially I was able to engage him using the "squiggle" technique that child psychoanalyst D. W. Winnicott developed to make contact with his very young clients. Milton held a thick marker between his two fingers and I requested that he draw a scribble. I then turned the scribble into a mouse. (Figure 17.1) On another page, I drew a line and asked him what he thought it looked like. He contributed his own graphic additions and by the end of the first session we had embarked on a joint effort of making pictures. (Figure 17.2) This was the manner that most of the drawings were done early in treatment. It was, in effect, a pictorial interaction going back and forth, from a

Figure 17.1   Mouse

Figure 17.2   What is This Man Thinking?

scribble to an image. Milton was able to use his imagination and in a sense "play," without the strong sense of self-judgment that other homebound clients, without a previous inclination toward art, often experience. Milton was truly willing to use the capacities he did have, his two fingers, to the fullest extent. This eagerness allowed the squiggle technique to evolve into an active, dynamic therapy situation.

The symbolic aspects of the drawings gave our visual dialogue a special function. For example, in a picture of a figure I asked Milton, "What would this person be saying?" and he replied, "What dog did this?" referring to the facial expression of the figure. He interpreted the figure in the drawing as having stepped in some dog droppings. This could well be a way for this individual to state, How did this happen, this crappy life

I've had to lead for the last nine years? To be able to express notions of this kind symbolically is especially important for homebound individuals, for they have few acceptable channels to express such feelings. Emotions that surround the consequences of their illness are often perceived as too overwhelming and threatening to vent. With a clientele that is capable of walking in and out of an office it may be appropriate to enlist the art process to directly work through feelings around intense anger and helplessness. For a homebound disabled population there are other considerations. As in this case, it has proven better to let the making of art serve as a connective path to the healthy aspects of the self, to use creativity to establish some defenses from the very real overwhelming helplessness that exists. Hence, the therapeutic plan was to highlight ego strengths rather than insight uncovering treatment. The drawings gave Milton a way of legitimizing feelings in symbolic form, protected and comprehensible.

The art therapists' expertise is called upon to help the client use the metaphor of artistic communication to address itself to the following areas:

- ... The transformation of complex affect into images by creating pictures that transcend the nature of words. Expressing the unspeakable, putting diffuse and amorphous feelings into symbolic form.
- ... The homebound client's limitation of outside experiences results in a lack of stimulation, both visually and spiritually. Using art materials to create original images provides the individual with something new to respond to in a way that is manageable. (Figure 17.3)
- ... A testing ground is created for perceptions. The drawing itself serves as a built-in feedback system, i.e., the body image is seen with its distortions, fantasies, and elaborations.
- ... Converting a sense of physical immobility into visual motility is of special importance to a disabled individual.

Figure 17.3 Coffeeshop

284

Milton creates a football game, has a figure ride down an escalator, and walks to a mailbox. (Figure 17.4)

- ... The art experience provides an imaginative piece of reality that affords an opportunity for experimentation with new adaptive solutions. Milton approaches conflict when he is unable to control his movements and an image not intended emerges. He learns to play with it and makes something else out of his mistake.

- ... Formats are created in which the person can experiment with a variety of cognitive styles. Portraying some notion in fantasy or in reality, impressionistically or in great detail, becomes an option. Milton did a series of abstract forms, one entitled "I defy."

The joint drawings not only encouraged Milton to exercise his imagination but provided him with a medium through which he could recapitulate and reexamine past experiences. For example, one "squiggle" turned into Lake Michigan where he grew up. Another drawing led into a discussion about what it was like to fly a kite, or watch the locomotives go by as a

Figure 17.4   Man Walking to Mailbox

young boy. Some drawings like these relate to old memories. Some, such as drawings of hospital scenes (Figure 17.5), connect to recent events, and other pictures developed as stories invented together in the present. (Figure 17.3)

Using a technique promoting interpersonal interaction on paper there often was a true merging of imagery. This process should not be confused with fusion or possible infantilizing wishes on the part of the therapist. The art therapist "plays" with the illusion of joining on paper, but remains individuated. The interplay of imagery proved to be a therapeutic necessity in order to meet Milton at a receptive psychological level.

Clearly in his physical situation, Milton has been greatly infantilized, and there do exist strong tendencies toward regression, especially in terms of psychic energy being directed inwards. But by encouraging our imaginations to work together in the making of pictures, I was able, on paper, to draw that energy outward in intense interactional form. There was a vitality in mobilizing energy around contact that provided valuable

Figure 17.5   The Doctor Comes

experiences for progression. Milton now converts energy into symbols and symbols into contact.

However, one consequence of this energy exchange was the eroticism of the therapy relationship. Several drawings around sexuality emerged. Some pictures depicted sexual themes in a disguised form, and others, such as the drawing of a naked prostitute were more direct. Such an image may not concern sexuality as much as it concerns issues around power. Portraying a woman as a prostitute may be a way for Milton, in fantasy, to gain a sense of mastery in the sexual realm. Other pictures, more indirect, depicted duality—two figures engaged in some activity. Motifs like these can help give Milton some form to the feelings around his body change and loss of physical interaction. At the same time, however, Milton began to transfer his energy away from art and into verbalizations around erotic and highly provocative material from television shows that he watches. These sexual overtures and pictures may have more to do with the loss of physical affection and touching than actual sexual activity, though that is a real loss as well. How to help Milton validate his need for recognition around his manhood became a major focus.

When asked to do a drawing around the theme of contact, Milton drew a picture of a couple dancing. This motif, like other pictures of this time period, were primarily conceptualized by Milton with only technical assistance required by me. This is in direct contrast to the early pictures where the themes were mutually developed. A subsequent drawing concerned a couple talking about their children. (Figure 17.6) This picture is different from his other work in that it was done entirely on his own. Just as it was natural for me to join with him in the drawing sessions, it was not appropriate and natural to keep a distance. The patient had enough power and use of imagination to initiate and carry through his own artistic production. This drawing also made it possible for us to explore notions of mutuality. Human contact had become so sexualized in Milton's thinking that he needed to reacquaint himself with other modes of interaction. He was able to do this by referring to his own drawing. In the drawings from the second notebook, one can see that Milton was able to internalize a more multidimensional body image and incorporate aspects from my own drawing in terms of body portrayal. In previous pictures I helped define the figures by adding form and substance to his fragmented figures.

What began as an aesthetic consideration on my part served an important function. I was, in a sense, repairing some of the fragmentation projected onto his creations. This technique, of serving as a model through a drawing, relates specifically to the loss of body integrity experienced by the physically disabled. In addition to feeling immobilized, the homebound often feel their bodies to be fragmented, not whole, their identity as complete sexual beings ruptured. In the techniques used, the self is not only nurtured, but is reflected with a greater degree of cohesiveness—the self becomes apprehended and symbolically begins to be repaired.

Figure 17.6   Couple Talking About Their Children

The fact that Milton's pictures progressively depicted more complete body parts serves as amplification of the theory that in order for therapy to be effective, the self must be healed and restored. In Milton's case, two major changes have occurred: His drawings indicate greater body awareness and he is able to work more independently. (Figure 17.7)

The art experience by its very nature is personal and the use of art therapy with a homebound clientele has value in helping the person gain a sense of intimacy. The disabled experience a tremendous violation of privacy. Their bodies have been invaded by disease and by ceaseless medical probing. There is invasion with respect to lifestyle, personal space. Due

Figure 17.7   Man Walking the Dog

to the needs of a chronic disability they often reside where convenient. Milton lives in the family room. The family is intertwined with the illness and inevitably reinforces the role of "the sick one." When emotional tension within the family becomes unbearable the homebound person cannot get up and take a drive to get away. He or she does not have the opportunity to physically create distance. The art therapy experience can help the individual conceptualize a sense of inner space, a psychological room within the self.

It is a day-to-day struggle for my homebound clients to consider that despite their real loss of control and mobility their sense of integrity and self need not be lost as well. With the usual connections to the outside world sharply severed, they must find other ways to get information about themselves so that they may feel whole. For Milton, the drawing sessions provided a feedback apparatus that reflected the alive and healthy aspects of his personality. With such great emphasis placed on the disability, these areas often become neglected. In the gradual symbolic confrontation of his situation, disassociative and repressive tendencies had the opportunity to become alleviated. Thus, our work achieved some partial neutralization of the intense affect of loss and rage, though Milton's anguish was never directly confronted.

The case of Milton demonstrates how art served as a transitional medium, reflecting various stages toward the restoration of ego mastery. A close relationship with the therapist, in which joint image-making allowed bound-up energy to find an outlet, served as a primary factor in treatment. Milton was able to move from a state of passive resignation to a position in which he no longer required symbiotic support on paper. The drawings indicate the enormous potential for self-regeneration and reconstruction of self-concept through creative expression. In the face of appalling reality limitations, art served to overcome pain and failure.

Chapter 18

EXPRESSION AND MEANING

Michael Eigen, Ph.D.

Human expression is the heart of human perception. While baby stares at mother's face during feeding, both mother and infant are exquisitely sensitive to variations in one another's expressive qualities. Soon the baby smiles at the mere appearance of a human face or even mask: a coherent, radiant smile expressive of awareness of self and other. The baby's sensitivity to expressive qualities suggests that early on the human subject exists primarily through its connection with another subject. It may be that for the infant the world often is a kind of fluid, kaleidoscopic mandala with the human face as its center. Self and other fluctuate through their sensitivity to one another with direct, immediate transparency (Arnheim, 1949; Spitz, 1965; Elkin, 1972; Eigen, 1980 a, b, c).

This open sensitivity to expressive qualities remains, in varying degrees, a central part of perception all our lives. For most of us, the keenest interest remains invested in our own and others' feelings, moods, or intentions. However, ability to sense our own or other people's feelings is not uniform. We learn to filter or dampen the potential impact of experiences for many reasons. We may need to tone them down simply in order to selectively distill, process, and digest their felt meanings. Then again, present emotional concerns or past experiences may blind us to the existence or distort the significance of imminent expressive meanings. In this vein, our conditioning or defensive patterns may bias or ward off a more open experiencing of our own or other's states of mind. In general, the kinds of attitudes with which we meet events affects our ability to perceive expressive qualities. A severely intellectually detached attitude may split the subject off from the object and result in immunizing the subject against immediate experiencing of physiognomic qualities. Wertheimer (reported by Luchins and Luchins, 1973) offers a simple demonstration of this. A few individuals, unseen by observers, placed samples of their handwriting on a blackboard. Observers who watched these individuals walk were correctly able to match walk with handwriting. Artists and dancers were able to do this better than psychologists. Apparently the former were able to process expressive qualities more directly.

The ability to sense and understand expressive qualities is especially important for the psychotherapist. Yet, it is often said that the way therapists are trained hinders, if not kills, the development of their inherent ability to experience and understand psychic reality. The moment-to-moment fluctuations in the therapist's sensing of his own and the patient's psychic reality have not received the detailed attention they deserve in professional writings. The present paper is a small attempt to indicate the importance of the therapist's ability to register and respond effectively to the shifting expressive qualities of the patient.

In this case presentation, the therapist's (my) remarks and interventions follow from changing perceptions of the patient's momentary psychic reality as expressed in the latter's verbal and nonverbal gestures. Although the patient used the couch for most of her analysis, no one "technique" or style of intervention was adhered to. The therapist must invent the means of "treatment" as therapy unfolds, making fresh use of old tools while fashioning new ones. The living word and gesture carry communication forward. The ability to do this is linked with the cultivation of metaphor in the service of tolerating and illuminating psychic reality. A blend of familiar and novel interventions spontaneously evolve as the patient moves from old to new regions of experience. However, the result is no eclectic chaos. Staying close to the psychic requirements of the moment has its own kind of rigor and order.

Jane announced herself as a "hopeless case." Her face seemed worried and accusing. "I don't think anyone can really help me. I don't know why I came. . . ." She paused, then continued, "I suppose I didn't have a choice. . . . I have to try to do something. . . ." She sentenced herself to therapy. Her nature and predicament offered her no other recourse, so it seemed.

Her skin was yellowish and tight, hard pressed and glistening. She seemed extraordinarily alive and driven, electrically so. I half expected the surface tightness to peak and burst, all manner of things tumbling out: strange animals, wild flowers, shooting stars. But the tightness was very deep, the constraint bitter. Its thoroughness gave every hint of leakage a propulsive force. I felt somewhat intimidated. Was her hopelessness a declaration of war? Did she offer herself to me as a begrudging dare?

I also felt worried, even hurt for her. For something important seemed to be lacking. In spite of her fierce gleam of chaos and need to explode, she described herself as blank and hollow. She had somehow gone away from herself and the person others thought she was formed a resentful shell. She anxiously appealed to others to fill the vacuum. But if they did she felt her disappearance all the more keenly and was driven to run still further away. She mocked all those who would venture near yet hated those who didn't.

She began telling her story, starting with her last therapist. He had been very warm and charming. He encouraged her not to give up. Someday, he told her, she would make it if only she kept trying. He gave her tranquilizers and friendliness. She commented, "He smiled more than you do. He made me feel more comfortable." She was offering bait. The battle lines were being drawn.

"Were you helped?" I was curious, frightened, and annoyed. Her face now scared me a little more. Her lips suddenly took on a crisp, metallic cast, stingy and hard. Her neck was rigid. She seemed a bit impressed with her own tone. But her expression was also fragile. She moved timidly and quickly with many little quivery spasms, something like a taut bird or quizzical rabbit.

"I felt better for awhile . . . but it didn't last." Her voice had an underwater, muffled quality. The room oddly became full with a hard to place sense of dull echoes.

In fact she was in a state of chronic falling apart. Buildings seemed to crash down on her, streets slanted, she often was dizzy and faint or scattered, nothing held together. She could not feel her body. Her limbs seemed to fall off or float or splinter. She had thoughts of murdering her daughter. She blamed her husband for her lot: "He's only interested in himself. He doesn't try to help me."

Her breakdown began four years before, following the death of her father. She had felt close to him. She had been deeply attached to what she experienced as his warmth and love. In some sense he had been holding her together.

She hated but felt enslaved to her mother. Her mother frequently abandoned her in infancy, apparently more attached to a gambling addiction than her child. This mother was consistently unreliable yet expert at inducing guilt and exacting obedience. Jane swallowed her rage and to a great extent even her fear. She pretended to get along. She felt deeply dependent and afraid to cross anyone she imagined to be powerful. She had been more or less successfully brainwashed and puppetized by her mother.

Her husband, Kirk, could not stand the way she gave in to her mother and fought with her about it. Her mother virtually had the run of their house when and as she pleased. Kirk was infuriated and, in part, blind to the progressive deterioration in his wife's condition. At times he was sympathetic but she could not truly respond. She could only weep helplessly, have fits of temper, or stare despondently. The sight of her helplessness enraged as much as frightened him. He often took it as a personal assault, something she did on purpose to thwart him. He would finally withdraw into drugs and ignore her, which increased her resentment of him, a vicious circle.

She spent much session time blaming him and expecting me to join her. In fact I felt sympathy with her in her pain. She had been and was suffering much. But I also was somewhat put off at her refusal to take any responsibility for her own life. Nevertheless, I knew such a failure was inevitable given her background and could not blame her for it. I could sense her deeper predicament. It was not just her inability to take responsibility that was bothersome. It was something of the amorphous yet peremptory quality beneath it. There was a threatening aspect to her helpless clinging, an adhesive formlessness that pushed and pulled. It made me want to keep a certain distance, far enough to feel safe, yet near enough to be able to keep sensing what was happening between us and not shut off.

She made of each moment of our session, of her life, a crisis and catastrophe and could not, would not understand why I was not swept away with her sense of urgency. She seemed to take my quiet pleasure in being me, my allowing myself the right to my own sense of life and private consciousness, as an act of cruelty. The fact that I did feel and convey a certain sympathy was not enough. If I did not become distraught and overtly anxious she felt uncared for. Insofar as I simply remained in contact with my own thoughts and feelings I risked provoking her rage and withdrawal.

"You're cold and hard," she accused. "'You don't really want to help me. You don't care."

"It looks like we're stuck," I said. "If I give you the kind of sympathy you say you want the way you want it, you will be coercing me like your mother coerces you. I will feel like little Jane giving in to mother. However, if I don't do as you want I will be the cold, ungiving mother who was not there and you will be furious and alone."

We ran through variations of such interactions any number of times. And at some point she began to break down and weep. She wept out of frustration, helplessness, anger, and also a deep sense of loss. For the moment she felt herself deeply, but it was more than she could take. Panicky thoughts of killing her daughter rose to the foreground and obsessed her, filling the space she almost gave herself.

She pictured using a knife, a certain long knife, which out of fear she hid away on the highest shelf of a closet. By the time she could climb up and reach it, she calculated, some modicum of reason might return and she would not have to act. These were not new thoughts but this time she spoke as though she wanted me to say something she could listen to. She had the need to show herself at her worst and be as frightening as possible. In the past she had hoped for the relief of finally being forthrightly judged and condemned and made manageable. If I had not tried to control her she saw me as uncaring and weak.

Her weeping with me made a difference to both of us, at least for the moment. The breakthrough of something soft made me less afraid of her, which, in turn, reinforced her touch of openness. Even so, something grating and tense remained, though with more subtlety and shading.

"You want to kill your daughter the way you feel your mother killed you," I interpreted. "You felt so barren and bullied. Something had to happen with your anger. You couldn't simply keep it tucked away all the time. Is it so surprising you have a killer in you? After all, you are your mother's daughter."

She protested with irritation, more frightened than offended. She wanted to be sure I grasped the gravity of her

situation for she did not really understand why I did not ad-
monish or threaten her. It seemed to her that my lack of disap-
proval of her thoughts was approval of the actions they
portended. She showed a sharp rise in the intensity of her
feelings to the point of seeming almost uncontrollable and I felt
compelled to let her know that I did not underestimate her
danger. At the same time, I wanted to convey trust in the
therapy situation, even if one could not possibly know the
outcome.

"You know, one can have all manner of thoughts," I said.
"Thoughts and actions aren't the same thing. One can learn alot
from all one's thoughts and feelings just by studying them or
talking about them."

She seemed quizzical but relieved. "I'm always afraid I'll
do whatever I think. I'm scared of my thoughts because I feel
I'll have to act on them. Thank God something has always held
me back. Maybe fear held me back. It never occurred to me I
could use them for anything. You're telling me they're worthwhile. Are you crazy?"

"They're you; they're part of you," I suggested. "They
must have something important to tell you."

"What they're telling me is I'm filled with hate. So filled
it comes out on the one I love most. More than anything I
wanted to be a good mother, a mother like I never had. But I
was terrible. I tried to be with her all the time. I couldn't let
her be. I thought I was being good, the opposite of my mother.
But it would end up awful. I was really frightened and used her
to cover up my fear. I was holding on to my daughter for my
life. I was too weak to show the hate I felt. I wasn't ready for
a family. I knew I was doing the wrong thing when I got
married but I couldn't help it."

Jane was sad, hurt and angry but mostly sad. It was a
conversation we had many times in different ways. Her sadness
gave her strength but she also tried to escape from it. Her
hatred for everyone in her life gradually increased, or at least
she felt and showed it more. At first her husband felt relief. He

had always wanted her to stand up to her mother. For the first time in their marriage Jane seemed to hate her mother more than him. But in time he, too, was threatened and periodically joined her mother's attempt to crush her unpleasant self-assertion. I felt that I was witnessing the preliminary states of a struggle that one day might have to be focused on me. In the meantime she had more moments of feeling stronger.

About six months into therapy Jane spoke about a dream that she came to find significant and that considerably deepened her. She had brought in dreams before but somehow they had not really clicked. Even when she seemed interested and momentarily moved, their effect appeared to be transient and they came and went with little trace. It is not entirely clear why she made the present dream her own. Perhaps her relationship to me and therapy had reached a certain resiliency and depth. Possibly she found that therapy could take more of her than she had imagined and that she could express more of her thoughts and feelings than she had hoped. She, also, had begun to test herself out vis a vis her mother and husband and found that she was not altogether helpless even though she often felt that way.

While such notions are likely true they do not really pinpoint with any exactitude why this dream and none before became "her" dream. It was not an unduly special dream from all appearances. Although it was dramatic enough it was not, by objective standards, necessarily the most dramatic she had produced up until then and not extraordinarily dramatic so far as dreams in general go. Nevertheless, for the first time she was able to own that, indeed, it was she who had produced it and that it was intimately linked with and reflected her. She could recognize herself in it as in a mirror—but a very special mirror. For before having the dream she would not have recognized herself precisely in the way that she was able to come to view herself through the dream mirror. The dream adds something new to one's reflection that one might not have imagined without its aid.

Jane dreamt that she lost her car on the street she grew up

on. While she wandered about looking for it someone told her that a little girl was lost. Jane looked for the little girl and found her on the roof of the building Jane lived in as a child. The girl was getting ready to jump off but Jane spoke with her and finally was able to take her down to the ground below.

The dream presented Jane with a summary and prognosis. It was like a puzzle in which she could recognize various parts of herself wanting to come together. As a child she lost her body self, her sense of body aliveness, her spontaneously-felt being. On the one hand she tried to survive by hardening herself, turning her body self into a machine, represented by the car. But this gesture at mechanization for the sake of functioning effectively could not be sustained. She sought safety by trying to rise above it all and live solely from her head, represented by going to the roof. If she could stay on top of things she might be able to look down on life without being wounded by it. However, the resulting dislocation between her body self and mental self led to suicidal wishes. In the dream Jane was able to face this situation and influence the lost little girl to come back down to earth again. She, of course, herself was the lost little girl caught between mechanization of the body self and escape into a cut off mental existence in which she would be reduced to a hopeless onlooker.

When she focused on the image of the little girl she could feel her body come more alive. It was as though she were reuniting with a part of herself that had gone blank and now was filling out again.

I suggested that she spend more time until our next session (we were now meeting three times a week) focusing on the lost little girl and allowing herself to think and feel whatever would come up. Apparently the more she stayed in contact with the image of the little girl the less lost she felt. She took to this little girl instinctively and felt sorrow but also excitement and relief in her presence. For it was clear to Jane that by seeking and saving this girl she had done something genuinely helpful for and with herself. With that came a new sense of her own felt depths and the possibility of making and sustaining contact with her own being. As she later put it, "I had a glimpse that someone was home after all. That there really was something going on in me. *I* was going on in me and *I* had many voices. I began to feel filled with the different parts of *me*" (see also Eigen, 1973, 1975).

Things, however, did not run smoothly. Her sense of bodily aliveness or presence would come and go. Her dream experience was more programmatic than something she could fully base herself on. It diagnosed the problem and set a goal. Our actual work was uneven and raw. Nevertheless, some underlying sense of the possibility of movement, however vague, never completely left her for long. In the matter of solidifying an unconscious thread of hope the dream was decisive. It was a hope she would have to test to the utmost to be certain of its genuineness. As a six-year-old she once dreamt she was in total blackness, except for a slight opening between two boulders through which a little light came through. It was, apparently, a light that had not been destroyed, surrounded by a blackness that had not been very much alleviated.

The feeling of strength Jane found in her little girl began to fade in the sessions that followed, and for awhile no further dream came to save her. However, she was able to continue to experience and articulate with far greater clarity ways in which she felt split or pulled apart. Her use of drawings helped her to express and try to heal distortions she felt with relation to her head and body.

In one set of drawings head and body were clearly severed. In these pictures they variously courted, fought, or ignored one another. Either head or body appeared more inviting, menacing or refusing. In some scenes they seemed to struggle more playfully. In another set head and body underwent distortions that made them virtually unrecognizable. In other pictures they seemed to amorphously collapse or melt into each other. Such scenes of fusion might appear chaotic, peaceful, or grimly oppressive. She was unable to draw with conviction or sincerity scenes in which head and body genuinely fit together.

After her drawings Jane's sense of being split was most dramatically focused in a fantasy she would have before falling asleep. "As I drift off I begin to fade away but catch myself just as I'm on the way out. Somehow I am not fast enough to catch my body. It seems not to be there anymore. I'm afraid I'll vanish if I look for it. When it reappears I feel like a small point somewhere inside it and it spreads around me, black and formless. I'm like a point inside a shapeless circle. I fear I'll die if the point vanishes or is suffocated. I feel lost inside the circle.

"I try to make the point move around and feel stronger. It can press against and trace the edge of the circle. If it lies on the edge and gets stuck it starts to push hard enough to break through the circle entirely. When it is outside I feel frightened and free and start to appreciate how comforting it was to feel surrounded. I begin to long to be inside the darkness again and feel if I found it I could drift in it forever. I imagine becoming totally passive and want to give up and fall back and not put any more resistance at all. I start to sink in it and disappear but once more think of struggling. Neither being in nor outside wholly satisfies me. I lie helpless and depressed, caught between my wishes. I feel exhausted.

"If I stay paralyzed long enough two figures, a witch and an angel, begin to rise above me and argue. They fight over my body. They both want it. The witch sends a cold feeling all through my body. She wants me to give up on my body so that she can grab it and bury it. The angel also does not want me to feel my body but he wants to protect me. Maybe he thinks if I don't feel my body I can't do anything bad. When I was a child, if I concentrated with all my might on not having a body it stopped me from doing dangerous things."

It seemed likely that point-surround and angel-witch not only referred to head and body but also to father and mother (viz., Eigen, 1980c, d). I suggested, "Perhaps head and body mirror mother and father's relationships to each other and you."

Jane concurred and elaborated. She had always maintained the stereotypes, mother-bad, father-good. Now she said,

"They (her parents) never got along. She'd fight and do what she wanted. He'd withdraw or placate her. I wanted to hurt my mother since I was a little child, really hurt her bad. I never showed any kind of anger until I broke down and lost control. All the things I kept in made me nervous and afraid. If I ever spoke to her she'd slap my face. She never stopped to ask, 'What's bothering you?' I hardly talked at home. Dad didn't hit but he'd ask, 'What's bothering you?' over and over until he started to yell it. He would always want me to talk. I could never answer him and when I wanted to tell him what was in my heart he wasn't there anymore . . . Now my head is light and floating. The witch is still flying in and out of me. . . . "

"The witch, once your mother, is also your own violence now," I said, somewhat amplifying and shifting her perspective, pointing to her own depths.

"I want to draw her now but I can't. No materials could do it."

"You can draw her with your mind, make her with the same materials that make you, your thoughts and feelings."

"I'm picturing carving her out of the blackness that surrounds me, my body blackness, my body hate. She is the outline of my body, made from the dark. Inside is the father angel point. The point is loving but cold. The blackness is warm. Hate is warmer than love. When the witch fades the blackness stays but is empty. I'm no longer frightened but lonely. I need to be filled, even by loneliness. Without the hate to stop it, loneliness sucks everything up. I tell it, 'Go ahead, take in everything.' "

"So, without the brakes of hatred, *vertige*," I found I said. Neither I nor Jane knew much French. Rimbaud was in my mind, *Je fixais des vertiges.* It was really an invocation, a wish to conjure up the sense of spinning height or depth without location and essentially unplaceable, like stepping off the edge of the world with no solid reference area to grip. I felt I wanted to send a psychic flare to light up the no man's land between the hate and the sucking.

In fact my remark unconsciously was linked with the lost

little girl on the roof for it spontaneously evoked in Jane a heightened awareness of her predicament, which took the dream further. The sense of groundlessness she evoked in me was sent back to her and she instinctively tried to grab it and rework it through the live wire of the dream. She only partly tried to fill her loss with hatred. She said, "I'm in my dream again and I picture the little girl falling off the roof and breaking into millions of pieces. Her face is deep in unhappy thoughts. There's a lot going on behind her eyes. My body jumped off the roof while my head watched it disappear from sight. My body got lost. I couldn't take any more pain so I got rid of it by not feeling it. I pushed it off. Now I want it to come back but it won't. I'm scared that it broke into too many pieces and won't come back. My limbs just float. They're not part of me. There's a big hole in my stomach where my father should be . . . I'm angry for feeling love for my mother since she took my body away. . . . "

She doubled up on the couch and cried, at first without tears. She made sounds that sometimes turned into shrieks. What seemed to be her limit point for tolerating agony gave way to still more pain and it was clear that she was touching something of the pure pain of her early years, pain within pain, the timeless pain she had long tried to ignore, hide from, go around, get rid of or outfox. She had feared that once experienced it would never leave and she would suffer it endlessly.

When the dreaded pain began to subside, new feelings and images started to appear. The relative relief she experienced had the momentary quality of a new found sense of freedom. It was not something she could hold on to for long but the fact such a clear sense of being could exist, however briefly, had a long-term heartening effect. It gave her a taste of feeling whole. Although at first she felt severely disappointed when this sense of wholeness began to disappear and regarded its loss as a bitter setback, her felt realization that it existed at all and that it could exist again helped her to face more ably what most frightened her about herself.

Her struggle toward self-repair in part required the repair of damaged images of significant others related to her. She began to have many more dreams about her parents in which she increasingly dealt with and repaired their traumatizing aspects. Apparently her pride at having been able to start to face the states that most frightened her permitted her to experience more thoroughly the gaps in her psychic structure that were tied to faulty relationships with feared-hated objects. The imaginative elaboration of thoughts and feelings that stem from contact with dream images allowed her to develop more precision in representing her psychic reality. Earlier she tended to find such work too disorganizing and she usually escaped by some variable combination of heightened vigilance, fragmentation, and global reactiveness, tendencies that remained present through most of her analysis.

In dreams, her parents at first most often appeared as attacking or depriving. Jane was usually persecuted or isolated. A number of dreams involving her parents in restaurants and supermarkets made their appearance, often exhibiting conflicts over bad food. Jane sometimes struggled and won and at other times gave in, overpowered or dispersed. A new dimension opened through dreams of cleaning (e.g., images of Jane doing laundry). Our sense was that the anger she turned against herself was cleaning her out. She felt fresh and able more often. Deeper, self-restoring parental images could now appear. In one dream Jane was in the water with her mother. They seemed to be holding each other up and giving life to one another. Her mother appeared more whole and benign than in actual life. Jane's capacity to generate her own good images was beginning to evolve.

This phase of therapy culminated in several dreams in which my face apeared more glowing than in real life. After these dreams she felt a sense of wellbeing that would last a good part of the next day or two. She said of my dream face, "Your face is heavenly, from another world ... yet still you, the you I know ... I had the feeling I could enter it or become one with it and pass through it and be more myself than ever ... We added to each other rather than took away. ... "

In the dream we were two yet one, within yet outside of each other, permeable yet distinguishable. The material world was not abandoned yet at the same time gave way to something ideal, ineffable. Both she and I retained our identities or, rather, rediscovered them but with a touch of the divine, a sense of perfect bliss. She had tapped an ideal realm of experience in which separation-union did not contradict one another but rather existed fully, simultaneously and made each other possible. For the moment she lived in a transparent world that was both immaterial and material, ideal and real.

Following this dream Jane produced her first drawing in which head and body fitted well together in an alive and convincing way. Together with this her sense of body life expanded. She could allow the vagueness of her body boundaries to give rise to "pillowy, foamy" feelings, a sense of "airy softness" evoked by her glimpse of tenderness. For a time she escaped the chronic contraction of stark terror. Her contact with the ideal imago opened a dimension deeper than both her parents and her previous body sense and offered a potential starting point for profound regeneration.

The fact of my sustaining and organizing presence in her dream signaled a new phase of therapy in which I was to be the focal figure. Previously her session talk was largely concerned with people in her life outside of therapy, particularly her obsessions with parents, husband, and child. In the dream she acknowledged the central role I was playing in her personal development. It was largely through our relationship that her capacity to generate good images was emerging and her dream emphasized this. It was only a matter of time before I became the persistent focus of many of her other feelings as well. For the curve of idealization inevitably carries over to disappointment or disillusionment, with correlated experiences of rage, grief, envy, and isolation—unless one falsifies oneself via seductive collusion in order to maintain oneself as an idol.

Jane soon felt forced to renew her early attacks on me for being cold and uncaring, lifeless or insensitive, not available or present enough, and the like. At times it did not seem as though therapy could survive such attacks but each therapy relationship must prove itself capable of embracing the necessary ruptures it generates within itself. One must hold out long enough for the patient to become disillusioned with disillusionment. In time, the patient comes to encompass his or her own capacity for polar oscillations between extremes of experience and evolves a deepening sense of attunement with his basic rhythms as they undergo development (see Eigen, 1977).

In Jane's case, idealizing moments and moments of depressive hurt and hate came back to back and often were intermixed. She continued to enjoy many positive gains from her unconscious idealizing use of me. There was a general rise of good feelings for herself and others and at times she became orgastic in sexual intercourse, a new happening for her. Her orgastic moments could be shown to be related to idealizing fantasies. When she was irritated or despondent in relation to me she could not climax, although several times she climaxed out of spite, hatefully. Our relationship, of course, was destined to fail her, if only in the sense that she could not totally fulfill herself in and through it. We did not live together or make love or hold each other. She could not have me for herself alone. At the end of sessions we parted regardless of the emotional intimacy previously stimulated. And even in sessions it became apparent I had my faults and defects and was something less than perfect: a hard-to-escape fact of life that she, for good reasons, had forgotten for awhile.

For a time she tried to maximize her use of idealization by viewing herself as like me and in me. In one dream she danced with her daughter in a man's dressing room. She saw the man's dressing room as something previously forbidden and fine. Feelings of exclusion and appropriation were present. I was one of the men she imagined the room belonged to. Here she and a female part were active in me. One could also sense a manic glee in her claiming male prerogatives. I, in part, represented her own male side that she was in the process of claiming.

In a second dream, a little boy and girl played with toys together in the therapy room as Jane and I looked on appreciatively. The dressing room led to the undressing therapy room and although this scene still carries an idealized glow and expresses a wish for us to be a couple, it also exhibits a maturing, accurate picture of the therapy situation. All real therapy is in a sense play therapy with the male and female children in oneself. Jane and I appeared to be forming a working alliance toward this end. This includes meeting all the ups and downs characteristic of the struggle of play and growth. The therapy relationship must eventually define itself as something capable of embracing, one way or another, the full range of reversals that makes one human.

Before long our first year of work together was drawing to an end. What did we accomplish with one another and where were we going were questions we had to face. Clearly, therapy assumed a mounting importance to Jane as the year progressed. Her tie to me had begun to take the place of gaps in her development. My impending six weeks vacation was bound to precipitate difficult upheavals, possibly even a state of emergency. The challenge also provoked her to mobilize her resources and tap or consolidate new-found psychic possibilities. Following are excerpts taken from a session as our time of parting grew near.

"For awhile yesterday I felt good thinking of not seeing you. I never felt better. I can do it on my own, I thought. I even convinced myself I was glad you were going. But I started hating you and tried to cover it up. I felt you didn't care what happened to me. I couldn't stop crying. I never felt so bad. I've been weeping on and off since . . . When I get like this I think to myself, 'He's got an easy session. All he has to do is listen.' You just sit there and I do all the work. The idea of you feeling good while I'm so miserable makes me feel sick. But picturing myself happy makes me feel sick now too . . . I get the feeling that you are really just playing with me, kidding around. You must be laughing at the way I'm behaving. I want to be able to laugh at you ... I was disappointed in yesterday's session. It didn't do a thing. Nothing new: zero. There was no stimulation from therapy. It made me tired. ... "

"Are you saying that if you don't get stimulation from therapy you don't get stimulation at all?" I asked.

"I want you to tell me what a good job I'm doing," Jane said. She continued "Alot of people must call you Mom and Dad ... I want to be praised by you ... This morning my mother and father were in a dream together. I never had a dream where they appeared together before ... My daughter was in a dream too. She was playing with three teddy bears and pretended the mother and father bear were kissing ... Something in me is coming together. I can feel my body more. But I'm still depressed. Am I really getting better?"

"You sound frustrated that your analysis isn't over in a year," I suggested.

"I want more than I've gotten," she said. "It feels strange for me to say that. I do feel good alot, even great sometimes. I feel myself sometimes. I'm not used to feeling I can want something more if I already have something more than minus ... It's a new kind of impatience ... Yesterday I felt like I was spinning. I felt like a rope, winding and unwinding. I stayed with that feeling for a long time. Afterwards I felt tremendous energy. I was full of life and wanted to do things. I talked to an artist friend about how he paints. He spoke about images as though they were music. He has flashes in his mind like I do. He does beautiful, beautiful work. It made me want to do more painting but I was afraid to try anything new. I don't like to do things I don't know how to do. I give up trying. ..."

"Aren't you surprised you stayed in therapy? You didn't feel you could do *that* well."

She laughed. "That's what I mean. You never take me seriously. You're playing with me. And I'm nervous about you leaving me. You don't really want to help me. I want to run out of here ... I dreamt I was driving a car down a mountain in reverse ... I want to leave you before you leave me. There's a part of me that wants to stop coming to therapy ... I'm frightened of discovering my mind. I'm scared of what I'll be like if I touch these things. It makes me feel like a seed that has to grow itself and start all over from the beginning. I'm all new and strange to myself. I feel alot of loneliness inside and I think I feel lonely because a part of me is leaving me. The part that's leaving me used to seem like a friend. Now it's an enemy. It's something that shouldn't be there and I used to think it was the real me. I feel like a mirror inside. Somebody else is there, someone mysterious. I'm afraid of the mystery. My mind is deep and going down like a mine shaft. I can't find the root of it: it's never-ending ... When I first came here I'd blame everyone for my misery. I felt everyone was doing things to me. Now I try to stay with whatever comes to me. It's another level. I can stay with all the blackness in my head ... I see designs ... colors ... faces ... animals ... attacking feelings ... two things punching each other ... spinning fast ... a whirlwind ... dancing ... violence...." After a long pause, "I feel refreshed ... When I'm home and frightened and tight I let the images come and feel them. After a while I usually feel better, like I do now. It's not easy...."

"You're telling me you are grateful to me for knowing *you're* there but at the same time it's both scary and comforting for you to know that too."

"It's like being let in on a secret I didn't know I had ... It's really scary to have a mind. But I was dead without it. At least now I know I'm running...."

Perhaps the most fundamental accomplishment of our first year of work was Jane's dawning sense of her psychic reality. However, our therapy work scarcely had begun. It was a full three years later that she could say that all her previous therapy work had been an attempt to make me love her. And it was only then she could feel the difference between what it might be like to work *with* me rather than *for* me. It was still a beginning, but the goal was genuine.

In the above case my responses included: (1) clarificatory and educational remarks about the nature of therapy work and psychic reality; (2) transference interpretations; (3) evocative reflections of the double-bind style of thinking, which seemed to be the atmosphere the patient lived in; and (4) evocative mirroring of the patient's basic assumptions, which inured her in narrowing, destructive circles. Whether drawing on or stimulating verbal or nonverbal expression, my responses were aimed at the barriers preventing Jane from making fuller contact with psychic reality in the therapy situation and life as a whole. A variety of therapeutic responses had the good effect of stimulating more varied ego functioning.

As Jane's awareness of her own psychic reality (thinking-feeling-sensation) developed, a sense of the mind-body splits she was caught in became more focused. Various ways the mental and physical aspects of her self-feeling fought against, escaped from or collapsed into one another were expressed, most pointedly in drawings and fantasy, particularly linked with dream work. Splits between the mental and physical self, to an important extent, mirrored or caricatured structurally similar struggles between parental images. Healing of mind-body dissociations went together with the gradual development of healthier inside parents and, ultimately, a fuller, more autonomous sense of self.

The fact that deep healing took place with reference to dream images of the analyst's face suggests that Jane's sense of self and other was being regenerated at very early levels. For the baby's early sense of self and other is given coherent expression through its smile to a human face or face representation (Spitz, 1965; Elkin, 1972; Eigen 1979a,b). The sense of self and other simultaneously giving rise to one another may form the basis of our early experience of wholeness, a dual unity characterized by overlapping areas of union and distinction. A distance element is crucial. The smile, expressive of self and other awareness, does not arise from touch alone. It involves a *seeing* of the other, a visually-rooted cognition (in analytic work on the couch the "seeing," of course, is done mainly in terms of images and thinking-feeling). It is likely that the infant relies more on an image of the mother's face than on her breast when in distress. Or, rather, visual experiences of the face and tactile experiences of the breast (and enfolding maternal body) refer to different aspects of infantile longing. The sense of self and other grows in an ambiguously shifting context involving both closeness and distance dimensions. The sense of wholeness undergoes maturation through an evolution of both these necessary poles of human experience, with varying degrees of emphasis. A certain structural dual-unity (of self-other and mind-body) characterizes human consciousness at every level.

The work described places much emphasis on the quality and power of the imaginative response of the therapist. Surely not all therapists respond alike and given the variety of practitioners the case discussed could have unfolded differently. This might also be said of the same therapist at different phases in his life and career. If Jane entered therapy with me now rather than five years ago, she could not have had the same analysis. However, responses do not have to be identical in order to be structurally similar. One can imagine sets of structurally similar enough responses fit to do the work that needs to be done. Nevertheless, responses by different workers or the same worker at different times will not be equal in quality. Responses do differ in effective power, for example in fertility of meaning. This in itself ought not be viewed as a defect in methodology. It is, rather, a testimony to the vastness of our subjectivity, to our possibility. For we are always subjects in the unique position of searching ourselves. As subjects we experience and cognize the basic structures of our subjectivity. We bring ourselves into accord with our discoveries, our meanings, while through them incessantly alter who we imagine we are.

REFERENCES

Arnheim, R. The gestalt theory of expression. *Psychological Review*. 1949, *56*, 156–171

Eigen, M. Abstinence and the schizoid ego. *International Journal of Psycho-Analysis*. 1973, *54*, 493–8.

Eigen, M. Psychopathy and individuation. *Psychotherapy: Theory, research and practice*. 1975, *12*, 286–294.

Eigen, M. On working with 'unwanted' patients. *International Journal of Psycho-Analysis*. 1977, *58*, 109–121.

Eigen, M. On the significance of the face. *Psychoanalytic Review*. 1980a, in print.

Eigen, M. Ideal images and instinctual fantasy. *Contemporary Psychoanalysis*. 1980b, in print.

Eigen, M. Ideal images, instinctual fantasy and creativity. *Psychoanalytic Review*. 1980c, in print.

Eigen, M. Abandonment threats and mind-body dissociations in the wish for suicide. 1980d, unpublished paper.

Elkin, H. On selfhood and the development of ego structures in infancy. *Psychoanalytic Review*, 1972, *59*, 389–416.

Luchins, A. S. & Luchins, E. H. *Wertheimer's seminars revisited: Problems in Perception II*. Albany: Psychology Department Reports, The State University of New York at Albany, 1973.

Spitz, R. *The first year of life: A psychoanalytic study of normal and deviant development of object relations*. New York: International Universities Press, 1965.

Part IV

A FINAL NOTE

In the final analysis, each therapist must be constantly discovering and rediscovering for each patient both theory and technique. Beyond this point we move from being merely technicians to being artists when we interject within ourselves an authentic self-representation in which feeling is intuitively interwoven with scientific knowledge. It is this balance that evolves with the accumulation of experience into a therapeutic style. Hopefully the reader can, by taking note of the various approaches we have presented, use this material as a springboard to the forming of his or her own unique artistic and therapeutic style. To accomplish this end, we have tried to present the tools, offer examples, and provide an open environment for learning and exploration. To those of you who believe in the value of creativity in the therapeutic process, we wish you good luck on your journey. We trust that we have offered you a few signposts along the way to help in your encounter with the inevitable confusion, frustration, and exhilaration that are part of this process of learning.

Arthur Robbins, Ed. D.

INDEX